PIM

596

IN THE SIXTIES

Barry Miles is the author of *Allen Ginsberg: A Biography*; *William Burroughs: El Hombre Invisible*; *Paul McCartney: Many Years From Now* and *The Beat Hotel*. He lives in London.

For Lija,
with love + thanks,
from
Richard

IN THE SIXTIES

BARRY MILES

PIMLICO

Published by Pimlico 2003

1 3 5 7 9 8 6 4 2

First published in Great Britain by Jonathan Cape 2002

Pimlico edition 2003

Pimlico
Random House, 20 Vauxhall Bridge Road,
London SW1V 2SA

Random House Australia (Pty) Limited
20 Alfred Street, Milsons Point, Sydney,
New South Wales 2061, Australia

Random House New Zealand Limited
18 Poland Road, Glenfield,
Auckland 10, New Zealand

Random House South Africa (Pty) Limited
Endulini, 5A Jubilee Road, Parktown 2193, South Africa

Random House UK Limited Reg. No. 954009

A CIP catalogue record for this book
is available from the British Library

ISBN 0-7126-8998-2

Papers used by Random House UK Limited are natural, recyclable
products made from wood grown in sustainable forests. The manufacturing
processes conform to the environmental regulations of the country of origin

Printed and bound in Great Britain by Bookmarque Ltd, Croydon, Surrey

To Hoppy

Contents

Acknowledgements

Memoirs tell a life from only one utterly biased viewpoint, and even one's closest friends might have trouble recognising themselves, or indeed the author. When I went to art college in 1959, we looked back enviously to Paris in the Twenties, a period impossibly far away in time, when James Joyce and Ezra Pound browsed at Sylvia Beach's Shakespeare and Company bookshop, Picasso dined at Gertrude Stein and Alice Toklas' salon and F. Scott Fitzgerald and Zelda played party games with Hemingway at the Dingo Bar. The decade had become mythic. For someone entering art college now, the Sixties are just as far away, though fortunately, many of the protagonists in this book are still with us. There have already been a number of Sixties memoirs from the people in my 'circle', as rare book librarians like to call it: Mickey Farren's *Give the Anarchist a Cigarette*; Richard Neville's *Hippie Hippie Shake*; Rosie Boycott's *A Nice Girl Like Me*; Tom Clark's *Who Is Sylvia?*; Jenny Fabian's *Groupie*; Marianne Faithfull's *Faithfull*; Jim Haynes' *Thanks For Coming*; Michael Hollingshead's *The Man Who Turned On the World*; *Burnt Bridges* by Charles Marowitz; *Jaywalking* by Jay Landesman; Florence Turner's *At The Chelsea*; Michael Abdul Malik's *From Michael de Freitas to Michael X*, and a dozen or so others. There is also Jonathon Green's excellent vox-pop style *Days in the Life*, with its wonderfully conflicting descriptions of many of the events I deal with here, which is essential reading for anyone interested in the underground scene of the Sixties.

Over the years there have been many differing accounts of the Albert Hall Poetry Reading, the founding of *International Times*, the UFO Club, the 14-Hour Technicolor Dream, the meeting of John and Yoko, Indica Bookshop and other underground activities that I was a part of. I offer the usual excuses for writing mine: a desire to set the record straight – at least as I saw it – and the flattering pressure from friends who encouraged me to do so. I have used letters, diaries and business papers from the period, and some journal notes made at the time. In the early Seventies I was encouraged by Allen Ginsberg to write it all down, and between 1970 and 1972 I filled a number of notebooks with the retrospective memoirs which form the basis of this book.

I'd like to thank Betsy Sandlin (née Klein) who kindly sent me copies of my letters to her from the mid Sixties; Ken Weaver, John Hopkins, Christopher Gibbs, Caroline Coon and Larry Lewis, who read through parts of the manuscript and made helpful comments and corrections; Felix Dennis for access to his valuable archives, and John Dunbar for jogging my memory. I'd also like to thank the following for their help and encouragement: Steve Abrams, Penelope Austin, Gordon Ball, Dave Bawden, Ann Biderman, Julia Bigham, James Birch, Victor Bockris, Peter Broxton, Simon Caulkin, Chris Charlesworth, Sherry Dashiell, Ingrid von Essen, Colin Fallows, Mick Farren, Hilary Gerrard, James Grauerholz, Michael Henshaw, Michael Horovitz, Graham Keen, George Lawson, Jean-Jacques Lebel, Paul McCartney, David Z. Mairowitz, Gerard Malanga, John May, Jenny Miles, Susan Miles, Lauris Morgan-Griffiths, Tom Pickard, Ed Sanders, Jon Savage, Andrew Sclanders, Peter Stansill, Bernard Stone, Simon Vinkenoog, Gordon Waller, Mark Webber, Mark Williams, Andrew Wilson, Damon Wise, Peter Wollen and Andrew Wylie.

Special thanks to Rose Gaete at the Wylie Agency and to my editor Dan Franklin at Jonathan Cape. And of course to Rosemary Bailey who, despite having heard all the stories many times before, read the manuscript in all its different drafts and provided countless valuable suggestions.

List of Illustrations

Introduction

The Sixties began in black and white and ended in colour. The Beatles were a black-and-white band; they dressed that way and their first film was monochrome. The print unions determined that newspapers remained that way throughout the Sixties, and unless you could afford the expensive colour receivers introduced in summer 1967 in time for Wimbledon, television was a black-and-white experience as well. (Even if you could afford it, colour was only broadcast for a few hours a day.) But late in the decade came an explosion of colour: the hippies in their velvet and lace, psychedelia, the Beatles in their *Sgt Pepper* costumes and in Richard Avedon's psychedelic posters, rainbow printing, *OZ* magazine, posters so drenched in colour that they were unreadable. Coloured family snaps were introduced and interior designers went berserk with paisley-pattern wallpaper and purple coffee tables. Apartments began to look like Indian restaurants. But for most of the Sixties you had to make the colours in your own head.

Unless you are old enough to remember, it is hard to imagine how drab and miserable life was in Britain in the early Sixties. Television was broadcast for only part of the day and closed down with the National Anthem at midnight. The BBC controlled all three radio channels, one of which, the Third Programme, played classical music by day and ran lectures and talks in the evenings. The BBC frowned on pop music, and chart records were only given three or four hours a week, on one channel. Pop music was classed as 'light entertainment' and much of this was provided by BBC in-house musicians such as the Northern Dance Orchestra, who cranked their way through the melodies of Elvis Presley and Frank Sinatra without a flicker of excitement on programmes such as *Music While You Work*.

It was a society as regimented as any East European police state. Everything was designed to get people to work and back, and to make sure that they were in fit enough condition to make money for their bosses. To this end the pubs opened at 11 am and closed again at 3 pm. They reopened at 5 pm until 11 pm, with shorter hours on Sundays so that the acquiescent population could attend church. Some councils still chained up the children's swings on Sundays. If you had wine on your table in a restaurant at closing time, the waiter had to pour it into your glass. It was illegal to have a bottle on the table after 11 pm, which was also the time when the buses and tubes stopped running.

Thanks to pressure from the Roman Catholic Church lobby there was no contraception available for unmarried couples (although this changed in 1965) and abortion was illegal. Homosexuality was also illegal. (In 1967 the homosexual law reform bill made it legal for persons over twenty-one.) At the beginning of the Sixties the Establishment ruled.

We wanted to change all that. We wanted the Church and state to have no part in personal relations. And once we had got rid of them, then would come the great experiment of deciding how to live.

Squalor in the Cotswolds

I arrived at Gloucestershire College of Art in Cheltenham at the age of sixteen, callow, utterly naive, wanting to live in a garret and dedicate my life to painting. My annual grant was £100. My parents were supposed to make up the difference, but I had quarrelled with my father and we were no longer in touch. His wage as an ambulance driver was, in any case, hardly sufficient to support me as well as my mother and sister. It was the summer of 1959. Connie Francis, Marty Wilde and even Gracie Fields were still in the charts. The students all looked like their mums and dads: fashion still dictated that an eighteen-year-old girl dressed like a thirty-two-year-old woman; some had permed hair, all wore make-up, and skirts were to the knee. Some of the men wore suits and ties, others came in blazers with shiny buttons. One student carefully wrapped himself in a full-length butcher's apron each morning to avoid getting paint on his suit. Some of the mature students, as they were known, wore artists' smocks and carried real kidney-shaped palettes. A number of the men had done their National Service and were consequently older and wiser than those of us fresh out of school.

I quickly noticed that Cheltenham had a population of ex-art-school students who still hung around, hoping to get some cheap drawing paper or oil paints, and that they, unlike the ones at the school, looked like proper artists. There was Pierre Berry – his real name was Peter, of course – who shocked the old ladies of Cheltenham by carrying down the Promenade a huge, very realistic nude portrait of his girlfriend. He wore his hair in a Dizzy Gillespie bebop cut, brushed forward over his forehead, as the Beatles did years later. Then there was Black John, a dark brooding character with a large overcoat, who later did very well selling his paintings from the railings on Bayswater Road in London. They both wore jeans, as did Colin Parker, who had joined the art school with my year.

3

Colin had been in the army before coming to college and was extremely knowledgeable about the ways of the world. He informed me that Levis were the only correct attire for a real artist, but unfortunately the only place they could be obtained was Lawrence Corner on the Hampstead Road in London. It brought them in from the States and they were not always in stock. It took two visits before I was able to get any. Colin was taking no chances and wore an entire Levi suit like the one worn by Peter Blake in 'Self Portrait With Badges'. It was a scene very much out of Joyce Cary's *The Horse's Mouth*, but fortunately we were aware of it and laughed at what we were doing.

But we *were* Gulley Jimson characters, with our sketchbooks and long hair, always talking about what 'worked' and what did not, discussing the light on a building, the framing of a patch of colour on a distant wall, the angles of rooftops and the shadow on a model's thigh, delighting in the golden section and enthusing over de Staël, Giorgio Morandi, Klee and Bonnard. In 1959 the American Abstract Expressionists had not yet penetrated Cheltenham Art School. For the most part the teachers painted Cotswold landscapes or Euston Road School nudes, with little crosses to show intersection points; they refused to accept that abstract painting was in any way valid, the subject of many a heated discussion. It was a traditional pre-war art education: every morning for four years we drew or painted from the nude. In the afternoon we painted figure compositions or still-lifes. The evening classes were in flower-drawing, anatomy, history of art and other classical subjects. For the first two years we learned basic techniques: wood carving, lettering, gold leaf, etching, lithography from the stone, the stretching and preparing of canvases, and so on.

I arrived at the college with Peter Broxton, known as Kipps, who had been with me at Cirencester Grammar School. We were the only ones to take double art classes with Miss Wyckham-Martyn, who once had an exhibition in London of paintings of cows done 'in the manner of Cézanne'. Kipps knew how to behave in public, having gone to a private prep school and been a Queen's Scout. They threw me out of the Scouts after one meeting; something to do with attitude. Kipps was solidly grounded in reality. He was a keen

4

amateur archaeologist, having helped excavate the Roman north gate to Cirencester, the Roman Corinium. Kipps was quiet and thoughtful and kept his opinions to himself, though in years to come he would sometimes advise against some of my more idiotic plans. At art school we continued as before, having paint fights and generally behaving like the teenagers we were.

Also from Cirencester was Howard Pearce, known as Duff, whose parents had let him have the tiny attic room of their tumbledown house in Cricklade Street. He called it 'The Buddha', not because he knew anything about Buddhism but more likely to annoy me, as I had read Suzuki's *Introduction to Zen Buddhism* and rather fancied myself as an expert on the subject. Duff had a red light bulb, which impressed us all very much, and Kipps and I, sometimes with others, would gather in The Buddha, bumping our heads on the sloping ceilings, marvelling at the red light bulb, and share a bottle of cider between us while discussing art. His father would sometimes yell angrily up the stairs, but Duff never appeared to take any notice. There was one serious fight when Duff couldn't be bothered to walk all the way down to the privy in the back yard and pissed out of the window instead. Unfortunately his father was standing outside and got splashed. The row was quite spectacular.

Duff was very keen on Toulouse-Lautrec and when we all went on to art college at the age of sixteen, he did a series of etchings that were essentially copies of Lautrec's work. No one could really see the point. Duff just laughed. To him, art college was a stepping stone out of the Cirencester working class. Duff didn't stay long. Kipps and I ran into him in Paris in 1966 in the Jardin des Tuileries. Duff looked tanned and handsome. He dangled some car keys in front of us and nodded over to an open-topped sports car. Seated in it was an attractive young woman with her sunglasses perched on her head. Duff gave us his most beguiling, wicked grin and was off. I have not seen him since.

I was called Miles then and throughout the Sixties, and still am by most people. The Barry got dropped when, working on an art-school project involving six of us, three of us were called Barry. I never liked the name. I was to have been called Peter, but the Alsatian dog next door was called that and my mother thought there would be some confusion when they called me in from the garden. So Barry it was, named after the hero in that month's serial in *Woman's Weekly*.

Aside from his sartorial influence, Colin also explained to me the importance of parties. By this he meant the kind of party given by wealthy young people, the sons and daughters of Foreign Office officials at GCHQ – then, as now, located in Cheltenham – with enormous tables of food and drink, and sometimes a catered buffet, rather than the art-student parties where, if you didn't bring a bottle, you didn't get a drink. Unfortunately Colin was already quite well known in Cheltenham and he and I were thrown out of a number of birthday parties for respectable young things as unwelcome gate-crashers, but usually not until we had consumed a meal's worth of ham and cheese washed down with a glass or two of Chablis. Sometimes he was the only one to be identified as a stranger to the proceedings and I would get to stay on. I would fill my pockets with comestibles to share with him later. With Colin's guidance I learned to identify the most expensive and desirable items on a buffet and home in on them quickly before some Hooray Henry started to graze.

One good place to go was the basement of 38 Priory Road, which was opened each Monday night as a jazz club for Jane Filby and her friends by her mother, who sat with her poodle watching television on the ground floor as some of the best musicians in Britain played below her. Bacon and eggs were served just after midnight for the members and there was the added attraction of hearing some very good jazz. The atmosphere was so congenial that musicians playing anywhere in the West Country would drive over after their gigs to jam. The music was mostly traditional jazz, of the English, West Country, variety, but I once heard a superb set from Shelly Manne there. It was sometimes hard to get in as Colin and Jane Filby did not always see eye to eye.

Colin had thinning blond hair and a short neat artist's beard. He was from Nelson, Lancashire, and was a paid-up member of the Communist Party. He was full of tales of the iniquities of the system and I soon realised that gatecrashing the parties of the rich was not only right and proper, but could in fact almost be regarded as a revolutionary act. He educated me by explaining how society worked, how the people who manufactured a product were not in fact paid enough to be able to buy it, the price difference going to the owner of the factory as his profit margin. I was an eager student and he was soon drawing diagrams showing how the owners of capital ripped off the workers, and how the whole thing fitted together. He drew circles representing the car industry, the oil industry and the steel industry, then drew smaller circles in the spaces in between, which was where the scrap-metal industry was located and the makers of upholstery. The circles in between them contained even more specialist people, such as rag-and-bone men, feeding the scrap-metal dealers.

Sometimes Colin and I would get the urge to travel, and we would hitch out of Cheltenham on a whim, usually when the Restoration Inn closed and it was Saturday night and we knew of no parties, or couldn't get into any. We once hitched down to Cornwall and stayed with Colin's friend, the painter Paul Francis, in St Ives. It was like arriving on the Riviera, with the palm trees and an intense blue sea like the Mediterranean. We spent a few days exploring rock pools and collecting interesting bits of sea-sculptured wood, before heading back. Another time we hitched to Liverpool, arriving first in Manchester as dawn broke. I had never been to the North before and was shocked to see it was just as Colin described it: there actually were people walking to work in wooden clogs, clomping along over the cobblestones, huddled in shapeless over-coats against the biting wind. We enjoyed Liverpool, although most of the places that Colin knew had been torn down by property developers or the council – the whole area near the cathedral was a wasteland. The wind died down and it was a bright clear day so we continued north, to Blackpool, where I saw a stall selling peppermint-flavoured cockles. Then on to Nelson, where one of Colin's obliging aunties kindly put us up, though she made it plain that she disapproved of spontaneous jaunts such as this and that, in future, arrangements had to be made in advance.

My grant of £2 a week obviously did not go far and during the holidays I was obliged to get a job. Across from the college was the Black and White bus station, so I asked if there were any jobs going.

I became a server at the coach-station shop, selling bags of toffees, Wagon Wheels, Penguin bars and fruit. The oranges were from South Africa and I was a supporter of the campaign to boycott South African goods. 'They're from South Africa,' I would tell the customer if they showed signs of buying one. Most people reacted with indifference, but one old lady replied, 'Thank you for telling me, young man. It hadn't occurred to me that they've had nasty black hands all over them. I shall have an apple instead. They are English, aren't they?' Well, at least she didn't buy South African.

Stroud

Gloucestershire College of Art was split into two parts, one in Cheltenham and the other in Stroud. For my second year I had to attend the branch in Stroud, so Colin Parker and I decided to get a place together, and to look for two or three other room-mates to share the expense. We found an old sweet shop with accommodation above. It consisted of two houses, about 400 years old, at numbers 4 and 5 Hill Street, joined by the addition of a kitchen at the back. There were two staircases and eight rooms. Colin and I made ourselves look as tidy as possible and went to see Stroud council about renting it, as they were the owners. The rent was £3 10s a week, which we thought was feasible with enough people living there. The American painter Larry Lewis took an attic room and Don Braisby, another Cheltonian who was working in a local mental hospital, had the main room over the shop, which he shared with his girlfriend Kate, though she didn't stay over that often. Colin had the attic room above Don, and I had the room over the living room, below Larry.

The shelves of the old sweet shop were still filled with sticky tins of congealed acid drops and toffees. We broke up the counter and the shelves with their paper linings, and burned all the brown paper bags, commercial literature and mess left behind, stripping the room down to its bare stone flags and plaster walls. We painted it pure white and scrubbed the stone floor. A man from the council came to inspect while we were still cleaning up. The place looked good: we had already painted part of the outside wall white and in the brilliant summer sunshine the Cotswold limestone glowed golden and the fresh paint was dazzling.

We stood outside admiring our work. Suddenly puffs of smoke could be seen coming from the top right-hand window. Was the house on fire? The window burst open and Larry, engulfed in the dust of centuries, pushed his head and shoulders out and hung, coughing and gasping for air, cobwebs in his beard, clouds of dust swirling around him. When he recovered, he climbed halfway out and smashed a metal advertisement for Cadbury's chocolate off the wall with repeated blows of the broom. The man from the council clearly had his doubts, but he was impressed with our labour and signed the lease.

Half the kitchen was filled by two huge iron trays the size of a professional pool table, where the sweets and toffee had been rolled out. There was no way we could get them out, for they must have been cast there in the nineteenth century. We had to smash them. A gypsy scrap-metal dealer came with his horse and cart and, after a blunt exchange, took everything away, giving us five shillings. We argued long with him over the gas stove, which he wanted to take as part of the deal, swearing that it would not work. We used it the entire time we lived there.

We now had one room left to rent, but unfortunately the door to the bathroom led off it. Colin, who was a trained carpenter, soon partitioned the room, constructing a narrow corridor from the door to the bathroom and leaving a reasonable-sized living area. This we succeeded in renting to another painter, Pete Simpson, who had been expelled from Reading University Art School for sleeping with his girlfriend Ag. She was from Cheltenham and Pete had moved down to be with her for the summer. Now she was about to return to Reading for the new term, but Pete had elected to stay in the Cotswolds and paint.

Pete was subjected to a brief interview before being allowed to live in squalor with us. Larry and I met him in Ken Smith's El Patio coffee shop and we discussed Paul Klee over cups of frothy coffee in glass cups while Mose Allison played on the record player. Pete passed the test. He was to move in in a week's time.

Mike Cooper, one of Cheltenham's original beatniks, moved all of our stuff to Stroud in his family's Land-Rover, loaded down with my books and paintings, Colin's rucksacks and Pete's sea trunk. Mike was a tall lanky fellow and his knees seemed to stick up on either side of the wheel. He drove and talked as we imagined Dean Moriarty would. Pete didn't say much, just clenched his hands together until his knuckles were white as Mike took another blind curve on the wrong side of the road screaming, 'Death! Death! Death!', talking non-stop and roaring with laughter. Once we got to Hill Street Pete disappeared into his room and we didn't see him for a week.

On the eighth day, Colin, Larry and I decided to see how Pete was getting on. First of all none of us was sure of his name, so that was the first question. He treated the interview as an interrogation, which in a way it was, but finally showed us his watercolours and drawings. Most of them were of Lowestoft, and those that weren't looked like Lowestoft. They were all very much in the manner of Paul Klee, miniature worlds created with delicate gradations of line and subtle ink washes.

Pete was a large, shaggy sort of person with wild sandy hair and a full beard. He wore an unravelling oversize sweater and the same pair of jeans the whole time we lived there. At some time he ripped a large hole in the knee, and each day the knee itself got dirtier until eventually his knee and his jeans matched, and the hole could hardly be seen. He rolled his own cigarettes, and his tongue fretted over tiny strands of tobacco stuck to his lower lip. He drank tea all day, which he constantly knocked over. We used indescribably filthy plastic beakers with no handles that had teeth marks all around the top. Pete would brew up, pour a cup, bring it to the living room, sit down and kick it over. One day he kicked over four cups and the teapot as well.

His girlfriend often came to visit, though it was clear that they were breaking up. Ag was a thin, sexy, fiery girl with black darting eyes and a sharp tongue that made some people wary of her. She wore all-black art-school garb of stockings that were always torn or run, a short skirt – before the mini-skirt reached the King's Road –

that was also paint-stained, topped off with a woollen sweater. Her long, dark tangled hair fell across her eyes. She was without doubt much cleaner than the rest of us.

The living room, like the rest of the house, was very sparsely furnished. Most of this was Larry's doing: he had a very austere approach to life and wanted the place to resemble a monk's cell. His room was just that: a thin mattress on the floor and an easel – not even a chair to sit on. We had no chairs in the living room either; we had furnished it from the street with two large oak house-beams, one against each wall, propped up on bricks. A few cushions were arranged on them, donated by various sympathetic girls. There was a window seat – the walls were about four feet thick – and a huge fireplace. Over the fireplace was an axe, not for defence, but to chop wood. The floor consisted of bare flagstones, which in the winter had a coating of ice from the damp so that you could slide across them. The walls were panelled with boards of Russian pine and the door to the right of the fireplace concealed not a cupboard but the staircase leading to the rooms that Larry and I occupied. Most people didn't notice it because the whole wall over the fireplace, including the door, was covered by a huge mural painted by our friend Paul Francis. On another wall Larry had painted a long poem by Lawrence Ferlinghetti.

The building had very thick outside walls and my room had a window seat with a view out over the town. I laid a mattress on the floorboards, set up an easel near the window and arranged a few wooden packing cases for my clothes and paints. A copy of Gregory Corso's *Bomb*, a long broadside with the poem typeset in the form of an H-bomb mushroom cloud, was tacked to the wall next to CND posters and dozens of my own drawings and pages torn from my sketchbooks. I often worked in series, and pinned them in a row where I could see them from my bed.

I found a long plank to prop on piles of house-bricks as a bookshelf and unpacked my trunk: paperbacks, mostly Penguin editions, by Joyce, Orwell, Gide, D. H. Lawrence, Waugh, Wilde, Huysmans, Sartre, including the *Roads to Freedom* trilogy, the few Henry Miller paperbacks then legal in Britain, and a couple of hardbacks: Lawrence Lipton's *The Holy Barbarians* – 'the first complete story of the Beat Generation' – and Colin Wilson's *The*

Outsider, a book that was a tremendous influence on me when I was sixteen and introduced me to Camus; *L'Enfer* by Henri Barbusse; Hesse and William James. I also had, of course, the well-worn copies of *On the Road* and *The Dharma Bums* that had accompanied me when I hitch-hiked around the south coast in 1959. Each of these books had opened up new possibilities and new ways of living to me; they presaged a life beyond the Cotswolds, though as my friend Mickey Farren and I later agreed, James Garner in the TV series *Maverick* probably influenced us just as much as Sartre or Camus.

The lease required us to run the old sweet shop as some kind of retail concern, so we hung some of our paintings and displayed some of Kate's pottery. They looked fabulous against the newly white-washed walls and the scrubbed stone flagstones, but we soon tired of having to keep an eye on them and turned the door sign permanently to 'Closed'.

Larry would not allow Colin or me to listen to Radio Luxembourg: 'Shit! That's just shit!' he'd yell, complete misunderstanding on his face. 'I just don't understand you guys because on other levels you seem . . .' We would often put the radio on just for the hell of it. How he managed to hear it two floors up I don't know, but he'd come clattering down the stairs, red-faced, and we'd all laugh at him as he came bursting in.

He was in a very creative period, churning out paintings and drawings. Each evening, when Colin and I got back from art college, there would be a new picture hanging on the living-room wall. He was doing a series of abstracts called 'Peaceful Landscapes', which he seemed to paint over and over, never able to decide when they were finished. Instead of painting new canvases he would always change and develop the existing ones, so there was rarely any record of the changes in the development of an idea. Each evening he would stand and stare at that day's work with unbelievable concentration. Once, at the Rothko exhibition at the Whitechapel, I saw him sit before one of the canvases for more than half an hour. When he finally got up, his face was streaked with tears, he had been so moved.

Larry was involved with a girl called Ruth Doniach. They made love so noisily above my room that I usually put on one of my three albums to drown out the yelps and squeals. One day Larry came up to me in all innocence and asked me if I could hear them. He was quite shocked to find that I could and went away very quietly, deep in thought. It didn't seem to affect his performance, however, and I still had to get out my live recording of Ray Charles singing 'What'd I Say' whenever Ruth visited.

When Kate was staying we didn't see much of Don because they holed up in their room, which was by far the most comfortable in the house. Sometimes the floor would shake as they danced to rock 'n' roll records. Kate used to wear a red dress and they would put a red bulb in the light and really live it up. They may have even had alcohol in there – a very rare thing in the house, except at parties.

Parties were another thing. For these we stripped the house of all valuables, few that there were. There would be dancing in the living room, talking, drinking and socialising in the kitchen and art gallery. In my room people would look at books, relax and take a break from the frenzied partying. Larry's room, Don's room and Colin's room would all have candles burning and blankets over the beds so that people could have sex without messing up the bedding. We always took the precaution of warning the local police in advance that we were going to have a party and invited them to attend. Any scruffy-looking or long-haired person asking directions would be sent to Hill Street whether that was their intended destination or not.

The parties sometimes lasted for days. People living outside Stroud or Cheltenham would be sent postcards to invite them, usually with dried flowers, leaves or collages stuck on them. Literally hundreds of people came, driving or hitch-hiking down from Oxford and London. The police would usually stop in for a beer and a chat at some point in the evening while in the rooms above people would be taking pills and drugs that the local coppers had never even heard of. One young constable with a thick Gloucestershire accent, red face and blond hair took to dropping by quite regularly for a chat; he liked to discuss politics with Colin. At one party he was seized by a large lady potter in a floor-length hand-woven skirt and bursting blouse. The next morning we found his helmet in the cat's litter box. We took it to the police station and left it; he wasn't in that day. We never saw him again.

The local intelligentsia, such as sculptor Lynn Chadwick and the American painter Larry Rivers – who was going out with a local Stroud High School girl, Claris – would come to the parties and, knowing that supplies would be meagre at best, brought generous quantities of alcohol as their contribution to local beatnik life. Poets Michael Horovitz and Pete Brown would usually turn up from London with a bunch of people, and Nigelfred Young, another old Cheltonian beatnik, would come from Oxford, loading up his father's Cresta with students, imagining he was in *On the Road*.

One such carload of people delivered an old girlfriend of mine, who had since gone up to Oxford, and we had lost touch. I first met her under the table at a pub in Reading during the Aldermaston March – there was nowhere else to sit, the room was so crowded. This was before we got Hill Street, and Larry Lewis was then living in a room in Golborne Road in Notting Hill. She was eighteen, older than me, and we spent the night in my sleeping bag on the floor of Larry's filthy room. Periodically Larry would leap from his bed and tear more pages from a huge old Bible to throw on the fire. He had already burned all the furniture, including the table. Now, a year later, at the party, she wouldn't speak to me and was very moody with her friends. In the morning, when everyone who had stayed over added their names to the long list on the kitchen wall, she cursed dramatically, then drew a hammer and sickle instead of her name. I noticed she was still wearing my anorak.

One person who came to stay for a few days was John Bird, a skinny little cockney fellow whom I met while dancing at the Café des Artistes on the Fulham Road. Dick Heckstall-Smith and Laurie Morgan had a regular gig there at which Mike Horovitz and Pete Brown often read poetry and I would hitch up to see them all. I casually invited John Bird to stay, little thinking he'd come. He did come, but his somewhat loud, aggressive personality rubbed Larry up the wrong way and I was asked to get rid of him, as it was I who had invited him. Between us we managed to scrape together a couple of pounds to put John on the coach to London and he departed, laughing all the way. He later started the *Big Issue*, was given an MBE and now drinks champagne in Soho at 3 am, which just goes to show something.

Many people reciprocated by inviting us to their parties. One time we were walking up the long lane to Lypiatt Park, Lynn Chadwick's house, when he roared past us in a pea-green tear-drop Citroën. When we arrived he said cheerfully, 'I saw you on the lane

14

and I could have given you a lift, but I didn't because I'm a cunt.' Chadwick won the International Sculpture Prize at the Venice Biennale in 1956 and was consequently utterly ignored in Britain and sold only to the Europeans and Americans. He showed us around the mansion, which was where Guy Fawkes plotted to blow up the Houses of Parliament. Chadwick had turned the chapel, with its huge Gothic window, into his studio; it made a magnificent place to work. The greatest space of all was the dining room, the original Tudor hall. He had cast a long sculptural dining table out of marble chippings, long enough to seat a dozen people and heated to keep the plates warm. It ran from one of the support pillars of the Minstrels' Gallery towards the great Gothic bay window. The original oak floor was polished and his spiky, welded metal sculptures were everywhere in evidence, squatting like birds or tortured broad-leaf plants. There was a fireplace consisting of a stone platform with a black metal hood suspended over it from a long black smokestack rising to the ceiling, about twenty feet above. It was the height of Sixties modernity.

I encountered the composer Peter Maxwell Davies standing next to the grand piano in the music room. He used to be my music teacher at Cirencester Grammar School and was the first person I ever met who would fix you with an intense gaze while talking. The older boys at school would sometimes be invited back to the converted apple loft where he lived, to drink claret from eighteenth-century glass goblets. When the City of Birmingham Symphony Orchestra refused to record his *O Magnum Mysterium* on the grounds that it was impossible to play, he used the school orchestra instead, making the various percussion instruments in the school craft workshops. As music teacher, he was required to play piano for the hymns at morning assembly, and would place a lighted candelabrum on top, in the manner of Liberace, before he began.

I was pleased to see him again. He complained that most people in Britain walked around with their eyes shut and ears blocked. Larry misunderstood and thought he was saying this was a good thing and they talked at cross-purposes for a while. Peter played us a short piece that he had just completed. The music was wonderful and, as I listened, I could see Larry Rivers, a friend of Chadwick's, jumping over the big bonfire outside.

The girls who visited Hill Street often tried to clean it up, particularly Ruth, who was quite manic about washing clothes and scrubbing surfaces. She seemed to think she was the Jewish mother of us all and would break into our rooms while we were out and grab all the dirty clothes. One day she found evidence of another female in Larry's room. After several unearthly screams Larry came bounding down the stairs, taking both flights in four steps, followed closely by Ruth. Concerned that something was amiss, I pursued them to find Larry running round the kitchen table, with Ruth in hot pursuit brandishing the kitchen knife. Larry, genuinely scared for his life, was stuttering out an implausible explanation.

Each evening Colin and I would do the cleaning, and Larry and Pete cooked, the theory being that they both worked at home whereas Colin and I were at college and couldn't shop. We spent £2 a week on food for us all. We had a standing order with Jim Cant, the bewhiskered grocer at the bottom of the hill. He kept broken biscuits for us, and bacon offcuts that we ate with rice. We could never afford meat, though we sometimes had liver; mostly we lived on stew. We had a large battered pot to which was added new vegetables or anything that came along. It consisted mostly of lentils that had been reheated dozens of times and tasted awful.

What glimpses of modern art we did get during visits to London were immediately reflected in the paintings we did at Hill Street: mostly half-baked, ill-digested borrowings from Abstract Expressionism, happenings and Pop Art. Colin and I made a lot of pornographic collages, using images from girlie magazines that Paul Francis gave us (only breasts were revealed in Sixties men's magazines, everything else came later). It was based around a manifesto we had posted at college about obscenity being the only valid art, since it was the only thing that could shock the bourgeoisie into recognition of true reality, or something along those lines.

Inspired by Pop Art, I made collages, including an altarpiece of Helen Shapiro, even though I had none of her records. I knew 'Don't Treat Me Like a Child' and liked her deep fog-horn voice, but it was more her image I wanted: the beehive hairdo and pencil-drawn eyebrows. I sent away to Columbia for her photographs – in those days record companies sold pictures of their artists – and did a whole series based on her image. Then Larry, whose paintings were for the most part Abstract Expressionist in style, decided to try his hand at Pop Art and painted one of the most disgusting Baconesque portraits of the Queen imaginable. Unfortunately he hung it on the living-room wall right by the window and the police received complaints about it.

Larry painted a lot of nudes, most of them of Ruth, but much of the time it was too cold in his attic for her to pose. I did some nudes too, paying Jenny, the college model, to pose for me privately at weekends. She did it a few times, but stopped because I smoked marijuana when I was painting her – and because it was so cold.

Across the street was an area of waste ground on a steep hill, where the council had demolished a row of seventeenth-century stone houses. One morning, after staying up all night talking, Larry and I sat there among the trees to play music in the light that comes before the dawn. No colour. A luminescence of objects that denies perspective and distance. The lane was empty. The wasteland we sat in was shadowless. Above and behind us was an abandoned orchard, the trees damp and stunted, fruitless. In the rich, rotting earth at their roots small rustlings and the flap of wings indicated life awakening. The view extended right down the valley, through the small town centre to the River Severn about eight miles away, a silver shine, the perspective distorted by the pale morning light.

The first notes of the guitar sounded unnatural and jarring – a simple three-chord progression, taught me by Larry. Then Larry began playing the flute, pointing it at the fluttering birds. Pan notes emerging from a small forgotten orchard on the hillside leading to a small town with no colour. Smoke from the factory chimneys below the town just rising into the air. We played in the dawn, then sat and watched the sun rise for about an hour, the colour spreading at walking pace up the sides of the valleys, the sky turning from red to mauve above the distant white strip of the Severn, shadows being created, colours emerging.

Just as we were about to leave, the milkman came down Hill Street. We did owe him quite a lot of money, but it had just occurred to us that he might like his milk bottles back, so the night before we had obligingly washed them and put them out. There were about sixty of them, in a long line next to our wall extending

17

past the next-door house all the way down the hill. He paused in front of our door, looked both ways – couldn't see us sitting among the trees looking down on the street – then he kicked viciously at the row of bottles, sending them spinning everywhere. He banged his hands together and stamped on a few that he had broken, then charged off down the hill, preceded by a dozen or so that he had set rolling. Larry quite simply could not comprehend why he had done it. 'I don't understand why some people are violent,' he said.

Paul Francis, the only painter we knew who was halfway professional, was often in London or Cornwall, painting or on business. Whenever he was away, his pregnant wife Pat would stay with us at Hill Street. After the baby was born, we used to keep its nappies and milk in an orgone accumulator we had built in the art gallery. I was studying the works of Wilhelm Reich that I was able to get through the inter-library loan system from my local library. Only one of his books was in print in Britain, and one in the USA, where all the others had been burned six years before in the last official book-burning.

Larry and I got together enough money to have the local blacksmith build us a foot-square iron box with a round opening. This we surrounded with a thick layer of organic material – straw, twigs, leaves – held in place by cardboard. The final construction was quite ungainly and looked a mess. Once more there were complaints because it could be seen through the gallery window – we should have said it was art. We used it to conduct the temperature experiments that supposedly proved the existence of orgone energy, a measurable natural life force that is all around us, as outlined in the Wilhelm Reich–Albert Einstein correspondence. We also tried sitting with one hand in the box and the other out, held in a similar position for half an hour. It was hardly a scientific experiment, but the box did cause a tingling sensation and would open up the pores of the hand, making the skin feel smoother. If you did it for long enough, the hand developed a certain redness. A number of us experienced these phenomena, enough to suggest that Reich might be onto something, even if it wasn't the life force itself. In any case, we thought it would do no harm for the baby's nappies to be charged up.

Colin had a variety of girlfriends, including the sexiest girl in college. Everyone fancied Sally Hayward and she flirted outrageously. She had a huge rugby-playing boyfriend, who was exceedingly jealous and had vowed solemnly to do great damage to anyone who laid a finger on her. Colin decided to brave it and they had a good time together, but we were constantly worried that a gang of enormous rugby players would one day arrive and pulverise us. Despite this, Sally was very nice to have around.

It was inevitable that we would draw the attention of the local Teddy boys, who enjoyed throwing bricks through our windows. There was nothing for kids to do in Stroud: they left school and went to work in the pig factory or became policemen. On Saturday night they took on a bellyful of Courage ale and kicked the station-master's hat around the railway station or terrorised people at the coach station. But now they had beatniks to bait.

We nailed boards over the broken windows, but the next Saturday they attacked in full force wearing all their finery, drape jackets, suede shoes and bootlace ties. There was a skirmish in which the five of us inside tried to hold shut the front door, and about a dozen of them outside pushed it open. The door was broken off its hinges, a glass panel was broken and Colin's cheek was badly gashed. Pouring with blood and furious, he flung the door aside and screamed at them. They backed away at the sight of blood, but one of them was heard to mutter in a sinister voice, 'Scarred for life. Ha, ha, ha!' After threatening to come back and finish us all off, they departed, evidently pleased with their work. However, Colin had somehow acquired a First World War German Mauser, an ancient bolt-action rifle. We had no ammunition for it – nor did we want any – but the next time the Teds came round, Colin threw open the door and stood, holding it in his hands, his finger on the trigger. They turned and sauntered away, thinking they had finally pushed us too far.

We reported the assault to the police, and demanded protection. They did nothing, of course: the Teds were their brothers and cousins; they had all been to school together. However, the next time we had a party, they put four men in a police car in the car park across the street and had two more on the street. Though we felt more secure, this made us uneasy as by then we were conducting various chemical experiments. In fact, most of the drugs we were using were still sort-of legal: ephedrine, Benzedrine and the like were technical offences and we hadn't heard of LSD yet. We did have a little hash which, after much thought, we hid, well wrapped-up, in the cat's shit box. This was a pretty good hiding place because Monque never used it after it got too dirty, so there was no danger of it being accidentally dug up by her.

Monque had been named after Thelonious Sphere Monk, the great pianist, before we realised she was not a boy. When it got cold she took to sleeping in the hot ashes in the fireplace. This accounted for the curiously mangy, singed look she had. She soon gave up washing as well, but I took her in hand, gave her a bath and allowed her to creep down to the bottom of my bed each night.

We hadn't paid the rent. We had three eviction parties, one each week, until we were thrown out. The first was the biggest we'd ever thrown. A huge London contingent came and there were live musicians: John Keen's jazz band and other local trad men, including Squeak Brampton, the clarinettist, who used to keep a separate pair of false teeth in his clarinet case to use for playing: 'So's not to wear my good ones out.' He was a great player.

At midnight the booze was getting rather low, but the party was still in full swing. Suddenly a large party of Dickensian-looking Teds burst in. Our hearts sank, but they were in the kitchen before we could do anything. Their leader, a huge Ted in a purple drape jacket, absurdly pointed two-tone shoes and a bootlace tie, his hair immaculately coiffured into an intricate duck's arse, took charge. 'Right,' he said. 'Is dis where the party is?'

We assured him it was. Since it was happening all around him it would have been difficult to deny it.

'Right,' he repeated. 'We'll need some booze, won't we?'

'It's past closing time,' I ventured.

He dismissed this remark with the scorn it deserved. 'Do you know who I am?'

I didn't, but I didn't know how to break it to him, and fortunately he continued before I had time to reply.

'I'm the Undertaker! I've held parties in hay ricks, in barns, and last weekend I had one down the caves.'

'Oh, that was you, was it?' I said. I'd read about it in the local paper. The police had made the mistake of trying to close it down, resulting in a pitched battle.

The Undertaker produced a huge wad of money and counted off about £20, which he gave to someone called the Ferret who was wearing a yellow drape with a black velvet collar. The Ferret was dispatched for crates of beer from some late-night connection they both knew. 'This is gonna be some party,' said the Undertaker, beaming. 'I don't usually like beatniks, but I can see that you're really artists and that's different.'

We smiled back happily in agreement, assuring him that there was a world of difference.

He continued, 'I like a nice picture. Not this modern rubbish though,' looking at one of Larry's paintings on the wall, 'but I don't argue about it because it don't make sense, so it's a waste of my time.' We were having quite a conversation. He went on, 'I quite like you guys. In fact, I won't ask for a contribution towards the beer. After all, your contribution is the place and it's not often we get invited to a party indoors.' I felt rather sorry for them, having to party outdoors in all weathers. They produced a great pile of excellent rock 'n' roll records from their car, drank the beer and did a curious hopping country version of the jive until the early hours, without causing any trouble and without even going upstairs.

Meanwhile the weather grew colder and my aunt gave me £5 for some coal as the place was freezing. After much pressure from Larry I gave in to his suggestion that it would be a much better use of the money to buy a piano, which we did. It was an old upright that we put in the living room next to the window. Each day Larry practised J. S. Bach's *The Well-tempered Clavier* until we all knew the pieces by heart. It was wonderful to draw or paint in my room with the sounds of Bach drifting up from the room below. Instead of coal, we stripped the pine panels from the walls and burned them. Eventually we put one end of a house-beam that served as seating into the fireplace and slowly burned our way through it, all standing up to move it along a bit every few hours.

Snow blocked the shortcut through the park to the college and the water pipes in the house froze solid, then burst. We flattened the outdoor pipes that led to them, but our tight-lipped neighbour repaired them as we had cut off his water supply as well as ours. We cut away a section of pipe and flattened both ends, but he joined them again with the aid of a length of rubber hose. The local council refused to help because we had still not paid the rent and should already have moved out. Soon the kitchen was eight inches deep in water. It never rose much higher because it overflowed into the basement that led off the kitchen, running down the stairs and into an open gutter that ran through the old stone room and presumably entered a medieval drainage system somewhere outside. We used the wheels from Colin's Fiat as duckboards and abandoned the room except to cook. The damp froze on the living-room flagstones. Things looked bad.

It was bitterly cold. Huge icicles hung from the broken kitchen guttering outside and touched the ground, turning into ice columns as thick as small trees. My time-keeping at art college improved; it was warm there if you positioned your easel near a radiator. Poor Jenny the model had goosebumps, however. A two-bar electric fire arranged on the model's dais warmed her feet and legs while the rest of her froze. The art college closed for Christmas. There was one last college event that everyone attended, the legendary Art School Dance. I was in charge of the students' union, such as it was, and had booked the Ramrods, a Shadows imitation group in tight matching outfits, featuring the young Brian Jones on alto saxophone in his days before the Rolling Stones. Their tortured beaten-up amps delivered a very basic rock 'n' roll message, but everyone was dancing. Brian's playing had a distinctly jazz flavour to it. The group broke up when the lead singer choked to death on a chip on his wedding night.

Despite being in danger of freezing to death, we did have a fine Christmas dinner: a turkey roasted in a hubcap from Colin's broken-down Fiat, with all the trimmings. Larry cooked all the traditional American things like sweet potatoes, cranberry sauce and apple sauce – he must have received them from his parents in Cheltenham. We had bacon and roast potatoes. It was wonderful. The electricity ran out in the middle of it, but we finally found another shilling for the meter. We got to the pub just in time to buy cider before it closed. We had been going to bed later and later ever since college shut for the holidays. Eventually we were getting up at about 6 pm and staying up all night painting, drawing, sketching each other and talking and talking. Our meal was eaten at 2.30 in the morning.

In the New Year, people began to move out. Larry and Ruth moved to London, Don moved back to Cheltenham, Pete returned to Reading. Colin and I realised that this phase of our lives was over. Colin rented an ancient mill house in Kingly Bottom that was heavily propped up to stop it falling into the mill-race. He shared the house with an unspeakable ginger cat named Simon, which never washed its arse and was always trying to back into you. To get to Colin's you walked down a narrow valley and over some very rickety footbridges, green with lichen. At the bottom everything was dripping and damp and the mill appeared to be sinking slowly into the moist earth.

Toadsmoor Valley

In January 1961 I moved into Ron and Crystal Ludlow's cottage in the Toadsmoor Valley. Ron was away and Crystal wanted company. The cottage had no water, so you had to walk down to the spring to gather it, and we soon found that it was easier to brush your teeth and wash at the spring itself than carry water back up the hill. There was electricity, but something was wrong with the wiring, causing the stove and the whole flower garden outside the kitchen to be live. Crystal had to wear a huge pair of rubber wellingtons in order to cook without getting a shock, and after a few fur-raising incidents, Monque stopped using the flower garden to shit in.

Soon Pete Simpson came back from Reading and moved in, closely followed by Larry, who immediately carved Easter Island heads from the lumps of oolitic limestone that littered the hillside and lined the path up to the cottage, which we had now renamed 'Orgonon' in honour of Reich. Colin came to visit and the party continued. Ron was living in London at the time, but eventually he found out that we were living in his cottage. He had no objections to us being there and wrote to me, 'I understand that you and Peter are staying on at the cottage. Fine. You will understand that I have no objection to what you do on moral grounds or on any other

23

grounds come to that. BUT, Miles, you must be careful about the key. And for Christ's sake don't leave that door open because those little bastards from the farm and the village will be up in a shot.'

The rent was ten shillings a week and Ron was hoping we would all make a contribution. I don't recall that we ever did. There were some wonderful all-night talks, often culminating in a walk through the woods to watch the sun rise at a little pool near the head of the valley. We would all take sketchbooks and on a few occasions I tried to capture the changing light on the water as the colours brightened with the daylight. Orgonon was not a very satisfactory arrangement, however, because there was essentially only one room up and one down. There were a number of bedroom cubicles, but the thin wooden walls were only eight feet high and the rest of the room was open, giving no privacy at all.

At art college the year opened with the art students gathering in the basement each lunchtime by the counter where weak coffee and soggy egg baps were sold, to dance the twist to Chubby Checker's 'The Twist' and 'Let's Twist Again'; Sam Cooke's 'Twistin' the Night Away'; and 'Peppermint Twist' by Joey Dee and the Starlights. This wasn't really my kind of music, but you couldn't twist to Thelonious Monk, plunking his way through a deconstructed version of 'Tea for Two' on solo piano.

New Departures

Sue Norman was in the painting class at art college. She had been a model and had even appeared on the cover of *Vogue*, but gave it all up to study art. In addition to being beautiful, intelligent and glamorous, she had a car, a Mini-Minor, which immediately widened the horizons as far as parties were concerned. Thanks to her we were now able to range as far afield as Berkeley or Gloucester, and to show up – usually uninvited – at events held at country cottages deep in the woods, though when they saw Sue we were assured of a welcome. It was Sue who moved my trunk of books from Hill Street to the cottage in the Toadsmoor Valley. She became a good friend.

I was already friendly with Sue's ex-boyfriend, Fred Young, or Nigelfred Young as he was sometimes known, who was once more courting her, wanting the relationship to start over again. He had always come to our parties at Hill Street, but now I became more involved with his life in Oxford, where he was heavily involved in the Campaign for Nuclear Disarmament. He invited me to all the CND demonstrations, marches and parties, and I frequently spent the night on the floor of his room at 4a St Clements, just over the Magdalen Bridge. Fred looked rather like Oliver Reed, with a large round chin, an over-large smile and black hair brushed forward in the French manner. He often wore shades or thick black-framed glasses and clearly modelled himself upon Zbigniew Cybulski in *Ashes and Diamonds*, as did many of his friends.

The whole of 4a St Clements was filled with students, and may have been a squat. Staying at Fred Young's place, I quickly got to know Paul Pond, who also lived at 4a. He later changed his name to Paul Jones and became the lead singer with Manfred Mann, but then he was crooning to an electronic music backing and doing other experimental things. As well as being extremely knowledge-able about blues singers, he enjoyed the latest avant-garde poetry and had already assembled a large library of small-press books. I was there one evening when he came storming into Fred's room, clearly upset: 'I say, man, d'you know who's got my copy of *& I dreamt I shot arrows in my amazon bra*?' (a rare Piero Heliczer title). He recognised the importance of little literary magazines and made a point of assembling runs while they were still available. He even had a set of *POTH (Poor Old Tired Horse)* magazine in the days before its editor, Ian Hamilton Finlay, went into concrete poetry; it was a notoriously hard magazine to find even then. Paul had a definite awareness that the current literary scene was of the greatest importance, and communicated his excitement to his friends. Oxford was probably the best place in Britain to find the new books and magazines. I was amazed to discover that Blackwell's even stocked *Big Table* magazine.

It was in Oxford, in the autumn of 1960, that I first met the poets Michael Horovitz and Pete Brown. Michael read literature at Oxford, and then, realising he didn't want to be a teacher or a critic, continued with a postgraduate thesis on the influence of Blake on Joyce and published an article on 'The Blake Renaissance'. Just as he was making something of a name for himself in this area, Horovitz 'suddenly felt Blake saying, "Never mind my renaissance, what about your own?" . . . I departed from academia, and the kind of pre-ordained lines that had been laid down, and got in touch with writers such as Beckett and Burroughs and Ginsberg, who I admired, and gradually re-entered the land of the living.' Michael went to Paris, where William Burroughs and Gregory Corso were living at the Beat Hotel, and assembled the material for the first issue of *New Departures* magazine, which he published in Oxford in 1959. It featured work by Burroughs and Samuel Beckett, as well as Cornelius Cardew and Kurt Schwitters. Shortly after I met Michael, the second issue appeared with work by Allen Ginsberg, Gregory Corso, Jack Kerouac, John Cage and Raymond Queneau. As far as I could see, this was easily the most interesting magazine in Britain.

Michael affected a permanent stoop from which he looked up like an amiable tortoise. He had a long thin face with a wonderful horsey grin, and the slow, languid, exaggerated Oxford accent that only his generation seems to possess. Through him I discovered the true dimensions of the world of literature I had stumbled upon. He showed me how it all fitted together, John Cage's experiments with random sound, with William Burroughs' experiments with cut-ups. He put me in touch with poets in Liverpool and Edinburgh and Newcastle, suggested books to read and plays to see. He taught me a huge amount.

Mike's partner in crime was fellow poet Pete Brown. I assumed that they had been working together for a long time from their easy familiarity, but they had only recently met in a field at the August 1960 Beaulieu Jazz Festival. They had gone from there to put on readings at the Edinburgh Festival Fringe. I was very impressed because Pete had had his poems published in *Evergreen Review*. This magazine, the house organ of Grove Press in New York, was filled each month with the work of Ginsberg, Burroughs, Beckett, and all the Beat Generation luminaries. That someone in England should appear in its pages – moreover someone I knew – seemed remarkable. Whereas Mike was thin and stooped, the urban intellectual, Pete was solid like a brown bear or a hearty woodcutter, rounded but not chubby. He was very friendly and often let me stay on his floor. He took rooms here and there in a number of buildings in North London, never seeming to stay anywhere for long. Once, when we were both starving, he took me to his parents' home on Hendon Way, where a sullen overweight housekeeper made us endless kosher hot dogs and Pete showed me his collection of rare 78s by tenor saxman Chu Berry, and his father's collapsible silk top hat.

Pete sometimes stayed in a house on Regent's Park Road. The whole building was filled with artists and poets and little-magazine editors (this was the era of the little magazines, usually mimeographed, which provided the only outlets for experimental writing in the UK). Pete explained how they were able to have a telephone there. You had a phone line installed under a false name, then when the bill arrived – which was usually enormous, because many of the poets were Americans and liked to call home – the telephone was thrown into the Regent's Canal. The main junction was carefully unscrewed, the lines taken out and the top replaced. No trace of the phone remained. Meanwhile, someone in the next room was having a phone line installed, and the same process happened over again.

I liked the building, which reminded me of Hill Street only on a much grander scale. When they had a party at Regent's Park Road it was a serious affair. At one party there were gunshots and Pete fell the full length of the staircase without damaging himself. The drug of choice was Benzedrine, which obviated the necessity to find somewhere to sleep.

Michael and Pete believed very much that poetry should be performed live, and hitch-hiked all round Britain, giving readings in colleges, pubs, art galleries and jazz festivals, often augmented by jazz, experimental music, short plays or an on-the-spot Abstract Expressionist painting. I first saw them at the Bear Lane Gallery in Oxford, and from then on, whenever a *Live New Departures* event was scheduled within easy hitching distance, I tried to attend. Every two weeks or so I shouldered my sleeping bag and hitch-hiked to Oxford or London up the A40. There were no motorways yet and I was usually able to find a lorry driver who fancied a chat to relieve the boredom. Once Paul Francis and I were picked up by a Rolls-Royce; the chauffeur was transporting a bootful of logs to town from

27

a country mansion and felt sorry for us. We sat in splendour in the back as he complained about the 'idle rich'. Though we originally intended to go to Oxford, it seemed too good a chance to pass up and we went all the way to London with him.

In addition to 4a St Clements, where many of my friends lived, I got to know people in the colleges whom I could stay with if 4a was overcrowded. The colleges were closed at night, of course, but I soon became adept at climbing over the wall to spend the night in someone's room. At Magdalen, the Dean left his bicycle chained to the lamp post on the street outside so that people could use it to climb the wall and down over the bicycle sheds on the other side without waking him with their antics. I spent hours in book-lined rooms, talking with young men who sat around smoking pipes, making tea and wearing carpet slippers, and they were only twenty years old.

Not all the poets I met were avant-garde. There was Locker Madden, a student at Magdalen, who claimed to be related to Tennyson. He wrote in much the same way as his ancestor and affected the manner of a great poet, with a red kerchief and a silver-topped cane. Going for a drink with him could be a hazardous experience because he was always looking for an audience. Seeing a group of men from the Metal Box Company gathered to enjoy a few pints of beer after work, he would approach them and pipe up: 'I say, d'you know the *Morte d' Arthur*?' And, finding them ignorant of such a masterpiece, he felt compelled to recite it to them from memory. Given the slightest encouragement – they sometimes found him amusing – he would then produce the manuscript volume of his own verse that he carried everywhere and would read them some of his own rhyming couplets. There was always the danger of this type of encounter going wrong, and several of Locker's friends advised me to position myself near the door whenever he embarked upon one of these encounters. He was active in CND, as were many of the students I knew, and he and I went on a number of marches together.

Money was a perennial problem, so when Colin was offered a job by his friend Ken Smith, a scrap-metal dealer/builder, he suggested that I might come along. Ken had bought an estate of American-built prefabricated bungalows, surplus to American Air Force needs, for something like £20 each, and he intended to reconstruct them as housing for labourers on a large building site in Newport, South Wales. The bungalows would be put together as H-blocks, with a central section of bathrooms, shower rooms and a kitchen connecting two long corridors of bedrooms. The houses were superb; it seemed like vandalism to tear them down when so many people in Britain still lived in squalor. We took off the roofs, carefully disconnected the walls and lifted the floor units, which were made of hardwood boards. All the beautiful bathroom fittings had to be smashed to get the floors out. I thought of my aunt in Cheltenham, with her outdoor lavatory and lack of bath or washbasin, and of all the other old people living in similar conditions.

At the building site, where 17,000 Irishmen were constructing a steel works, we first laid foundations. These were rows of railway sleepers, which Ken had also bought cheaply from somewhere. Onto these the prefabricated sections of the bungalows were reassembled according to a set of architect's plans. Colin and I could just about carry one railway sleeper between us, whereas some of the Irish labourers working on the building were capable of carrying two at once. At the end of the second day, two of the labourers came to us with a deal. We were obviously 'gentlemen who could read the plans'. We were all on piecework, paid by the yard of housing block erected, but they had to wait around for someone to tell them the next thing to do. They proposed we get a sub-contract from Ken and employ the two of them to work for us. Together we made a good team, the plans were easy to figure out and we doubled our earnings. I could work quickly on the lighter work, such as nailing tar paper onto the roof, and marking out things in advance.

It was very hot. The building site stretched for miles on landfill of red shale, with no plants or shrubs in sight. In the distance, about a mile away, the cooling towers could be seen rising. There was a daily newspaper called the *Newport Irishman*, and an Irish priest wearing a hard hat rode around the site in a jeep with flashing lights, ready to give the last rites to anyone unfortunate enough to be blown off the scaffolding, something that happened about once a week. In the evenings we would go to the pub, another temporary building, one of many, with room for hundreds of drinkers, its floor awash with beer. I once made the mistake of innocently asking one of our drinking companions how long he'd been working in England. 'Twenty fucking years!' he spat, and stamped off. On payday, trucks would arrive from London, and East End conmen would sell vastly overpriced suits to the men. I managed about ten days. I was not used to this type of hard physical labour and was just not up to it. However, I made £38: enough to last me the summer. Colin stayed on while I headed up the A40 to London.

One place in London where one could always crash out, but which was usually already full of sleeping bodies, was Verina Johnson's flat on West End Lane in West Hampstead. Bunk, as she was known, was a wonderfully generous woman, and the Cheltenham gang tended to all be at her place at weekends. Bunk sensibly kept her own room out of bounds, but the other two bedrooms were first-come first-served. There was a piano there, upon which Larry Lewis once played a four-hour improvisation, and it was possible to listen out of the kitchen window to the marvellous sounds of Dick Heckstall-Smith and friends playing next door at Klook's Kleek. The toilet was downstairs off the stairwell, a common occurrence in flats in those days. The kitchen was where everyone gathered, and on the wall Graham Keen made a collage of images taken from the new Sunday newspaper colour supplements. We all picked up on his idea and the same images could be seen juxtaposed in different ways in a number of flats from the Cotswolds to London. I loved to lie in bed, with the neon sign of the ground-floor Italian restaurant lighting up the window frame, listening to the sounds of the city: the constant traffic on West End Lane, the car horns and the Metropolitan Line trains heading north from Baker Street. There was never any question but that my next move was to London.

Hoppy

In my early days at art school I never knew where I would spend the night when I hitch-hiked to London. I always had my sleeping bag with me and often finished up on a friend's floor or curled up in the corner as a late-night party raged. I met Hoppy, John Hopkins, through friends in Cheltenham and he generously suggested that there was always room at his place. From then on, every two or three weeks for the next couple of years, I would hitch to town and head straight for flat three, 105 Westbourne Terrace.

Hoppy's flat occupied the whole first floor of a large converted Regency row-house half a block from Paddington Station. Hoppy had the largest of the two front rooms, which both had access to a long balcony, overlooking the service road and trees of the terrace. He lived there with Gala Mitchell, a model who was still a teenager at that time; Hoppy met her when she was seventeen. They had a tempestuous relationship, and Gala rarely emerged from the room. I learned a lot from studying Hoppy's room: his filing system for negatives and boxes of prints, his methodical, scientific approach to his papers. He had studied science at Cambridge and worked for the Atomic Energy Research Establishment (AERE), first at Harwell, then at Winfrith Heath, down in Dorset. He left after going on a trip to Moscow with Colin Parker and a number of other friends of mine in a 1930 yellow hearse with a CND sign on the back. (I didn't go because I couldn't raise £12, which would have been my share of the cost, or get a passport; my father refused to sign the papers. The others were older and had savings or jobs, and had already travelled abroad.) When they returned, Hoppy found himself on the front page of the *Daily Mirror* – 'Atomic Scientist Propositioned' – which resulted in a five-hour security grilling somewhere in Whitehall, ending with them telling him, 'If you ever go anywhere abroad again, do let us know.' To which he replied, 'If I ever hear from you again I'm going straight to the *Daily Mirror*.' As Hoppy put it, 'I thought a change of occupation was in my own best interests. Anyway, the social life was marginal and my girlfriend at the time, Nicole Lepsky, was at Oxford.'

The other front room at Westbourne Terrace was occupied by Alan Beckett, always known as Beckett, a motivational research analyst whose greatest interest was jazz. There was one other large room leading off the hallway, lived in by Peter Wollen, who had recently returned from a year teaching in Tehran. Peter was studying film, and his marked-up copy of *What's On in London* usually had three-quarters of the films listed scratched through, meaning that he had seen them. Anything of the slightest interest would take him to far-flung suburbs as he methodically absorbed the complete works of director after director. He was also reading Freud, and I remember being amused as Beckett's face fell visibly when Peter, having finished the final volume of the Standard Edition of Freud's works, turned to him and asked, 'Now, man, tell me what *you* think Freud means by transference.' Beckett's degree was in psychology, but he had forgotten most of it.

A staircase led from the hallway up to a bathroom and another smaller bedroom. During the years I hitched to London this was variously occupied by Adam Ritchie, John Howe, Alexandra Weston Webb and Larry Lewis. The telephone was on a small shelf attached to the banister at the foot of the stairs and everyone was particularly pleased with the phone number: PAD 6876, further proof that it was indeed a 'cool pad'. For some reason, largely to do with Hoppy and Gala's relationship, the receiver was often broken, smashed to pieces with its innards arranged along the shelf, although it still worked, the relevant pieces being held together with masking tape and rubber bands.

Another staircase led down to a small kitchen. The large hallway served as the living room and had a low table surrounded by several comfortable armchairs, as well as a long cushioned bench, which was where I unrolled my sleeping bag. This was also where the record player was, so it was the natural gathering place of an evening. As this was the main floor of the original house, the ceilings were very high, which was pleasant in the main rooms but made the hallway/living room oppressively high. Hoppy solved this problem by suspending an old double bedstead from the ceiling, its coiled springs breaking the space and providing a place for postcards and other items – if you could reach it. I came in one day to find Larry Lewis cowering in the corner, obviously terrified. 'There's someone here, man,' he whispered, 'I can hear them talking.' He visualised robbers or the police, but no one could be seen. He was correct about the voices, though, I could hear them myself and began to feel his anxiety. Hoppy arrived just after me and we all bravely investigated. It transpired that the bedstead was receiving police radio messages, like a crystal set, and Larry's paranoia was at least half justified.

Thanks to Hoppy I was now able to spend more time in London. Instead of Easter and summer jobs in Cheltenham, I could work in the capital. Ron Ludlow had a job in the garden-furniture department at Harrods and suggested that I apply. I was given a job in the perfume department, working in the stockrooms and occasionally replenishing the shelves. My boss was a Mr Gay, who swished about the room, fussing with this and moving that. My biggest job was to fill the mail orders for face-cream. Each customer had a card, on which was typed the percentages of various ingredients in their prescription. There were only two, as I recall, or maybe three. I ladled some of the goop out of a huge tub and stuck it in a jar, then did the same with some other goop, in roughly the proportions indicated by the card. I gave a stir and stuck a Harrods label on it. Each jar cost more than my week's wages. I also put the powder puffs into their Harrods bags. The powder puffs appeared to me to be no different from those at Boots. They came in a huge sack and it was my job to put each one in a cellophane bag with 'Harrods' written on it.

The workers were not allowed into Harrods through the shop doors. We entered across the street, clocked in, and walked through the ceramic-tiled tunnel connecting the various Harrods buildings. There was a series of roadways beneath the store, down which West Indian porters drove forklifts and other trucks loaded with refrigerators and beds at breakneck speed. There was a staff canteen and, all told, it was a fairly easy life, with many opportunities for cigarette breaks in between unpacking industrial-sized crates of Elizabeth Arden and Helena Rubinstein cosmetics. I soon found where the West Indians gathered in one of the delivery bays, but friendly as they were, sadly no one passed me a joint.

American London

One weekend there was a CND demonstration in London and Mike Cooper knew of a party afterwards at Christie Johnson's basement flat in Cadogan Square. Christie's best friend was Sue Crane, and Sue and I quickly became good friends. She had long hair, wore cowboy boots and spoke with an American accent. Sue turned out to be British – the accent came from having attended Beverly Hills High, and after that the Dalton School in New York; her father, Lionel Crane, had been the Hollywood correspondent for the *Sunday Mirror*, and was then based at the *Mirror*'s New York bureau. He was the *Mirror*'s 'Man With a Passport to the World'. Sue was completing her final year in high school at the American School in London in Regent's Park. She grew up surrounded by stars: Jayne Mansfield washed the dishes after parties; she had met Elvis Presley and Marlon Brando on film sets; Zsa Zsa Gabor advised her to collect diamonds; and Elizabeth Taylor gave her a tiny Yorkshire terrier, which her mother still had in her London apartment. Despite all this, Sue herself had no interest in celebrities.

Her parents returned to the States that summer, leaving Sue in charge of their large apartment in Chiltern Court, above Baker Street underground station. A whole group of us promptly moved in. Sue and I holed up in her bedroom and the Cheltenham contingent – Graham Keen, Mike Cooper and Larry Lewis – had other rooms. Larry spent his time building a harpsichord on the living-room table. Unfortunately none of us noticed that he had neglected to protect its highly polished surface, and some of the deep scratches and gouges could not be disguised afterwards.

Christie often visited, and got very friendly with Graham. We sometimes went with her to visit her parents and sister Roxy. The Johnsons had two huge apartments on Grosvenor Square, next to the American embassy. Her father, Nunnally, was a well-known screenwriter and director. He made *The Man in the Grey Flannel Suit* with Gregory Peck, and wrote the screenplays for such classics as *Grapes of Wrath*, *The Dirty Dozen* and *The Three Faces of Eve*. He was Marilyn Monroe's favourite scriptwriter and wrote a number of her films, including *How to Marry a Millionaire*. Entering the apartment was like being transported to California. A huge kidney-shaped table dominated the living room, all the furniture, books, tableware, fabrics and curtains had been shipped from the States, and even the salt and pepper was American. Nunnally was only in Britain for tax purposes and didn't trust anything that was not made in the USA. Somehow he got all his food through the PX or the embassy. Nunnally had a whole apartment for himself to use as his office. He was very sedentary and at one point, after his doctor became insistent that he get more exercise, he had the toilet moved to the other end of the corridor so that he would have to walk further to take a piss. I enjoyed being there, leafing through the leather-bound volumes of his scripts, which filled several bookshelves. Nunnally himself was gruff and offhand, though not unfriendly. He always seemed vaguely surprised to find that he had two teenage daughters.

At the end of the summer Sue moved to Cheltenham with me, having applied, and been accepted for, a place at the art college. Her parents thought that she was sharing a flat with two other girls. In fact she and I had a cold draughty flat together on the top floor of a building in Pitville Crescent, with such a dilapidated roof that a pile of snow a foot high gathered in the corridor from the holes in the ceiling. The lower parts of the building had already been condemned by the council and boarded up, but it was apparently quite legal to continue renting the upper floors. We made it as cosy as possible and even managed to acquire a very out-of-focus black-and-white television on which to watch *That Was the Week That Was*.

Colin Parker lived a few doors down, in a slightly better abode, though it seemed to me that the whole of Cheltenham was falling down. It had been built in Regency times by speculative property developers who paid architects to design impressive façades, with columns and pediments, but the buildings behind the façades were made from the cheapest brick at as low a cost as possible. The buildings had reached their sell-by date and were literally falling apart.

Edinburgh High Society

Sue and I arrived in Edinburgh during the Easter 1963 college break, having arranged to stay with Adam Parker-Rhodes. He was a friend of Pete-the-Rat, whom I knew from Oxford, and although we had not met him, he had very kindly replied to my letter to say that we were welcome. Hitch-hiking to Edinburgh from Cheltenham took some time in the days before motorways and it was about 2 am when we arrived at 112 Nicolson Street. Rhodes didn't mind being woken up and insisted on vacating his bed for us. He was going down to London the next day, which was why we were able to use his place. The wind blew so powerfully under the door of his one-room tenement flat that the thin doormat actually flapped and shifted position and the room was viciously cold. In his letter he had told us, 'I can't stand things busted & flogged etc', and before we retired to bed he pointedly showed us where he was hiding his good coffee, saying, 'The last people who stayed here *stole it all*!' as if he actually wanted us to strip the place.

As he spoke he was rolling a small ball of opium between his fingers. He said he was experimenting with various solvents to see if one could get high from skin contact with the drug. He also showed us some before-and-after photographs of monkeys dosed with LSD, the subject of his thesis at the University of Edinburgh. He gave us the addresses of a few like-minded people to look up, and bedded down in the armchair for the night. When we woke up the next day he was gone.

Jim Haynes

Adam Parker-Rhodes told me that I would like Jim Haynes very much, and this proved to be true. It was an unusually bright and sunny day when we walked over to the Paperback, Jim's bookshop at 22a Charles Street. This was the first paperback bookstore in Europe, an idea taken from Lawrence Ferlinghetti's City Lights Bookstore in San Francisco, and ideally suited to a city filled with impoverished students. An extremely large, very battered rhino's head hung on the wall outside a small shop, which looked promising from what we could see through the window. However, despite the optimistic opening times posted on the door, the shop was closed. We explored the neighbourhood and when we got back Jim was in. He was tall, casual, with the faint drawl of the southern states. He was ten years older than me, from Haynesville, Louisiana, and had finished up in Scotland when the US Air Force posted him to their base at Kirknewton outside Edinburgh. Jim talked about books and writers and insisted that we visit the Traverse Theatre, which he also ran, where Alfred Jarry's *Ubu roi* was playing. We bought the New Directions edition of the book that he had in stock and that evening saw the show. The audience sat on bleachers on either side of a small stage and, in the role of the entire Polish army, threw balls of cotton wool at each other.

Afterwards we met the director, Jack Henry Moore, whom Jim clearly thought was a complete genius. I thought at first his extreme devotion indicated a sexual involvement, but apparently not. Jack was short and round, openly, campily gay at a time when it was unusual to be so. He had been a dancer in the *Fantasticks* in New York and had a fund of stories which he told with outrageous exaggeration in what I assumed to be an arch southern accent, rather how I imagined Tennessee Williams must have spoken. When Jim first met him he was running a private detective agency in Dublin. His enthusiasm was infectious and his bitchy put-downs hilarious. We got to know them both, and Jim introduced us to his friends, including his Swedish wife, Viveka, whom we met in his huge apartment on Grassmarket in the New Town.

I enjoyed hanging round the Paperback, which was more of a literary salon than a conventional bookshop. People dropped by for coffee and conversation as much as for the books. Jim ran the shop on a trust basis. If a customer looked as if they were going to be browsing for some time, he simply asked them to look after the store while he stepped out. Some people got fed up with waiting for him to return and went on their way, leaving the shop unattended. Others hung on, frantic, arriving late for appointments because they were worried that the shop would be robbed if left with no one in charge. Jim did the same to us. Almost as soon as we walked in, he was off and we didn't see him for an hour.

In an effort to repay Jim's kindness, we offered to do a stock-take for him – something he had apparently never heard of. The store had been open since 1959 and, going through the boxes of books in the basement, I found that many of the invoices were still in them. When I showed a pile of Penguin invoices to Jim, he was shocked. He hadn't realised that was what they were. He'd seen the column of titles and thought they were packing lists. I must say it didn't seem to worry him.

A distressed young woman arrived at the door of Parker-Rhodes' apartment looking for somewhere to hide from the police. Her parents had obtained a court order to stop her from living with her boyfriend, but she had run away. It was through Ash, as she was called, that we met the occupants of Society Buildings. This was a 300-year-old tenement block that had long ago been taken over by squatters. There were a number of them in residence, but the ones we got to know were Red, Robin-the-Poacher, the Rubber Man and Limpy. There was also a dog called Wizard.

Red was a full-blown Scots baron and celebrated the fact by wearing the complete Highland rig: a clan kilt, a sporran, tartan sash, shoes with shining buckles and a dirk in each sock. He got his name from the ferocious red beard and moustache and the thicket of red hair that gave him the appearance of looking out from a burning bush. The second time I stopped by he was busy chopping up tripe with his claymore. 'Och, I'm sorry, Miles,' he said. 'but we only ha' just enough for us.' I looked at the seething mass of cow's stomach and was pleased that I had already eaten. A claymore is a rather unwieldy instrument for kitchen work, being a large two-edged broadsword, designed to cut people in half in battle. The floor was littered with plaster dust from the impact of the claymore on the ceiling, caused when Red swung it over his head to chop the tripe. Judging by the rather large hole in the plaster and the missing laths, I assumed that this was a regular occurrence. Everybody had sensibly removed themselves from the kitchen, since Red was regarded as a danger to other people, and probably to himself.

'I dinna know why he'll na' use the wee dirk instead,' moaned Ash. 'He'll use nothing but his claymooore!' She was small, slight and very young. She was busy separating out the seeds from a large pile of very twiggy grass on a tea-tray with a picture of Edinburgh Castle on it. She normally lived in Society Buildings with Robin-the-Poacher.

Robin was tall and thin, and wore his hair long, lank and in unwashed strands down his back. He used an Indian blanket as a jacket and the ends trailed on the ground behind him. His two great loves were hunting and getting stoned. He boasted to me that he had once hitch-hiked to London in only two days. Since this trip normally took about eight hours, I concluded that it was probably the double-barrelled shotgun that he carried over his shoulder that inhibited people from giving him rides. The gun was quite legal; he had a licence for it, which he needed since the police stopped him constantly when he was on the road.

He had been caught poaching on a number of royal game reserves, but such was his knowledge of the countryside and of animals that they had all asked him to come and work for them. He had even been offered a job as a gamekeeper at Balmoral, the Queen's Scottish residence, but he thought this would have tied him down. He wouldn't have been able to go hunting in the Highlands with Red.

He and Red, armed with various guns and swords, liked to go pig-sticking in the remote Highlands of the north. Having found a wild boar, they would provoke it until it turned and charged them. Pigs are not known for their eyesight and cannot see a spear if it is pointed straight at them. The pig runs straight up the spear – and there you have it. There is a small crossbar to stop it from running all the way up and biting your hand before dying. They would load their catch into Red's ancient Rolls-Royce and drive down to Edinburgh. Back in Society Buildings, they used every scrap of the animal, tanning its skin for leather and even feeding its blood to the dog, Wizard. (I'm now told there were no wild boar left in Scotland, so quite what they caught I don't know, perhaps some domestic pigs that had escaped and gone wild.)

Limpy had a gammy leg, which he dragged behind him like a character out of Dickens. He wore a long black cape and was incoherent on drugs for most of the time. The others made sure, however, that he straightened up when it was time to work what was known as the Glasgow Traders con. They would study the commercial columns of the local newspaper until they found details of freighters arriving from promising places. The sailors would all come tumbling ashore on twenty-four or forty-eight hours' leave and immediately try to sell whatever drugs they had smuggled in with them. By mutual agreement, all the local dealers and dopers near the docks would decline to buy any of them. Eventually it would be only a matter of an hour or two before the sailors were due back on board and they would get desperate. This was when Limpy and the boys would come shuffling out of the shadows with the most ludicrous offers you ever heard, but the sailors would have no choice, since they didn't want to take the risk of bringing drugs ashore again in some other port.

I was shown the previous week's haul. It included four tins of raw opium and a variety of blocks of hash, most with the official Lebanese government stamp on them. They would sell most of it and keep the best for themselves. This was where the Rubber Man came in. Though they were all experienced dopers, the Rubber Man *really* knew his stuff. He was reportedly an earl, but no one knew for sure and he wasn't saying. He certainly had a fine Etonian accent that he could not disguise and, like most of the others, was probably the black sheep of his family. He knew what to buy and where to sell it, and as such was invaluable to the community.

He was called the Rubber Man because of his propensity for smoking dope through very long lengths of rubber tubing. Since he never knew when he might fancy a joint or two, he took to carrying the tubing with him wherever he went. As it was rather bulky, he found it necessary to wrap it round his middle, a solution to the problem that made him look rather like Bibendum, the Michelin man. He would fold a number of rolling papers into a chillum-shaped joint, stuff it in the end of his tube and light up. As everybody watched in delight, he would pull and suck on the rubber tubing until, quite suddenly, the joint would burn down very quickly and there would be a short period where everyone waited expectantly as he emptied his lungs in anticipation, as the fumes span in circles around his waist. Then the dope would reach his mouth, and with eyes bulging, the Rubber Man would collapse coughing in a huge cloud of smoke. It was a curiously moving performance to watch.

The occupants of Society Buildings rarely went out, partly because they attracted such hostile looks from the good burghers of Edinburgh, and partly because they seldom had any money. They were so far outside the normal economy that they even made their own ink. Their favourite excursion was to the local museum, where they would gather in the costume department and admire the long hair on the eighteenth-century models. 'People dinna always ha' short hair,' Red told me. 'It's just a recent aberrrration!'

Their main occupation was to sit around and think up truly imaginative places to hide their stash. This was of vital importance since by their very looks they attracted an enormous amount of attention from the police. Not for them the lavatory cistern, though they did once seriously consider keeping the dope in the ballcock. On one occasion, while I was visiting, they were very pleased with themselves, having just thought of a foolproof hiding place: inside the oven door. If the police came, they would quickly turn on the oven. The hash would be thickly wrapped in silver foil so that it would not smell. Brilliant! Of course, they had hidden dope all over the building and by now had forgotten where several of the stashes were, so another frequent occupation was searching Society Buildings for drugs. When we returned to Edinburgh that summer we found that the council had demolished the building and most of the occupants had dispersed.

Jim had found us a place to stay in the village of Dean, the extraordinary little settlement built by French prisoners in the gorge cut by the waters of the Leith, just below Charlotte Square in the New Town, and within walking distance of everything. The village is a series of tenements, with a clocktower and a bridge over the river. We stayed in the flat of a BBC producer who was away for the summer. The floors were piled with books as he had not yet built shelves and I spent hours browsing through his New Directions editions of Henry Miller.

We had gone to Scotland to get married as Sue was still only seventeen and her parents had refused us permission. I can quite understand why. I had only met them a couple of times, briefly, and when I showed up to ask for her hand I had unfortunately not been to bed the night before and was looking rather the worse for wear, unshaven, sweaty and dishevelled. They tactfully suggested that we wait a year. In the early Sixties it was almost inconceivable that an unmarried couple should live together; the pretence of marriage was essential. Now that we were moving to London, and Sue was transferring from Gloucestershire College of Art to Goldsmiths, her parents naturally assumed that she would return to her old room in their enormous Baker Street flat. The only way we could live together was to marry.

My only memory of the ceremony was that one of the ex-Society Buildings people acted as a witness, but insisted on signing the register with a quill pen using handmade ink. We wrote Sue's parents a carefully reasoned letter, presenting our faits accomplis and hoping they would understand. The letter, unfortunately, was on the mail train that the Great Train Robbers held up, and it never reached them. They did understand, and were very magnanimous about it; in fact we stayed with them for a short period when we moved up to town.

Westbourne Terrace

That summer Peter Wollen took a flat with Laura Mulvey, so Sue and I were able to take his room at Hoppy's. I built my usual rickety shelves for the books, set up the hi-fi and a large table for painting and drawing. Hoppy gave me all his reject prints, so I did a series of photographic collages featuring whomever or whatever he had been shooting: the Beatles, the Stones, Harold Wilson, the mayor of Paddington, portfolio portraits of pretty models, the medina in Tangier.

It was wonderful having our own room at Hoppy's, which, though not a commune, often engaged in group activities. There was a period, beginning a little before we moved in, when Beckett or Peter Wollen would read aloud to a gathering of five or six stoned friends. I remember the reading of Flann O'Brien's 1939 classic *At Swim-Two-Birds*, the story of Finn Mac Cool, and how the descriptions of how to become one of Finn's people reduced the company to tears of laughter and coughing at virtually every paragraph: 'If he sink beneath a peat-swamp or lose a hog, he is not accepted by Finn's people. For five days he must sit on the brow of a cold hill with twelve-pointed stag-antlers hidden in his seat, without food or chessmen . . .'

Most evenings were spent listening to jazz in the hallway/living room. Beckett had been the chairman of the Liverpool Jazz Music Appreciation Society and many evenings were spent listening to Sonny Rollins, John Coltrane, Charles Mingus, Eric Dolphy or Thelonious Monk. Sometimes several of his jazz-critic friends would come over and a new release by Cecil Taylor or Gil Evans might be played ten times before they began to discuss its merits and more importantly, its faults. Beckett's 'sounds', as he called them, were the most important thing in his life. They were kept in a row on the floor of his room, arranged according to how much he valued them. Those most cared for were in the centre of the row, with less-prized albums ranging away from them. This was so that, in the event of the house catching fire, he would be able to grab an armful from the centre and make his escape, knowing that he was saving the most significant items in his collection. It was always interesting to see what held the coveted spot; over the years it included: *Free Jazz* by the Ornette Coleman Double Quartet, *Into The Hot* by Gil Evans, *Looking Ahead* by Cecil Taylor, *Out There* by Eric Dolphy, all the Impulse John Coltrane albums: *Africa Brass*, *My Favorite Things*, *Olé*, *Coltrane*, Mingus, of course, and lots of Thelonious Monk. There was little else in his room, save the mattress, which was inconveniently situated on the floor just inside the door, the place where it

landed when Hoppy threw it into the room while helping him to
move in. One day Hoppy and I thought we would do Beckett a
good turn, and moved the mattress over by the window, giving him
much more living space. Beckett came home from work, opened his
door and threw himself on the floor.

Beckett's moods were legendary. Occasionally he would poke his
grinning florid face around the door and enquire politely, 'Would
you mind staying in your room for the next twenty minutes, man?
I'm going to have a controlled release.' We would all retire to our
rooms while outside we could hear Beckett kicking the broom up
and down the stairs, howling and cursing. Then he would once
more knock on the door and announce, 'I'm all through now, man.
Thanks very much.'

In those days, before he became successful as a photographer,
Hoppy augmented his income by selling marijuana. As a generous
gesture to his flatmates he kept a large bowl on the living-room table
filled with pot. One day Beckett came in with an old friend from
Liverpool whom he had just run into on the street. They sat down
and began talking about the old days. Then Beckett asked, 'What do
you do now, man?'

'Oh, I'm a policeman,' said his old friend.

'Let's go and have a drink!' said Beckett, panic in his eyes.

When he returned later that evening he said that he had brought
the conversation round to drugs and asked if the police had any
special training in how to identify marijuana. His friend said, 'They
showed us a photograph of a pot plant and told us, if you see anyone
with one of these, bust them.'

Peter Wollen still lived in the neighbourhood and would often
drop by. He was there on 22 November 1963 when one of his
relatives, who worked at the Foreign Office, called to tell him that
President Kennedy had been assassinated.

Another regular visitor to the flat was Priest, the leader of the
West London Rastafarians. He kept his dreadlocks safely hidden
inside a woolly hat and in every other respect looked quite
conventional. West Indians were continually stopped by the police
and he was not going to encourage them further. He would settle
himself into one of the armchairs and roll up a seven-paper spliff. He
often stayed for days, charming everyone with his conversation. He

expounded on the correct ritual for smoking pot: the joint should be passed to the left, unless the man on the left is wearing a hat, and so on. Presumably he ate and used the bathroom, but even if one came out in the middle of the night to piss he would still be there, sitting in the darkness, the room faintly illuminated by the glow from his huge spliff. Then he would suddenly say, 'Is that the time, mon? I mus' be goin'. People be expectin' me', and he would formally take his leave. He worked as a sometime hairdresser, but was famous for turning up a day late. One of his friends joked that dreadlocks were invented by people waiting for Priest to come and cut their hair. He lived by his own time.

It was through Priest that Hoppy got to take the official portrait of the London Rastafarian leadership. Larry Lewis painted their banner for them, but ran into difficulties looking for a picture of a lion as a model for the Lion of Judah. Then he found the Egg Marketing Board lion – a smiling cartoony lion with a little crown, which was stamped on every egg you bought. This he enlarged and painted on the banner. The leadership assembled beneath their banner with its jolly emblem, a number of symbolic objects before them including a large pile of ganja, 'Put on Earth by God for the Black Man', and an old-fashioned alarm clock with a bell on each side, 'To show the time when the white man will be driven out of Jah!' Hoppy had to turn over the negatives as well as the prints of these wonderful pictures.

I designed a cover for their magazine, *Teamwork: West Indian Affairs*, and Hoppy, Sue and I took it over to the Mangrove Restaurant for their approval. The pot smoke was so thick that you got high just from breathing, and virtually everyone in the place had an opinion, which they took considerable time to air with much scrutiny of the artwork from different distances and discussion of proposed colours. Then fried plaintains, pork, beans and red wine were produced and I had my first taste of soul food. Very good it was too.

When we first moved to London, in 1963, I took a summer job in a typing pool, then for the next year I attended the University of London Institute of Education, with the vague idea of becoming a teacher if nothing else worked out. I was still on a grant, so I could live and pay the rent. The University Senate House is next door to the British Museum, and I was able to spend some time studying in the museum library. When I ordered up a set of back issues of the *Continental Film Review* to read some articles by Antony Balch, I had to sit in the front-row seats of the North Library, where all the researchers into sexual perversion sat, in case I tore pages out or jerked off because the magazine published stills from 'Continental' movies. A stern-looking lady librarian glared at us from her desk in the front.

A Taste of Soho

I had always cherished shops like Pete Russell's Gallery Bookshop on D'Arblay Street, Soho, where one could pick up both Ezra Pound's weird pamphlets on economics and a copy of *The Naked Lunch* by William Burroughs. In those days the latter was an under-the-counter item, since British customs confiscated all Olympia Press books as a matter of routine.

When I was an art student I had always made a point of visiting Better Books on Charing Cross Road every time I hitched up to London. It was the only place that stocked City Lights and Grove Press books, and always had the latest issue of *Evergreen Review* in stock. Adam Ritchie, who then lived at Hoppy's flat, worked there in the basement of the corner shop, which was where the paperbacks were kept until they expanded around the corner to numbers 3, 4 and 5 New Compton Street in 1964.

In the late Fifties, when I first visited Soho and the area to the north of Oxford Street, known these days as Fitzrovia, there were still echoes of the bohemia that had characterised it before the war. It was still possible to find someone propping up the bar at the French Pub or the Round House on Wardour Street who would begin a story with the line, 'When I was drinking with Dylan . . .' Quentin Crisp preened his long, wavy mauve-rinse hair in his corner seat at the French café on Old Compton Street, and once offered to buy me a cup of tea. At Jimmy's Greek restaurant the chef slouched in the doorway to the kitchen, puffing at a Capstan Full Strength under the 'No Smoking' sign, and you received a great wedge of bread with your meal; it had never occurred to me that a loaf could be cut any other way than in thin slices. Schmidt's on Charlotte Street retained the old European custom of the waiters buying the meals from the kitchen to sell to their diners, so the service was always attentive even if it was often slow and not always polite. On several occasions we witnessed terrible altercations among the staff: 'Hans, you haff been taking my dessert spoons, again!' as the hapless fellow's arm was pinioned behind his back and he was frogmarched into the kitchen, from which then came shrieks and bellows. The whole staff had been interned during the war, but their food was so good and cheap that their customers soon returned when they reopened.

The Partisan café on the dead-end bit of Carlisle Street off Soho Square was filled with bearded men playing chess; there was a short-lived craze for chess cafés in the late Fifties, presumably modelled on those in Greenwich Village. It was also an unofficial headquarters of CND and the large noticeboard just inside the door was covered with leaflets and flyers for demos, marches, poetry readings and benefits. Peggy Seeger was sometimes there with her guitar – she once showed my cousin Stuart the fingering of the claw-hammer pluck – and in the evenings folk singers sang of mining disasters of long ago, heads thrown back, one finger in the ear for better tone. The music was usually superior at Bunjie's Folk Cellar on the other side of Charing Cross Road, where I saw Sonny Terry and Brownie McGhee give an impromptu set on my very first visit.

I loved Soho, and still do. It was urban and sophisticated, yet run-down, shabby and without all the formal dressing up of Mayfair. To me it was the intellectual and cultural centre of London, with the Charing Cross Road bookshops, the jazz and pop clubs, the bohemian pubs and drinking clubs and its mix of race and cultures. It was the only place to work.

In the summer of 1964 I took a job at Joseph Poole's bookshop on Charing Cross Road, next door to Better Books. There was no Joseph Poole – the owner made up the name, thinking it sounded bookish. The used-book section in the basement was run by a young man called Paul, not much older than me, who had connections in

Soho. He spent much of his time fumbling with Sylvia, the boss's secretary, when she came downstairs to make the tea: 'You make me so confused . . . Now I can't go upstairs till I stop blushing.' He bought books from the public, from book runners and book thieves. The same thieves would return week after week carrying unopened copies of the works of Gurdjieff or Sartre: 'Oi'm disposin' of me library.'

I visited Paul at home a few times. He had a stuffed rhino in his room that he liked to sit on with one of his girlfriends and smoke a joint. There was enough room for four people, sitting one behind the other, though it made conversation rather awkward. Sometimes Paul would do an evening job as stage manager at the Phoenix strip club just across from the shop on Old Compton Street. The first time he mentioned the Phoenix, I thought he was referring to the Phoenix Theatre and imagined that he moved in theatrical circles. Much to Sue's amusement, I launched into a discussion of Harold Pinter's *Birthday Party*. I was soon set right.

His job was to get the girls on and off the stage and make sure no one from the audience jumped on them, which they never did. I went to see Paul at work a few times and was offered the job when he was indisposed. I decided against it; I was interested in the underside of Soho but did not want to get involved with the Maltese gangsters who ran it. The girls would arrive, do their act and disappear to the next club, appearing at six or seven each night. They were poorly paid, obviously had no security and almost inevitably finished up on the game. Some of them were alcoholics, but few took drugs. Most of them were friendly, poorly educated, working-class girls who made more money stripping than working at Woolworths. A number of them were single mothers and the other girls would sometimes look after the baby while its mother was on-stage, if she had not been able to find a sitter. One girl, Veronica, jumped to her death from the top-floor window of the club.

Better Books

Hoppy moved to a five-bedroom flat at 115 Queensway, and Sue and I decided to get a flat of our own. We moved to a small garret at 6 Gilbert Place, a half-block from the British Museum. The rent was only £2 a week, but the place had a major disadvantage, for there was no electricity. The entire street was gas-lit and none of the buildings had electricity yet. In the small yard at the back of the building, a sculptor worked on an enormous tree trunk, hacking away at it, trying to turn it into a nude torso, but the wood was not seasoned properly and seemed to develop new cracks each day. The sound of him thwacking away, with only the occasional muffled curse rising to the top floor where we lived, was quite restful as one sat reading by the window. That autumn Jim Haynes and Jack Henry Moore presented a season of plays from the Traverse Theatre at the Jeanetta Cochrane Theatre in London, on the corner of Theobald's Road and Kingsway. Jack came to stay with us in the windowless room that led off our bedroom, but he was stymied by not being able to use a tape recorder. At one point he tried to get us to act out a new play he had written, but Sue and I were so purposely bad at it that he never asked again. The lack of electricity was a major disadvantage at Gilbert Place and early in 1965 we moved again, to a big airy flat at 15 Hanson Street, near Broadcasting House, and were able to play records once more.

Working at Joseph Poole's, I was only two doors away from Better Books and spent all my spare time there, getting to know the owner and staff. The manager was Bill Butler, a tall American poet from Missoula, Montana. Everything about Bill was huge: even his fountain pen was fat like a torpedo and his handwriting was twice as big as mine. He had two large Alsatian dogs and lived with his boyfriend in a flat over the archway entering Gloucester Mews from Craven Road at the end of Westbourne Terrace. Sue and I sometimes visited him there; it was the first time I'd seen black silk sheets. Bill showed me his poems in *Beatitude*, the legendary mimeographed San Francisco Beat Generation poetry magazine, and I was suitably impressed, and by the letter from Allen Ginsberg he had pinned to his bedroom wall. Bill decided to move to Brighton for his boyfriend's health and started his own bookshop there, the Unicorn. In January 1965 I took over his job at Better Books as the manager of the paperback division.

Tony Godwin, the owner, was the editorial director of Penguin Books, the man who replaced the original orange covers with coloured graphics and photographs, to the outrage of founder Allen Lane (though he retained the orange spines and Penguin logo). Tony's ideas about bookshops were extremely utopian. He saw them as a kind of Research and Development division of the publishing industry. He hired Germano Facetti, the designer at Penguin Books, to create an environment where books 'floated in a silver mist'. The idea was that the shelves would be invisible and the books would seem to float in thin air. Facetti's brief had also been for the shelves, other than those against the wall, to be mobile so that they could be arranged to create different spaces. Accordingly he constructed huge free-standing double-sided shelf units made from expanded perforated steel, sprayed with silver paint, which, far from being invisible, were immense eyesores. Unfortunately he used the small Penguin format as his module, so anything much taller was damaged by the metal, as staff and customers tried to jam books in and the silver paint rubbed off, marking the top and bottom edges of the books with a black smudge that was impossible to remove.

The units were on castors so that they could all be rolled away to leave the rooms free for events, and every month or two one would topple over if a customer struggled too hard to remove a jammed book. In the far room there was a small stage for readings and a machine that dispensed undrinkable coffee, tea and hot soup, all made from powder – possibly the same powder – delivered through the same nozzle. We had chairs and wobbly wooden tables with uneven surfaces made from artistically arranged wooden shapes like bad Joe Tilson sculptures. On these, the customers balanced their tea or coffee which came in very thin leaky plastic cups that split down the sides if you gripped them at all firmly – while they browsed through the stock. The damage levels were enormous, as was the degree of theft. In the basement, Tony had thoughtfully provided a set of tables equipped with second-hand typewriters that visiting authors were encouraged to use if suddenly struck by the muse. The staff were not exactly keen on the idea of 'writers' roaming the basement unsupervised – particularly if the writer was Alexander Trocchi – as stock tended to disappear, and they discouraged the practice. Tony eventually concurred.

Better Books specialised in European design magazines, books on film, *Cahiers du Cinéma*, photography and the arts. The literature department imported American paperbacks, in particular those published by Grove Press, New Directions and Alan Swallow, and Tony had an arrangement with Lawrence Ferlinghetti's City Lights Bookstore in San Francisco, so that a complete line of City Lights publications was available in return for regular consignments of used Penguin paperbacks.

With Tony's blessing, I ordered Henry Miller's *Sexus* from the States in lots of 100, always keeping it in stock. It was a $1.25 retail book, which we sold for ten shillings. I took half of each consignment to a dirty bookshop a few doors away on Old Compton Street. It was run by Charles, a pallid-looking ex-military man with a ramrod backbone and small dyed moustache. At first he only took ten copies. 'Not much in there for arse-hole peepers, is there, I arsk you? Not much fladge.' But they quickly sold and he upped his order. He paid us £2 10s each and retailed them for a fiver. This way Miller fans could have the thrill of buying it as an expensive dirty book, or they could buy it from us as literature at the published price. Tony liked these kinds of deals because they helped pay for the difficult-to-sell American small-press books from Diane di Prima's Poets Press, the Auerhahn Press, Oyez, LeRoi Jones' Totem Press, White Rabbit, 'C' Press and the publications of Ed Sanders' notorious Fuck You Press, 'published at a secret location in the Lower East Side', that I imported.

I worked out a similar stock-swapping arrangement with Ed Sanders' Peace Eye Bookshop in New York as we had with Ferlinghetti, in which UK books were exchanged for small-press books and magazines. Naturally Sanders also gave the address of the shop to Americans planning to visit London; they were often surprised to find a better selection of underground literary magazines such as *C, Lines, Mother* and *Kulchur* than was available in most big American cities.

We also carried every British small-press pamphlet and mimeo magazine we could get. The editor of *Anarchy* complained because we sold so many copies. Each issue was printed at a loss, and the more we sold, the more deeply into debt he went.

Gustav Metzger, the auto-destructive artist and theoretician, used to come in regularly to see if we needed more copies of his single-sheet 'Destruction in Art Manifesto'. We usually bought a half dozen or so from the complete stock of thousands that he hauled around with him in a large plastic bag, ripped and rubbed from being dragged along the pavement. We never figured out why he did not just bring a few dozen with him when he did his rounds. Gustav had a gloomy expression, but sometimes you said something that caught his attention or imagination and his face would light up. When construction work was being done on the South Bank exhibition complex, Gustav staged one of his performances: he erected a series of huge sheets of plate glass and invited the construction workers to smash them. They were initially wary of this strange little man and the crowd of art critics and avant-garde enthusiasts who had gathered to watch the event, but they soon got into it, swinging away with sledgehammers at the same kind of glass they spent their days installing, venting their frustration and rage. Gustav's face had an enormous smile as he watched, rubbing his hands together in satisfaction.

We had regular poetry readings and events, many of which were organised by the concrete poet Bob Cobbing, who later took over as manager in 1966 when I left to start my own shop. Diana Rigg, then playing Emma Peel in *The Avengers* TV series, read the poetry of McGonagal to launch a new volume of his excruciating verse. She looked gorgeous and the shop was packed out with smooth-looking actors wearing cravats and chukka boots, as if they had just stepped out of the Chelsea Cobbler, all panting after her. Stevie Smith read from her latest book in a wonderfully matter-of-fact way. I particularly liked the line: 'I am Miles, I did not die!' Basil Bunting launched *Briggflatts* there, published by Stuart Montgomery's Ful-crum Press. 'The spuggies are fledged,' intoned Basil in his Geordie accent, peering in vain through his half-spectacles for young girls in the audience.

Though I have been accused of only ever promoting American poetry, Beat poetry in particular, this is not the case. I was always fascinated by the Surrealists and made a point of carrying copies of the Grove editions of André Breton's *Nadja* (also the name of our cat), Artaud's *Theatre of the Absurd*, the New Directions Lautréamont, and any books in that area, most of which had to be special-ordered or imported directly from the States. I very much liked Cocteau, having worn out two copies of *Opium* since grammar school, and we always stocked everything of his that was in print. We celebrated a new collection of Alfred Jarry's work with a reading and a window display of rare first editions surrounding a four-foot circular photograph of His Magnificence the Baron Jean Mollet, the head of the College of 'pataphysics, eating a cherry. This portrait revolved once an hour. For this and other 'pataphysical activity I was made a member of the college and I still hold the order of the Grand Gidouille (the spiral drawn on Père Ubu's stomach).

Allen Ginsberg

When Allen Ginsberg walked through the door of Better Books in June 1965, asking for me, I at once asked him to do a reading. I first encountered his work in 1959 when I sent away to City Lights Bookshop in San Francisco asking for a catalogue. I received a typewritten card, listing, among other things, Bob Kaufman's *Second April* and *Abomunist Manifesto*, Gregory Corso's *Bomb* and Allen Ginsberg's *Howl*. I had not heard of any of them, but I ordered them all on the strength of their titles alone, which all sounded great; the poetry taught at my grammar school stopped with Siegfried Sassoon. Of the four – three were just broadsides – *Howl and Other Poems* was the one that impressed me the most. It put into words all my ill-formed sixteen-year-old thoughts and feelings in a way that came as a complete revelation. Ginsberg expressed everything I was feeling, and he did it in a way that was totally new to me, so to actually meet him, six years later, was very exciting.

Though not advertised, Ginsberg's reading was so jammed that many people listened from the street through the open door. The audience included the singer Donovan, who earlier sat on the doorstep and sang 'Cocaine, cocaine, going round my brain' accompanied by his roadie Gypsy Dave. Andy Warhol came, accompanied by his assistant Gerard Malanga, and his new superstar Edie Sedgwick, who wore a white fur coat. The reading was taped by Ian Sommerville, William Burroughs' boyfriend, whom Allen Ginsberg already knew from Tangier. I knew Ian socially before Better Books, as he was a friend of Hoppy and various of my Oxford friends.

I had seen a lot of Ian that spring because he was my contact for the spoken-word album *Call Me Burroughs*, recorded by him in the basement *cave* of Gaït Frogé's Librairie Anglaise in Paris, which she pressed and released herself. Ian had brought Gaït to meet me and we got on well. I later learned that he had charged her £5 for the privilege. Inspired by *Call Me Burroughs*, I hired a Ferrograph and had Ian record Allen's reading. We released the album in a limited edition of ninety-nine copies. (100 copies or more would have attracted purchase tax, whereas books were tax-free. Tony Godwin did not want to get involved with the tax man.) It was called *Allen Ginsberg at Better Books* and Tony got Penguin's cover designer Alan Aldridge to do the sleeve.

Earlier that year, Ginsberg had visited Cuba for a conference, but he made himself unpopular with the authorities and was deported. Because of the American embargo of Cuba, they flew him to Czechoslovakia with an open-ended air ticket to New York. In Prague he got on so well with the young people that, during the May Day festival, 100,000 students elected him *Kral Majalis*, the King of May. After this the secret police 'accidentally' acquired one of his journal notebooks and were horrified to read an account of Allen having a thrilling time all by himself in his hotel room with a broom handle. Clearly the man was a dangerous pervert as well as a threat to the security of the state, and he was once again deported, this time to London.

He was made welcome by Tom Maschler, the editorial director of Jonathan Cape, whom Ginsberg had met in Cuba. But Allen grew tired of travelling in from Tom Maschler's house in Hampstead, which he described as 'like living in Queens', and moved in with Sue and me at Hanson Street, ten minutes' walk from Better Books and Soho. From then on Allen made Better Books his unofficial headquarters for appointments and interviews.

It was wonderful to have Allen stay. He sat in the big broken-down old armchair and talked for hours at a time, telling us stories about Jack Kerouac, Neal Cassady and William Burroughs and his recent adventures in Cuba, Poland, Russia and Czechoslovakia. Though still in his thirties, he already had his full Sixties guru look: long curling black hair and a full beard, which made him seem a venerable old bard and, as he was seventeen years older than my twenty-two, he seemed to me a very old person indeed. Allen had been to Britain before, on two brief visits in 1958, but he knew little about day-to-day English life and was interested in everything.

One curiosity that he had not previously encountered was the meters for electricity and gas: shillings and florins had to be fed in each day to get power and gas. When the man came to empty the gas meter, I let him in and went back to whatever I was doing. It was necessary to climb on a chair to reach the meter and I heard the man call out, 'Excuse me, sir, I'm finished now, *sir*!' in a high-pitched, rather hysterical manner. Allen was standing next to him in the hallway, wearing his wristwatch, socks and shoes, but otherwise stark naked, enquiring earnestly about the business of meter reading while the man remained balanced on the chair, trying not to look. He was clearly not going to come down as long as Allen had him inadvertently cornered. I manoeuvred Allen back into his room and the man shot out of the door without even saying goodbye.

It was Allen's thirty-ninth birthday on 3 June and a party was planned. It was organised by Barbara Rubin, Allen's sometime girlfriend – there are pictures of her fooling with Allen and Bob Dylan and a top hat on the back of *Bringing It All Back Home* – who also happened to be in London at the time. I had expected him to want to meet young poets or artists, but the first people he suggested we invite were the Beatles. They had first met in Dylan's suite at the Savoy a few days before. We sent amusing hand-drawn invites round to NEMS and hoped for the best. Barbara borrowed someone's basement flat and more invitations were sent out.

At the party Allen got completely drunk and stripped off his clothes, putting his baggy underpants on his head and hanging a hotel 'Do not disturb' notice round his cock. It was at this moment that two of the Beatles arrived: John with Cynthia, and George with Patti. John and George quickly checked that no photographers were present. Allen kissed John on the cheek, and John told him that he used to draw a magazine at art school called the *Daily Howl*; they were friendly enough and accepted drinks, but then made quickly for the door. I asked John why he was leaving so soon. 'You don't do that in front of the birds!' he hissed in my ear. However, the next year, hearing that Allen was in the audience at the Beatles concert at the Portland Coliseum on their 1966 American tour, John called out a greeting to him from the stage between numbers. Of course John himself was to appear naked on an album sleeve four years later. When *Two Virgins* came out, I couldn't resist reminding him of his meeting with Allen, and his revised attitude towards nudity. 'That wasn't my problem with Allen,' John snapped at me. 'The trouble with Allen was that he always got up real close, and touched you, and shouted in yer ear!' Then he laughed. Allen was always ahead of his time. By the end of the evening he was so drunk I had to wrap his arms round a lamp post in order to keep him upright while we looked for a taxi.

The next day Barbara was angry with Allen because he had not come to find her to tell her that John and George were there. She paced about our apartment shouting, ate all the food in the fridge and then departed. It was the habit of helping themselves to the contents of the refrigerator that most irritated English people about visiting Americans. No one could afford much food, and the shops kept peculiar hours. If someone drank all the milk, it would be hard to find any more because it was normally delivered by a milkman, and the few dairies around only opened in the mornings. People quickly developed a habit of leaning against the fridge door whenever Barbara or her friends came to visit.

World Declaration Hot Peace Shower

One afternoon Allen, Barbara, Sue and I were sitting around the rickety tables in Better Books discussing the success of Allen's reading in the shop. Allen informed us that Lawrence Ferlinghetti would be arriving in a few days, and that Gregory Corso was in Paris. He also knew that Andrei Voznesensky was about to arrive in Britain from Moscow, and proposed that they all get together for a big group reading. There had never been a large-scale Beat Generation reading in Europe, and the idea was too appealing to resist. Better Books was out of the question as a venue because it only held about fifty people. Several other places were proposed, then Barbara Rubin demanded, 'What's the biggest joint in town?'

Sue understood it to be the Royal Albert Hall. Barbara strode through to the cash desk, grabbed the phone and returned a few minutes later, having booked the hall for ten days' time. The rent was £400. I was then earning £13 a week – the idea was terrifying. It needed American chutzpah and knowhow to think that big.

Another person sitting at the table with us was Dan Richter, an American poet with a bushy moustache who had recently published the first issue of *Residu* magazine from Athens, where he and his English wife Jill had been living. They were now in London, and Jill's mother was persuaded to put up the deposit money for the hall. (Dan later went on to star as the lead ape in Kubrick's *2001: A Space Odyssey*: he threw the bone into the air that becomes the spaceship.)

The original plan only envisioned a reading by the internationally known poets, but it seemed disingenuous not to include British poets as well. Ginsberg proposed Harry Fainlight, who had recently returned to London after a season on the Lower East Side, where he was part of the *Fuck You/A Magazine of the Arts* crowd. He also suggested that Christopher Logue and Alexander Trocchi be involved. Logue he knew from Paris and Trocchi, author of *Young Adam* and *Cain's Book*, from New York. Alex had lived near him on the Lower East Side where he had run his 'methadone university', where speed freaks sat around under intensely bright lights meticulously painting pieces of driftwood and garbage with intricate proto-

57

psychedelic patterns in garish colours that Alex called *Futiques*: antiques of the future. I knew Trocchi because he often came into Better Books, hoping to borrow money to buy drugs. In fact we had a few *Futiques* there for sale. Alex and I became quite friendly after one incident when he walked into the shop with his flies open and his shirt sticking out through them. When I pointed this out, he was extremely grateful: 'Thank you very much, Miles. You know, people never tell you things like that, important things.'

The Poets Co-operative, an ad-hoc committee of poets, all of whom wanted to read, took over the organisation of the reading. Photo sessions and press conferences were called and the list of poets scheduled to appear grew alarmingly, finally reaching nineteen, many of whom had not previously read in anything larger than the upstairs room of a pub. A press conference that included both Ginsberg and Ferlinghetti was held across from the Albert Hall, on the steps of the Albert Memorial, watched over by a life-sized statue of Shakespeare. Later that day, at Alexander Trocchi's flat in Observatory Gardens, Notting Hill, a collaborative poem was conceived spontaneously in honour of the occasion (though it was clearly directed and edited by Ginsberg):

> England! awake! awake! awake!
> Jerusalem thy Sister calls!

... World declaration hot peace shower! Earth's grass is free! Cosmic poetry Visitation accidentally happening carnally! Spontaneous planet-chant Carnival! Mental Cosmonaut poet epiphany, immaculate supranational Poesy insemination! ...

The Royal Albert Hall is a vast circular building from 1871, seating 8,000 and named after the Prince Consort. On Friday 11 June 1965 people began arriving at the hall for the biggest poetry reading ever held in Britain. At the door they were handed flowers by Kate Heliczer, Barbara Rubin and friends, all wearing long, flowing granny dresses, their faces painted with psychedelic paisley patterns. (The flowers were salvaged that afternoon from Floral Street when Covent Garden flower market closed for the day.) The centre circle of the arena was filled with friends of the poets and organisers. Incense and pot-smoke wafted into the dome, bottles of wine and chillums were passed around. A dozen or so bemused schizophrenics brought along by anti-psychiatrist R. D. Laing danced to music heard only in their own heads and blew bubbles from pipes. One girl in a short white dress waved her arms above her head in what later became an archetypal psychedelic dream dance. For a while Allen Ginsberg joined the future Prime Minister of India, Indira Gandhi, and Nobel Laureate Pablo Neruda in the audience, but he was unable to persuade the latter to read.

Allen opened the event with a deep-voiced Tibetan mantra, accompanying himself on Indian finger-cymbals. Six or seven thousand people, many of them high, some with wine or picnics, settled in for the evening. Lawrence Ferlinghetti read 'To Fuck Is to Love Again', alarming the elderly hall attendants, one of whom told a reporter, 'I don't understand it, he's shouting a load of four-letter words and they're just lapping it up!' Adrian Mitchell read 'To Whom It May Concern (Tell Me Lies About Vietnam)' to an enthusiastic response, and Ernst Jandl performed explosive sound poetry. Gregory Corso, who had not read in public for four years, was uncharacteristically low-key, and instead of one of his more amusing, crowd-pleasing poems such as 'Hair' or 'Marriage', he chose a new poem, 'Mutation of the Spirit', which he read while seated at the podium.

The eccentric artist 'Prof' Bruce Lacey – who appears out of a manhole in the Beatles' film *A Hard Day's Night* – attempted to get one of his robots to enter the hall, but it got stuck backstage. The more cerebral artist John Latham planned one of his 'Skoob' ('books' backwards) happenings with poet Jeff Nuttall; he covered himself with paint, then stuck pieces of torn paper all over himself, but something went unexpectedly wrong and he passed out because his pores could not breathe. The Albert Hall attendants thought some horrific homosexual orgy was going on when they stumbled upon Nuttall and Latham naked in the bath together in Sir John Barbirolli's dressing room, trying to scrub the green paint from Latham's body.

Alexander Trocchi 'compered the proceedings with schoolmasterly firmness' said the *New Statesman*, but he had a difficult job on his hands keeping the flow of poets moving, as few of them wanted to leave the podium; they stood transfixed by the spotlight in their moment of fame. Harry Fainlight read 'The Spider', a long difficult poem about an LSD trip, delivered in a low mumble. People in the audience shouted that they couldn't hear and some began to heckle; in 1965 few people had heard of LSD and Harry's poem made no sense to them. Harry stopped, frozen, his mouth twitching, traumatised with pain. Trocchi helped him from the stage, but then Harry decided he should return and explain to the audience what the poem was about. Trocchi was decisive. He took away the microphone and told him firmly, 'Thank you, Harry, I think we've all heard enough of that now.' (At a poetry reading at the ICA that I organised a few weeks later, Harry Fainlight again read 'The Spider' and stopped once more at the same place, unable to continue.) Meanwhile the audience continued to shout. Dutch poet Simon Vinkenoog had come from Amsterdam for the reading. He was tall and thin, and high on mescaline. Thinking to calm the bad vibrations in the audience, he began to shout 'Love! Love! Love! Love . . . !' – a huge smile on his face. It seemed to do the trick and the audience quieted.

There was a unique, high-intensity energy in the hall, caused not so much by the poetry as by the audience; the gathering together of a new generation, a new constituency of youth, not yet distinguished by dress or length of hair, but a new community of spirit that was soon to manifest itself, seeing each other for the first time *en masse*. The hall has three tiers of private boxes, and in each one a party was going on. However, there were too many poets – nineteen in all – and Allen was once more drunk when the time came for him to read and close the event. He was irritated by the volume of bad poetry that had eaten into his stage time, and by the fact that Andrei Voznesensky had refused to read.

Voznesensky was in the audience in defiance of orders from the Soviet Embassy – his minder sat watching him – but he felt that he could not actually take part without endangering his ability to tour abroad in the future. Allen grew increasingly angry with him over this (he thought) act of cowardice, and made up for it by reading one of Voznesensky's poems, 'The Three Cornered Pear/America'. Allen slurred the introduction and many in the audience thought it was by Allen himself; they heckled him for the lines criticising Voznesensky, thinking they were insults, not realising they were by the Russian. Voznesensky, annoyed at Allen's American arrogance and his incomprehension of the poet's circumstances in the Soviet Union, left the hall as soon as Allen began to read. The last poem of the evening was Allen's 'Who Be Kind To', addressed to Harry Fainlight and written three days before at Hanson Street.

The reading has assumed enormous importance in the history of British popular culture, and thirty-five years after the event there was an hour-long documentary about it shown on the BBC. At the time, however, Allen was very disappointed in both the reading and his performance. Eight days later he composed a letter to the editor of the *Times Literary Supplement* (it was never published) in answer to their largely sympathetic coverage of the event:

A participant in the poetry reading, I woke up early next morning depressed, disgusted by almost all the other poets and disgusted most by myself. The audience had been summoned by Blakean clarions for some great spiritual event, there was a hint of Jerusalemic joy in the air, there were great poets near London, there was the spontaneity of youths working together for a public incarnation of a new consciousness everyone's aware of this last half decade in Albion (thanks to the many minstrels from Mersey's shores & Manhattan's), there was a hopeful audience of sensitive elders and longhaired truly soulful lads and maids. The joy, the greatness of the poets, & the living spirit coming to consciousness in England, have never been adequately defined in public, and here was an opportunity to embody this soulfulness in high language . . .

There were too many bad poets at Albert Hall, too many goofs who didn't trust their own poetry, too many superficial bards who read tinkley jazzy beatnick style poems, too many men of letters who read weak pompous or silly poems written in archaic meters, written years ago. The concentration & intensity of prophesy were absent except in a few instances . . .

By the time I got up to read I was so confounded by (what seemed to me then) the whole scene turned to rubbish, so drunk with wine, and so short of time to present what I'd imagined possible, that I read quite poorly and hysterically . . .

Allen didn't read as badly as he imagined, but afterwards he was in a foul mood and attacked George Macbeth, as a representative of the 'bad poets' who had eaten into his time, in a slanging match that ended with a picayune 'Fuck off!'

A few days later there was a small party at Julie Felix's place in King's Court North, Chelsea. Lawrence Ferlinghetti was staying with her at the time and he and Gregory Corso were both there when we arrived with Allen. Gregory immediately attacked Allen, accusing him of being a drunken slob at the Albert Hall reading and of 'letting down the ideals of the Beat Generation', which he spoke of in terms of a crusade. Ferlinghetti tried to calm him down, but Gregory turned abruptly to him, saying, 'You, Ferlinghetti, you're so goddamn naive I'm surprised you're able to get by at all.' All this Lawrence took with equanimity; like Allen, he was used to Gregory's vituperative tongue. Barbara Rubin arrived with Kate Heliczer and her Dutch friend Pam, carrying several movie cameras. Before Barbara was fully through the door, Gregory was yelling at her, 'One peep out of that camera, lady, and I'll break it over your head. You just put them over there!' Later in the evening Barbara was winding film into the camera when Gregory saw her and leaped to his feet screaming, 'I told you, lady! No filming!'

This spiky demeanour was characteristic of Gregory. A few days later Gregory, Allen, Lawrence and I came out of a pub on Tottenham Court Road when Gregory suddenly saw the Post Office Tower, rising high above the other buildings. 'Hey!' he yelled, stopping pedestrians in their tracks. 'Who put that there?' He seemed outraged that something had been built in London without his knowledge. To his irritation, we all found it very amusing.

Allen, Gregory and Lawrence were going to Paris on 28 June, their season over. Gregory arrived at Hanson Street when Allen was out and we sat around talking. He described a film he had made about gravestones, which he was very pleased with. We were about to eat lunch and invited him to join us, but first he needed to take some medicine that Dr Martin Bax, the editor of *Ambit*, had given him. He asked for two glasses, one filled with water. As we were eating Gregory began to babble. He talked about a girl he'd met the previous evening and how she was married and he had spent the evening with her and her husband. When the husband was out of the room, he had persuaded her to remove her panties and most of the evening was spent with Gregory and the unsuspecting husband arguing over politics while Gregory had four fingers inserted in his wife. In the end the girl could handle it no longer and had an orgasm, to her acute embarrassment, her husband's horror and Gregory's amusement, at which time he made a hurried, gleeful departure. By the end of the story Gregory was shouting, had pushed back his chair and was standing up, gesticulating. He pointed dramatically to the fireplace and said, 'Look at that crazy little waiter, see his little apron . . .' and passed out. I managed to catch his head before it hit the fireguard.

Sue and I carried him into the next room and laid him on Allen's bed. We were just wondering what to do when Allen and Lawrence arrived. Allen was furious: 'That bastard, he does it on purpose! We've got a plane to catch in four hours.' All summer Gregory had been taking chloral, just to knock himself out. Catching the plane was impossible unless they left Gregory behind, something Allen would not do, so we all went to a pub. I pinned a note to Gregory's chest, telling him where we were. They managed to get away the following day.

Lawrence came back a week or so later and spent a week staying with us at Hanson Street. He did a reading at Better Books, which we also recorded and released in an edition of ninety-nine copies, complete with a sleeve by Alan Aldridge to match the one we did for Allen. The record included a song that Lawrence and Julie Felix did together. Lawrence got half the albums, but one box of twenty-five never made it to San Francisco, so it is now a very rare item.

Lovebooks

While all the excitement of the Albert Hall reading was happening, Hoppy and I, together with Hoppy's accountant Michael Henshaw, were quietly starting a company. Lovebooks Limited was incorporated on 24 June 1965, with Hoppy and me as the directors and Mike as the company secretary. We had our friend Binn Tivy print some headed paper, which had to read, bizarrely, 'Lovebooks Limited, printers, publishers and stationers'. Inspired by the small-press booklets and mimeograph poetry magazines coming out of the States, the idea was to publish alternative poetry and underground texts. Our first release was a record: a spoken-word recording of a reading at the Architectural Association on Bedford Square, which featured Allen Ginsberg, Lawrence Ferlinghetti, Gregory Corso and Andrei Voznesensky: the line-up originally intended for the Albert Hall. This was a magical reading, described by Allen as 'a substantial presentation of joy', and everything in terms of poetry that the Albert Hall was not. Everyone was on top form and Gregory read his most popular poems, 'Marriage' and 'Bomb'. I did a collage of the poets for the cover, using Hoppy's photographs, and added a slightly wobbly title using Letraset.

Next we published *Darazt*, an anthology featuring a long poem by Lee Harwood, and named after his mimeo magazine, *Tzarad* (*Darazt* being *Tzarad* backwards). Lee was particularly fond of Tristan Tzara. There were some collages, by me, inspired by Max Ernst, some photographs of Gala Mitchell naked by Hoppy, inspired by Bill Brandt, and a long three-column text by William Burroughs. I wrote to him in Tangier in 1964, asking for material, and we began a correspondence. He was interested in Wilhelm Reich and whether or not magnetised iron would improve the efficacy of orgone accumulators. It was pretty heady stuff. I first read Burroughs in *New Departures*, which printed two fragments from *The Naked Lunch*. (It dropped the definite article when it was published in the USA.) I read the book itself at Hoppy's. I remember Peter Wollen commenting on 105 Westbourne Terrace, 'What a cool pad this is, man. There's always a fresh copy of *Naked Lunch* on the living-room table.' It was true; everyone who went to Paris felt it was their duty to smuggle a copy back through customs. Ginsberg's 'Howl' had given form to my disconnected ideas, but *The Naked Lunch* was a real eye-opener. It was to see reality clearly, naked, stripped of any confusing disguises. To quote Burroughs: 'The title means exactly what the words say: NAKED Lunch – a frozen moment when everyone sees what is on the end of every fork.' It is still my favourite book.

William had been an invisible participant at the Albert Hall reading. He was in New York at the time, but a tape recording made by Ian Sommerville boomed out over the PA during the interval, though the hall acoustics were so bad you couldn't understand a word. Burroughs returned to London in September 1965 and lived there until 1974, when he finally returned to the USA after twenty-five years of voluntary exile. His presence in London throughout the latter half of the Sixties was low-key but noticeable.

101 Cromwell Road

A tall, thin New Zealand poet named John Esam had been on the London scene since the early Sixties: he had performed at the ICA in the summer of 1965 with William Burroughs, Brion Gysin and Daevid Allen (later of Soft Machine). In 1965 he moved into Nigel and Jenny Lesmore-Gordon's flat at 101 Cromwell Road in West Kensington, near the West London Air Terminal where the coaches left for the airport. There was no actual room available in the flat so he built an airless, windowless shack in the corridor to sleep in. Esam, sometimes known as 'The Spider', was one of the main organisers of the Albert Hall poetry reading, which was how many people first got to know him. If Michael Hollingshead was the first person to proselytise acid in London, John Esam was certainly the second. He had straight black hair worn like a skullcap and intense, piercing eyes. He approached his task with an evangelical zeal and had thousands of trips at his disposal, brought over for him by a friend from America.

Nigel and Jenny Gordon were from Cambridge, friends of Syd Barrett, Roger Waters and the other people later associated with the Pink Floyd. They were recently married and had moved to London because Nigel wanted to be a film-maker. They continued to rent out parts of their flat for many years and throughout the Sixties an extraordinary mixture of people lived there, including Peter Roberts, known to his friends as 'Pete the Rat', and George Andrews, an American friend of Dan Richter who had reached

London via Tangier. Andrews was a poet, heavily involved in the drug culture. In 1967, together with Simon Vinkenoog, he edited *The Book of Grass: An Anthology of Indian Hemp*, probably the best anthology ever assembled of essays on marijuana.

The whole building was filled with people associated with the underground scene. On another floor lived Christopher Case, a smart young American, educated at Oxford, who worked as Robert Fraser's assistant at the Fraser Gallery. Another notable resident was Syd Barrett, the lyricist and lead guitarist for the Pink Floyd, who had been playing together, off and on, under that name since the autumn of 1964 when Syd first arrived in London to attend Camberwell Art College. He came up with the name Pink Floyd by joining the Christian names of bluesmen Pink Anderson (1900–74) and Floyd 'Dipper Boy' Council (1911–76). Syd later told reporters that the name was transmitted to him by a UFO while he sat on the ley line crossing Glastonbury Tor. By then he may have believed it. Syd moved into 101 in the spring of 1966 to room with his friend Scotty. They were both from Cambridge, which was how they knew Nigel Gordon; one of Nigel's earliest films was of Syd on a trip. Syd had a gaunt hungry look, pronounced cheekbones, dark unruly tousled hair and deep expressive liquid eyes. He seemed to experience life with an overwhelming intensity. Girls seemed to find him immensely attractive as he already had the look of a tormented artist.

Indications

In August 1965 Tony Godwin announced his intention to sell Better Books to Hatchards of Piccadilly, an Establishment bookshop owned by William Collins, publishers of the Bible and other religious books. It seemed unlikely that the poetry readings, the American small-press books and the copies of *Fuck You/A Magazine of the Arts* would continue in Better Books for long after the change in ownership, so I decided to open my own shop. I knew an American poet called Paolo Lionni, a friend of Gregory Corso, whom I first met through Dan Richter and the people at 101 Cromwell Road where he was staying. I had given him a reading at Better Books back in June and he was often in the shop. I mentioned the idea of opening my own shop to him and he told me that John Dunbar, the art critic for *The Scotsman*, was thinking about starting an experimental art gallery and suggested that we get together.

I liked John the moment we met. We shared the same sense of humour. He combined an impeccable urban cool – he had been brought up in the West End of London, where his father ran the London School of Film Technique – with a curious Dickensian absent-mindedness accentuated by little granny glasses and a fondness for waistcoats. He was born in Mexico City of a Russian mother and a Scottish father, but his earliest memories were of Moscow and playing in the streets as snow fell all around. His father worked for the British Embassy there as a cultural attaché.

We were well matched. I had been through four years of art college and a postgraduate year at the University of London and was familiar with the current developments in art – at that time I was still painting and making collages. John had done a two-year science degree at Churchill College, Cambridge, followed by a Fine Arts degree. He was widely read in modern literature, particularly the Beats, and was already friendly with Gregory Corso and Lawrence Ferlinghetti, whom he had met in Paris. We would probably have met anyway as we were moving in the same circles. It seemed a good idea to combine forces.

John was married to Marianne Faithfull, whose first record 'As Tears Go By' had entered the charts in July 1964; now, at eighteen she was a seasoned performer, oblivious to the stares of recognition she received on the street. She had long straight blonde hair and girlish freckles. Her manager, Andrew Oldham, always described her as 'an angel with big tits', something she herself quoted, since it was accurate. I was very impressed when she told me that her great-uncle was Count Leopold von Sacher-Masoch, who gave his name to masochism by writing *Venus in Furs*.

It must have been very strange for John the previous year because there she was, his new girlfriend, still at school in Reading, suddenly a pop star. They had had an argument and he had taken off to

Greece for the summer without her. While he was away she had cut 'As Tears Go By' and it was already in the charts when he returned. John knew nothing of this. She met him in a café to try to explain this surprising new development in her life, but before she could bring it up, the record came on the radio and they both sat listening to it silently. John took it quite well, though he had always been a bit sniffy about the pop-music scene.

John, Marianne, Sue and I met for dinner upstairs at Leoni's on Frith Street, the 'literary' restaurant where everyone seemed to be a publisher, editor or sometimes even an author. The place had a rickety charm, and TV producers liked to sit at the table beneath the brass plaque announcing that in this room Logie Baird had first demonstrated television. It was here, in August 1965, between the avocado prawns and the sambuca, that we agreed to work together and start a combined bookshop and art gallery.

Despite making a reasonable income from her career, Marianne – wisely, as it turned out – refused to finance our venture, so we had to look elsewhere for the money. John's best friend was Peter Asher, who was having considerable success with his group Peter and Gordon: their first record, 'World Without Love', had been number one in both Britain and the States. John knew Peter because one of his sisters was going out with Gordon Waller, the other half of the act. John, Peter and I had many excited meetings at Marianne's luxurious new flat at 29 Lennox Gardens, off Pont Street, discussing what we were going to exhibit and sell and preparing different costings for the venture; figures that turned out to be entirely meaningless. In the end Peter agreed to put up the £2,100 we thought we needed to start the bookshop and gallery by loaning John and me £700 each, and putting in the same amount himself. After many thoughtful pot-filled evenings, we decided to call the bookshop-gallery venture Indica, after *Cannabis indica*, a name suited to the times. Interzone, from Burroughs' *Naked Lunch*, was used as a working name for several weeks, but we didn't really like it. Indica worked for an art gallery as well as a bookshop: John called two of his group shows Indications. One magazine even suggested that our name derived from the word 'syndicate', which was inventive on their part.

Peter and his sister Jane had the same intense, thick red hair and they were equally pale; they resembled each other very much, with the same even teeth and round cheeks. He looked earnest, and at times slightly petulant, but his face broke easily into a wide smile. His seriousness was accentuated by glasses with thick black frames, rather similar to my own. Peter looked every inch the Sixties pop-star, always immaculately turned out in narrow, dark pressed trousers and elastic-sided Beatle boots from Anello & Davide in Covent Garden, who supplied footwear for stage productions. Sometimes they would have a sale of medieval pointed shoes in various colours, which meant that a pantomime or musical production had closed early and the chorus-line costumes had been returned. Later in the Sixties the hippies sought out their knee-high pointed boots in yellow suede for street wear.

Peter had gone to Westminster, but in addition to being a public-school boy, he had the tremendous self-confidence that comes from being a child-star; he was in his first film at the age of eight – *The Planter's Wife* starring Claudette Colbert and Jack Hawkins – and the same year he was in Harold French's *Isn't Life Wonderful?* with Eleanor Summerfield and Donald Wolfit. He had appeared on the stage and done a lot of radio drama, including *Jennings at School*, a long-running series which I used to listen to on *Children's Hour* when I got home from school. His mother, Margaret Asher, was very much a stage mum, highly ambitious for her children, and clearly envisioned a show-business career for all of them: Jane was in her first film at the age of five – *Mandy*, starring Mandy Miller – and her younger sister Clare, who was still at school, had a part in the daily radio soap *Mrs Dale's Diary*. They seemed to know everyone and to have been everywhere, but they were very nice with it.

The Ashers of Wimpole Street

Over the next few months I assembled the stock for the bookshop. Tony Godwin allowed me to order books for Indica alongside those for Better Books so that we could get the trade discount before we had established accounts of our own. He seemed pleased that his concept of a bookshop as a centre for experiment would continue at Indica. The boxes began to pile up, and Peter suggested that we keep the stock at his house, where there were numerous rooms in the basement that we could use.

Peter lived with his parents and sisters at 57 Wimpole Street, a five-storey eighteenth-century terraced house in Marylebone. Peter had a large L-shaped room in the attic, facing the street, done out in modern style with shelf units made from pale Norwegian wood holding books, gold records, trophies and awards and large gold keys to various American cities, from his career in Peter and Gordon. Being on the top floor meant that it was light and airy and, being the full width of the house, he had room to entertain. There was a hi-fi and records and even a selection of drinks. It was the ideal set-up. In the much smaller room next door, adjacent to the top bathroom, lived Jane's boyfriend, Paul McCartney.

Paul's window looked out to the west, over the rooftops of Browning Mews. The room was crowded: a large brown wardrobe, a single iron bed and a cabaret piano – smaller than a standard upright – on which he first played 'Yesterday', a melody that came to him in a dream. There was a shelf littered with interesting curios: guitar picks; a couple of original Jean Cocteau *Opium* drawings, one in a cracked frame where it had fallen from the wall; a pile of first editions, books of Victorian curiosities and rare books from the Times Bookshop on nearby Wigmore Street; backstage passes; bass strings; and a bundle of correspondence. Once, at Peter's request, Paul showed me a letter that had recently arrived. It was from his accountant, Harry Pinsker, who said, 'I thought you might like to know that you are technically a millionaire.' Paul seemed slightly embarrassed, as if he was flaunting his wealth, yet here he was living in what used to be the maid's room.

Spilling out from under the bed was a pile of gold records and his framed MBE. He told me that the Beatles had turned on in a bathroom at Buckingham Palace before meeting the Queen because they were all so nervous, but years later he changed the story and said they only slipped away for a cigarette. John Lennon told the same original story in an interview; probably no one really remembers what happened any more. In the corner by his wardrobe stood a battered black case with white stencilled letters: BEATLES. It contained his violin-shaped Hofner bass.

One day I was waiting for Peter while he got ready to go out. He needed some clean socks so we went next door to Paul's room to borrow some. Peter pulled open the sock drawer in the wardrobe, and thousands of dollars, wrapped in paper bands, fell out onto the floor. Paul had obviously been given them by Brian Epstein to bring back from their last American tour and had tucked them in the sock drawer and forgotten all about them.

Because his room was so small, Paul's instruments and his tape recorders were kept in Peter's room; a pair of Brenell tape recorders sat on top of a chest of drawers just inside the door. These were the machines on which he devised all the backwards tapes and tape loops that feature in the later Beatles work. He discovered that his own name, when played backwards, came out as 'Ian Iachimoe' and suggested that if I ever needed to write to him I should use that name. Mail arrived by the sackload and he rarely opened much of it, and then not until months after it was delivered, so a letter addressed that way would be more noticeable. I did write a few times, but I don't know if he ever opened them because he never seemed to write letters. (The original manuscript of 'Paperback Writer', which is written in the form of a letter, is signed 'Ian Iachimoe'.)

There was no space for records or a hi-fi in Paul's room. He kept his albums with Peter's and his singles were stacked in a wire rack on the chest of drawers on the landing at the top of the stairs. The Beatles' office in New York sent each Beatle all the new entries in the *Billboard* charts each week, many of which were never released in Britain.

Also at the top of the stairs with the 45s was an old black Bakelite telephone and next to it an electric bell with its wires trailing down the stairwell, attached here and there to the banister, undoubtedly Dr

Asher's handiwork. Whoever answered the phone could let people in the house know who the call was for by ringing the bell a different number of times. No one had their own phone line. The stairwell was painted in various pastel colours; Dr Asher had picked up a cheap mixed job lot of paint. A crack ran up one of the walls, over which he had pasted a slip of paper that read: 'When this paper tears the house will fall down.'

Dr Asher was the first neurophysician to identify Munchausen's syndrome, a condition in which people invent medical problems in order to draw attention to themselves. It was entirely typical of him that he did not call it Asher's syndrome. He was rather eccentric. Once at dinner he suddenly leaned over to me and signed his name upside-down, perfectly. 'A little trick I learned in hospital, jolly useful too when nurses are handing you things to sign.' Another of Dr Asher's party pieces, guaranteed to get a rise out of his family, was to reach behind his head and inject himself in the back of the neck, smiling delightedly as they recoiled in horror. Paul was clearly fascinated by him. Dr Asher's small bald-headed frame was often to be seen in the blue boiler suit he wore to do odd jobs. Once he gathered all the redundant metal objects in the house to melt down and cast into another knob for the front railings, to match the one broken off and stolen by Beatles fans. Mrs Asher was not impressed as some of her favourite kitchen utensils had disappeared to achieve his purpose.

He usually did this kind of work in the early hours of the morning and Peter told me that he and his then girlfriend, the singer Millie Small – who had a hit with 'My Boy Lollipop' – were in the kitchen late at night, making themselves sandwiches, when his father walked in wearing his boiler suit and bearing a carving knife. He announced that he was sharpening all the knives in the house. Noticing that Millie was black, he muttered, 'Hmm. Some black blood in the line would strengthen it and maybe get rid of those wretched red hair genes.' He was not happy about his family's red hair.

Peter shared some of his father's eccentricity. Paul told me that he once found him sitting in a chair without his glasses. He was concerned that if he got up, he would stand on his glasses and break them, so he was waiting for someone to come along and find them for him. It was typical that when he earned money from Peter and

Gordon he should invest in Hovercraft, the curious half-boat, half-plane that shuddered its way across the Channel on a cushion of air.

One of the things I liked about the Ashers was the way in which they felt completely at home in London and treated it almost like a small town. When the Post Office Tower was near completion, and articles began to appear about it in the press, Dr Asher wrote to say that he had followed its construction with great interest from his window, and asked if it would be possible for him to visit the top of the tower with his family. The GPO agreed, and a few weeks before the official October 1965 opening Dr Asher, accompanied by his family, including Peter, Paul and Jane, were shown around by a surprised GPO staff.

They were a musical family; Margaret Asher taught oboe at the Guildhall School of Music, and often had her students over for lessons in the basement music room. George Martin, the Beatles' producer, had been one of her students, as was Paul McCartney. She taught him how to play recorder and it was Paul who played the solo on 'Fool On the Hill'. She was tall, warm and friendly but businesslike. The children's red hair came from her, inherited from her Cornish ancestors, the Earls of Saint Germans of Port Eliot.

The search for premises suitable both for books and art exhibitions continued. In those days a gallery virtually had to be in Mayfair or else critics and buyers would not visit. We often went to Mason's Yard, a small square containing an electricity sub-station and a men's toilet notorious for cottaging, reached by two covered passageways leading off Duke Street St James's in the art-gallery district. The Scotch of St James was there, a trendy 'in' club for the new rock aristocracy. Marianne needed to be seen, and it was also a pretty good place to hang out, except that the music was so loud that talking was virtually impossible. One night in September John Dunbar, Marianne, Sue and I were leaving the Scotch when John, with a big grin on his face, announced that he had found premises for Indica. Next door to the Scotch, the other side of the narrow alley leading to Gerard Mankowitz's photograph studio, was 6 Mason's Yard, one of the few shops in the yard. The rent was £19 a week – John had already contacted the estate agents – and we pressed our noses against the cold 3 am glass to see the space inside.

We decided to open the bookshop first, to provide income from the very beginning and so that construction work would not impede exhibitions in the basement. While we waited for the lease, I began to assemble the stock in the basement of Peter's house, sometimes going straight there from Better Books. There was a series of small rooms in the basement, one of which I took over for my boxes and card indexes of rare books. Next door was the music room where Margaret Asher gave music lessons, and where Paul and John Lennon sometimes wrote songs 'eyeball to eyeball', as John once put it, including 'I Wanna Hold Your Hand', their first American number óne. I soon spilled over into the music room as the piles of books grew ever higher. It was pleasant and quiet there, well away from the rest of the house, in a room filled with wobbly metal music stands, piles of sheet music and an upright piano. I separated out rare and out-of-print books from new paperbacks, listing those that were to appear in our first catalogue. I had noted how much attention Ed Sanders received from his catalogues and wanted to get our own out as soon as possible as a form of advertising. Sometimes when Paul got in late from a nightclub he would browse through the stock and leave me a note of what he had taken: one night he selected *And It's a Song*, poems by Anselm Hollo; *Drugs and the Mind* by DeRopp; *Peace Eye Poems* by Ed Sanders; and *Gandhi On Non Violence*. This showed both his range of interest and the type of stock I was buying. He was Indica's first customer.

One evening in late summer I closed Better Books and headed home up Charing Cross Road with Stuart Montgomery, who had reached proof stage with Basil Bunting's *Briggflatts*, the first title from his newly launched Fulcrum Press. We talked excitedly about our projects, Stuart's press and my ideas for the new bookshop. Stuart came back to Hanson Street for coffee. We walked down the hallway into the narrow kitchen and there, sitting on the draining board, was Paul, nibbling on hash brownies and talking with Sue. Looking back on it, I doubt if she was all that pleased to see us. Sue had casually invited him over a few days before, after mentioning that she had baked some of Alice Toklas' famous cookies, but it was somewhat unexpected to find him sitting in our cramped little kitchen.

Though Sue and I had flirted at the edge of trendy London for some months, many of the people we met were condescending or arrogant or both, so it was a pleasant surprise to find someone like Paul who was as down-to-earth and unpretentious as you could get. He said that he was exploring London 'with his antennae out', educating himself in the arts. He seemed to know nothing about underground literature, music or radical politics, but wanted to learn. I lent him some copies of *Evergreen Review* and played him *Call Me Burroughs*. He became a regular visitor to our flat, hanging out, smoking pot and playing his way through our shelf of records. Favourite stoned listening included electronic music by Luciano Berio; the IBM computer singing 'Daisy, Daisy'; John Cage's *Indeterminacy* – some stories were longer than others, but he read each one in two minutes, some speeded up, others very slowly; a two-volume Folkways recording of a Japanese Zen ceremony – on one track a bell rang once a minute, and it was always great when it finally rang; and lots of the latest squeals and shrieks from the ghetto: Albert Ayler's *Bells* and *Spirits Awake*; Ron Blake; Pharoah Saunders; Sun Ra and his Solar Arkestra; Eric Dolphy's honking bird imitations; *Free Jazz* by the Ornette Coleman Double Quartet: two reeds, two bassists, two drummers, two trumpets, thirty-eight minutes of spontaneous collective improvisation with no preconceptions. It was while discussing this album that we came up with the idea that if you were in complete control of your consciousness, you would be able to differentiate between audio sounds so completely that you could release a record with Beethoven on the left stereo and the Beatles on the right, playing simultaneously, and the brain could decide which one to listen to, or to flip between one and the other.

If I introduced Paul to a few things, I in turn learned about pop music from him. He gave me records he thought I should know, like 'Rescue Me' by Fontella Bass. He showed me how to identify James Jamerson's characteristic bass work with Motown – a player he regarded as his only serious rival – and recommended other artistes such as Smokey Robinson.

One time we were driving through Bayswater in Paul's brand-new Aston Martin DB4 and he turned on the radio. Listening to the BBC was normally like tuning into the early Fifties, so I was astonished to hear all kinds of amazing new R&B records and American releases. Not only that, but the DJ was really funny, presenting the records in a slick, humorous way that combined a parody of American flash with *Goon Show* jokes and humour. I asked which station it was, thinking it must be some new pirate ship I hadn't heard of.

I was slow. It took me a while to realise the DJ was Paul and we were listening to a tape, made using all the records sent to him. The Philips cassette player had just come on the market and he had had one installed in his car. Paul was such a good mimic that, even though I now knew it was him, I just couldn't associate that smooth delivery with the man at the wheel. It was uncanny.

He enjoyed doing impersonations and did a brilliant one of Little Richard, complete with the coy little wave to the boys in the band. 'We didn't know he was gay when we first played with him. We hardly knew what gay was. And there he was onstage blowing us kisses and saying, "This one's for *you*, boys!" and we thought, "Ah well, things are different in America!"' Paul loved to ham it up; he even did Al Jolson's 'Mammy', dropping to his knee, rolling his eyes and waving his outstretched fingers, throwing everything into the part. Privately he performed a cruelly accurate rendition of his friend Mick Jagger, perfectly capturing his facial expressions. 'He stole all the gestures from Joe Tex, you know,' Paul maintained.

Derek Taylor, the Beatles' publicist, once told me he was sure that no matter how Paul was standing or moving, he always knew just how the crease at the back of his trousers was falling or how his jacket was hanging at the waist. This was not a narcissistic thing as Paul wasn't a dandy; it was just an incredible level of show-business professionalism.

The Avant-Garde Studio

Paul lived in a world of sound, and his reaction to the issues of *Evergreen Review* and *Big Table* that I lent him was to envisage an audio equivalent, a sound magazine. The idea came up one evening in September 1965 when Paul and Peter Asher were visiting. He saw it as a fortnightly or monthly survey, except that instead of a review of a poetry reading there would be extracts from the reading itself, the highlights of that month's cultural activity. Paul: 'Instead of reading in *Melody Maker* that there was a great jam session down the Bag O'Nails and that Eric Burdon and Georgie Fame were playing together, there would be a recording of it . . . We could even have really important things from the Third Programme that people might have missed. Have it available on subscription as cheap as it possibly could be. We should be able to put it out really cheap, what with the vast resources of EMI and NEMS!' So it was decided that what was needed was a small studio somewhere that people could use, so that a modern jazz group could do something for that month's issue or a visiting writer could read, or a scientist record a short lecture. It should all be very easy and relaxed. But of course someone would need to run it.

A few days later Peter, Paul and Jane, Sue and I, with Ian Sommerville, were in the living room at Hanson Street, very high. The room was uncomfortably brightly lit with a huge fluorescent fitting because I used it as a painting studio – we had no other lights. Ian, looking rather nervous, was calculating what was needed for the studio and, to both Paul and Peter's minds, not being very clear about either the minimum amount of equipment required or what it would cost. His hair stood on end and he constantly ran his fingers distractedly through it. Eventually he finished writing his list in careful copperplate and gave it to Paul. Paul gave it a quick glance, returned it to him and said he should call Brian Epstein on a certain number and the payment would be taken care of. Ian was nonplussed: he had expected to have to justify every item. Earlier he had explained the principles of floating equations, a subject that seemed to interest Peter more than Paul, but at least it demonstrated that he probably knew how to wire up a tape recorder and some microphones.

Brian Epstein bought an office building just one block from the Indica Gallery and Paul announced great plans for it: he, Peter, me, John Dunbar and Ian Sommerville were to have the top floor. It had a reception room already furnished with a television and a carpet, an office to write in and prepare events, and Paul had plans for a recording studio leading off that, which Ian estimated it would cost about £9,000 to install. There was even a fast, smooth lift leading only to our floor – a rarity in Britain. We calculated that the first issue of the magazine-album would be out in about eight weeks and made a list of people who would receive free copies: Ferlinghetti, Warhol, the Fugs, *East Village Other* and the other underground newspapers. The first issue was to have a long electronic piece by Paul, a 'mutter' poem by Pete Brown and probably a story.

A hold-up over the office building meant that we would first have to move into an old flat of Ringo's while the building was fitted out, and just use temporary equipment for the first disc. Ringo's flat was in a basement at 34 Montagu Square, not far from Wimpole Street. It was a good location for the studio: central, easy to get to. Ian was to be allowed to exploit the equipment for his own use, making tape copies, recording demos – anything to compensate for the time spent as a recording engineer. He bought a pair of Revox tape machines, amplifiers, a huge pair of Braun speakers, various microphones, stands, booms, boxes of tape, several editing blocks, a cassette player, a record player and other equipment, all of studio quality and at a small discount from Teletape on Shaftesbury Avenue.

The audio magazine project itself never got off the ground because no one was actually in charge of it, though I could and should have assumed that role. I just did not have time to take on another time-consuming project: I was already working on the stock for Indica; Hoppy and I had various Lovebooks projects that demanded part of my time; and I was still managing my department at Better Books.

Ian naturally regarded it as Paul's studio, while Paul regarded it as some kind of 'people's studio', Peter had no use for it, and John used it mostly as a place to hang out and 'bang pots and pans' with his friends. We did this quite often as, with full reverb on the Revox, it sounded rather good, even if one was totally inept as a percussionist. Ian had been effectively homeless since breaking up with William Burroughs so he had moved into the flat along with his boyfriend, Alan Watson. This was a good thing because it meant he was always there, ready to record something. Burroughs visited them frequently and became the only person other than Paul himself to get much use out of the studio, recording hours of tape with Ian, exploiting the stereo separation and editing facilities.

One evening in late October John Dunbar, Sue, Peter and I

visited Bill Burroughs and Ian at Montagu Square. Ian was in the strange situation of playing host in Ringo's expensive apartment, fixing everyone drinks, fussing about, cautioning everyone not to lean against the green watermarked silk wallpaper in the sitting room. Then Paul arrived, very excited, bringing with him acetates of that day's mixing session at EMI. He put them on the record player: 'Norwegian Wood', 'In My Life' and some others. It was amazing stuff and we were all excited, convinced that this was a complete breakthrough in music. He said that the album was going to be called *Rubber Soul*.

None of us liked the title; it was a typical Beatles play on words: the rubber sole of the shoe, and 'soul' music. John Dunbar immediately dubbed it *Rubber Scene* and that was what we all called it. How many people got the original joke is hard to tell. (The Beatles did it again with *Revolver*, which was supposed to be both a gun and a record – something that revolves.)

None of the experimental musicians ever used the recording studio, largely because no one knew about it. Paul himself recorded most of the early demos for 'Eleanor Rigby' there, and had some amusing talks with Bill Burroughs and Ian Sommerville. Once, memorably, Ian put Paul down, calling him a 'tea head'. Since Ian was constantly stoned, and had been for many years, this was not much of an insult. One of Ian's fondest memories was that his pillow in Tangier had been stuffed with marijuana: 'Gives you great dreams, man!' After a number of evenings of everyone sitting round banging cups and rubbing the rims of wine glasses, Paul abandoned the experimental studio as unworkable. Ian eventually moved out, taking the equipment with him to Burroughs' flat on Duke Street St James's. Years later someone turned up to take away one of the Revoxes; Paul gave the remaining tape recorder and the rest of the equipment to Ian.

Three Go MAD in Mayfair

The company, called MAD (Miles Asher Dunbar) Limited, was incorporated on 20 October 1965. We all had equal shares. The first formal business meeting had been before Sunday lunch at John and Marianne's flat in Lennox Gardens three days earlier. The money was discussed and I was relieved to find that the book stock I had built up over the years would be counted as part of my capital at cost price. We were so naive, we hadn't the slightest idea how to start a business. Some of Colin Parker's lessons would have come in useful, considering that I had no knowledge of how the financial side of a bookshop actually worked, having dealt only with day-to-day administration at Better Books.

We got the lease on 6 Mason's Yard and found to our surprise that we had a lot of work to do before we could open to the public. The premises had a large ground floor with a small windowless office at the back and a basement that extended out beneath the street into what was once a front area. The basement floor needed replacing, but we filled in the holes with cement and covered it with thick blue industrial carpet bought second-hand from the Olympia exhibition hall; many people we knew carpeted their flats with matting from the Motor Show or the Ideal Home Exhibition. I was surprised how many people offered to help us build the place.

Paul's driver Taffy, who claimed to be a getaway driver, ran errands for us, usually in Paul's Aston Martin, though he preferred a Bristol himself: 'Very nippy they are!' One day at Philip Weisberg's wood yard on Goodge Place we were discussing the relative cheapness of the wood when the owner finally spoke his mind: 'Listen! I really don't understand you blokes. You arrive in a car which must cost four or five thousand nicker, then argue about the cost of two by three for 'alf an hour. Whose car is that, anyway? Is it hot? Why doesn't *he* buy the wood?' It seemed a lot easier to tell him, since it couldn't hurt Paul in any way, and he was very pleased and helped us strap the planks on the roof.

Pete Brown did some of the carpentry, all the time muttering oaths – 'God's teeth', 'By Saint Hilda's toenail', and so on – as he hit his fingers with the hammer. I think his principal motivation in working for us was to catch a glimpse of Jane Asher, the object of his admiration. Later in the Sixties he wrote most of Cream's material, including 'Wrapping Paper', and made a sizeable amount of money. At this time, however, he would arrive most days shortly before lunch, asking, 'Any chance of a nosh?' and we'd all go to Sid's Caff, a horrible greasy spoon on the corner of the yard, for sausage and chips with lots of tea and slices. Sid had the biggest, greasiest black tomcat I have ever seen, which would rub against your legs under the table, leaving a smear of tacky fat mixed with cat hair on your trousers. The café was mostly patronised by the labourers working on the new Cavendish Hotel on the corner of the yard, who regarded us with great suspicion.

Ian Sommerville spent several days cleaning the piece of wall that his electrical cables were going to run along. He carefully painted a lath of wood in red and blue stripes before attaching the wiring to it in a position behind some deep shelves where it would not be seen. Ian was very much the sort of person who liked to keep his pencils in a row. Although he and Bill Burroughs had effectively broken up, Ian and his very camp boyfriend, Alan Watson, were then living *à trois* in Bill's flat overlooking Mason's Yard and so Burroughs, too, became a frequent visitor. I got the feeling that sometimes he came over just to escape the sexual tension in the flat; he was still obsessed by Ian, but Ian wasn't interested. Bill hated Alan Watson, but his feelings were ameliorated somewhat by the fact that Alan was a fine cook. He worked in the canteen at Scotland Yard, where the bored detectives would encourage him to dance on the tables. Alan was what Quentin Crisp called a 'flamboyant homosexual', who wore hipster trousers cut so low that they were little more than two tight trouser legs and a belt. The labourers working on the new Cavendish Hotel would often kick a football around the yard during their lunch break and Alan loved to mince across Mason's Yard, hand on hip, flip a limp wrist at them and call out, 'Score a goal for me, boys!' while they hooted and catcalled.

John Dunbar carved an elaborate banister for the basement stairs, which would disassemble to allow large works of art to be carried down the stairs. It was like a piece of sculpture itself and he polished it lovingly. Whenever Paul had the time he would join in:

hammering and sawing, filling in the holes in the plaster and helping to erect bookshelves. The walls were made of concrete and the shelves were fixed either by using a nail gun – John became highly skilful with it – or by drilling out a hole and filling it with a fixative to take screws. This filling became known as 'grey gunge' and Paul became adept at mixing it up in a small pot. When the workmen realised who was working at Indica they became a terrible nuisance, pressing their faces against the window, staring at Paul as if he were in a zoo, and attracting passers-by who wondered what was going on. John spread Windowlene all over the front window to prevent them seeing in, but the rumours spread and soon everyone in the nearby shops and galleries knew all about the Beatles' new art gallery.

Sometimes the place got quite crowded. There was one day when Paul was putting up shelves, Ian was installing the spotlights with Alan 'assisting', John was polishing his banister and I was unpacking the rare books in the back office. Peter Asher always used Indica as a venue for interviews to get us some publicity; pictures of the shop appeared in *16 Magazine* and various Swedish and French teen mags. This day he was promoting Peter and Gordon's latest single. The interviews appeared to all be the same: 'What is your favourite colour?' 'What colour hair do you like best?' This last question he answered diplomatically – 'black' for Asian readers, 'blonde' for Scandinavian ones. Peter was beginning to wish that he had chosen another venue as he sat on the settee, surrounded by sawdust, trying to answer these inane questions while everyone giggled and chuckled, making him feel very self-conscious. Pete Brown went hopping past holding his foot, while Ian Sommerville played Ian Whitcomb's 'The Turn On Song' over and over on his Philips cassette machine.

Peter's third interview that afternoon was with a young Japanese woman, who suddenly realised that it was Paul McCartney wielding the screwdriver and could hardly take her eyes off him. Paul, who was standing behind Peter, winked at her and raised his eyebrows. 'Do you prefer blondes or brunettes?' she asked Peter. Ian Sommerville, wiring up a plug, smirked and Alan asked, 'Man or woman?' as Peter despaired over his uncouth friends.

Sometimes Jane helped out, on occasion bringing along her mother. Mrs Asher brought us a pre-war till made from polished wood, with a drawer for the money and a simple square hole through which passed a roll of adding-machine paper, wound on manually. Jane had played shops with it as a girl.

We carefully entered all the sales on the till roll, but when we received our first set of accounts we found that the accountants had included all the figures written on the earlier part of the roll in Jane's nine-year-old writing when playing shops – 12 eggs = £1.8.6d – giving us a tremendous turnover. When we refused to pay for such shoddy work our accountants tried to sue us, and we couldn't understand why our lawyer tapped the side of his nose knowledgeably and advised us simply to wait it out. Sure enough, the next week the accountant left the country in a hurry a few steps ahead of the police and the court case was dropped.

Mrs Asher introduced us to her bankers, Coutts & Company, who regarded us with some suspicion, but as Peter already had an account there they were far too polite to mention that it was not really the right bank for shopkeepers. I had rarely set foot in any bank, but I knew this was something exceptional when a footman in a frockcoat brought us our company cheque book on a silver salver. Coutts were still a little old-fashioned. Shortly after we opened, Sue took the takings in to deposit. The teller raised his hands in horror when she produced a bag of coins – something they presumably rarely saw. 'Just give it to me and we'll write and tell you how much is there!' he exclaimed.

Cavendish Avenue

After a while Paul was forced to complain about Taffy's use of his Aston Martin DB4, or 'the DB far-out' as Taffy used to call it. Apparently Taffy had borrowed the car the week before to pick up Marianne at the airport. He had been late, so he hurried out there, caught Marianne just as she came through customs and nipped back into town. Paul thought at the time that Taffy didn't seem to have been away long. This was confirmed in the shape of two tickets that

Paul received in the mail. The police hadn't even attempted to catch the speeding car, they just timed it between checkpoints. Taffy had been travelling at 128 mph on the way out and 135 on the way in. He was delighted, 'And I 'ad an extra fazzand revs on the clock as well, but I faught I saw the fuzz and cooled it.' Paul was none too pleased. He told the police that he had lent the car to someone but didn't know their address. This was not a lie because no one knew Taffy's address. No one knew his real name, either. But he certainly could drive.

One day Paul had one of his surprises to show us. He was grinning like a Cheshire cat when we got into the Aston. We drove through Regent's Park and came out by Lord's Cricket Ground, then drove down a quiet road at the back of it. The road was lined with large detached houses, each with its own grounds, with mature trees overhanging high security walls. Paul stopped in front of one and told us that he owned it. He had bought 7 Cavendish Avenue back in May and was now getting ready to do it up. He had hired John and Marina Adams – Marina was John Dunbar's older architect sister – to put his plans into effect. John Adams later told me, 'It was the strangest briefing I've ever had. Paul said he wanted to have the smell of cabbage coming up from the basement, which was obviously something he associated with the Asher house.'

Though the Ashers conveniently turned a blind eye to the fact that Paul and Jane slept together, it was still not possible for them to entertain friends at home or live as a normal couple. Although they had been together for three years, Paul had never really committed himself and the move to Cavendish Avenue would be the first real test of the relationship.

His new house was regency, like the Ashers', only much larger and with a substantial garden. A pair of columns flanked the porch, with steps leading to the door. A garage to the left would house the Aston Martin and the souped-up Mini. The living room occupied the full width of the house and had French windows looking out over a patio to a long garden with an orchard at the end. It was like being in the country, and yet London extended for miles around. Many years later Paul and Linda kept chickens and a horse there. The neighbours objected to the cock crowing.

Paul was filled with ideas for the place: a huge steel-faced clock, made for the Great Exhibition, was to be built into the wall between the two front windows of the dining room, and the kitchen was to be fitted with all kinds of new gadgets, such as eye-level ovens and spits. The wall in the living room opposite the fireplace was to be one vast bookcase housing two record players, tape equipment and with a built-in movie screen that would appear from the top of the unit. On the top floor, in what were originally the servants' rooms, Paul had his music room. He wanted the door of the built-in cupboard painted 'Like those old artists used to do', and asked if we could recommend anyone. We both immediately suggested Pete Simpson, my old friend from Hill Street, Stroud, with his great knowledge of gesso and ancient wood-painting techniques. Paul wanted little scenes in the panels and a decorative border. We said we'd organise it.

We drove away, but Paul stopped at the end of the street and we got out to look at the original Victorian pillar box. It leaned at a slight angle and the old Queen's 'VR' monogram was thick with official red paint. As we examined it, we were approached silently by a policeman who surprised us with his sudden appearance. He wanted to know what we were up to as he had seen us snooping about. Then he recognised Paul and became very curious. Paul explained that he had bought a house in the street and asked the policeman not to tell anyone and, rather jokingly, to keep his eyes open for robbers. The policeman seemed very pleased to be privy to this secret information and actually touched his helmet to Paul, like Jack Warner in *Dixon of Dock Green*, as we scrambled back into the car.

A week or two later Sue and I were just about to go to dinner at Pete Simpson and Kate Wallhead's flat when Paul dropped by unexpectedly. We thought this was a good opportunity for Paul to see Pete's work and discuss the painted door. Shortly afterwards we pulled up at St Stephen's Gardens in Notting Hill and rang the bell. Pete was a little taken aback at the idea of an extra guest for dinner – any extra guest would have shaken his carefully made arrangements – but they soon got over their fluster, and Kate's main problem was whether to wear her glasses and see what Paul looked like or take them off and feel beautiful. Kate was small, slender, with light blonde hair hanging straight to her shoulders. She was a sculptor and wrestled with giant metal armatures, dripping with white plaster. Pete, in contrast, was as big and bumbling as in our Stroud days, and his work was more miniature than ever. They made a wonderful couple.

Dinner divided easily into five and Paul was soon chatting about the old days in Liverpool, how his cousin was a redcoat at Butlin's Holiday Camp and how he used to work at the post office during the Christmas rush and so on, making them feel completely relaxed. Afterwards Pete and Kate said that they had been charmed, but had been most interested in their own reactions to being confronted with someone whose image they knew so well from newspapers and magazines, yet whose reality as a person was unknown.

Paul looked at Pete's work: meticulously painted electric arcs, strange cornucopias and Victorian engravings brought to life in modern colour; a commissioned portrait of a headmaster whom he had chosen to pose against the background of a hedge, with each leaf carefully painted. Paul liked what he saw and in due course people from the Beatles' organisation delivered the cupboard door to Pete.

Pete approached the job in true Renaissance manner and spent weeks sanding down the door by hand before he applied coat after coat of gesso white, sanding each layer flat until the work surfaces were impeccably smooth. Kate worried that he was even going to polish the surface with a shark's tooth in the traditional manner, but I think she stopped him in time. It took many months, and Paul often asked when he was going to have his door back. Finally each panel had a Klee-like, Dürer-esque scene of air balloons and strange scientific instruments standing surrealistically on seashores or in lush formal gardens, all surrounded by a monochromatic floral motif. The gesso gave the door a luminous depth of colour and it was very good work. Paul also bought a small watercolour of a pleasure garden, which he had beautifully framed.

The Man Who Turned On the World

Late in the summer of 1965, in September, we were introduced to a smiling young Englishman called Michael Hollingshead, who arrived in London from Timothy Leary's headquarters in Millbrook, NY, wearing a long coat, pink glasses and bringing with him 300 copies of *The Psychedelic Experience* by Ralph Metzner, Richard Alpert and Tim Leary, 200 copies of the *Psychedelic Reader*, edited by Gunther Weil, Ralph Metzner and Tim Leary, and half a gram of LSD, enough for 5,000 sessions. It was Hollingshead who first turned Leary on to LSD in 1961, and he had been resident at Millbrook for several years, guiding visitors through trips.

It had originally been intended that Leary would join Hollingshead in London in January 1966. Inspired by reports of the poetry reading, they planned to rent the Albert Hall – or Alpert Hall, as Leary dubbed it, after his colleague Dick Alpert – for a psychedelic jamboree, inviting the Beatles or the Rolling Stones to perform, with Tim as the main act of the evening, the 'High Priest'. This gave Hollingshead three months to set things up. Hollingshead was, to say the least, unpredictable and seemed to spread chaos wherever he went. When I visited Millbrook in 1967, Leary told me, 'When Dick [Alpert] and I stood on the dock in New York waving him goodbye, I said to Dick, "Well, that writes off the psychedelic revolution in England for at least ten years."'

In 1965 LSD was not yet illegal in Britain, but it seemed likely that the authorities would soon make it so. It was thought that the best tactic was to introduce as many influential people to the drug in as short a time as possible to inform the public debate. Hollingshead opened the World Psychedelic Centre (WPC) in a large, expensive flat in Pont Street, Belgravia, paid for by a wealthy friend. The president of the WPC was an old Etonian Lloyd's underwriter called Desmond O'Brien, who was joined a little later by Joey Mellon as vice-president. Mellon was another old Etonian, a graduate in law from Oxford and one of the first people in Britain to follow the example of Dutch professor Bart Hughes and trepan himself in the belief that he would revert to a naturally high state when the volume of blood in his brain had room to expand. Bart Hughes himself often visited the WPC, as did folk singer Julie Felix, who, though she had not undergone trepanation herself – a hole in the middle of your forehead does not look good on television – did set to music one of Joey Mellon's songs, 'Brainbloodvolume', a little-known psychedelic classic.

During its brief life, the WPC attracted a huge number of visitors. It was inevitable, given the number of old Etonians on the board, that the aristocratic Chelsea set would be well represented. Fellow old Etonians such as art dealers Christopher Gibbs and Robert Fraser, and members of the aristocracy such as Viscount Gorman-stone and Victoria and Julian Ormsby-Gore, the children of the British ambassador to the USA, were among early visitors. The word soon spread down the King's Road, and LSD became the new talking point in literary salons and art galleries. In Sixties Britain the class structure was still very much in place and this was reflected by the people who visited Pont Street: they tended to be the black sheep of aristocratic families, visiting Americans, celebrities, profes-sionals and, of course, anyone in show business or the arts. There was no likelihood of seeing an ordinary working-class lad at the WPC, just as you would never see one anywhere on Pont Street, unless he was digging up the road or delivering something.

Other visitors included the Surrealist artist Sir Roland Penrose, who was also a director of the Tate Gallery; 'Anti Psychiatrist' Ronnie Laing and his assistant at the Philadelphia Association, the American psychiatrist Joseph Berke, who in 1967 would co-found the Anti-University of London; film-maker Roman Polanski and his girlfriend Sharon Tate; William Burroughs; Ian Sommerville; Alexander Trocchi; and millionaire Victor Lownes, who co-founded the Playboy Club with Hugh Hefner. Workshops in 'Consciousness Expansion' were held at the Institute of Contemporary Art and St Martin's School of Art. Musicians who were to visit the WPC included Donovan, Eric Clapton and Peter Asher. Paul McCartney was the only member of the Beatles to attend, taken there by John Dunbar.

The centre quickly fell apart when Hollingshead began shooting speed and becoming progressively more unbalanced. Or, as he put it in his autobiography, 'There was a problem, a self indulgence of mine which earned me some social suspicion, if not also social ostracism, and which led me – though against all my instincts – well over that line which divides the normal from the abnormal. I refer, of course, only to my taking of methedrine.' He was shooting speed seven times a day, smoking pot and hash continuously and taking acid, in doses in excess of 500 micrograms, three times a week. He would often drift into a zombie-like state of catatonia and would have to inject himself with dimethyl-triptamine to jolt himself back to life again.

The Pont Street flat became squalid and people began to stay away; it was obviously going to be busted in the near future – not for LSD or for methedrine, which Hollingshead had legally on prescription, but for the pot and hash that were lying around in every room. Britain's gutter press had already 'exposed' him: under the headline THE MEN BEHIND LSD – THE DRUG THAT IS MENACING YOUNG LIVES, a reporter from *The People* wrote, 'The Centre was deserted and in a state of considerable chaos when our investigator gained entry on Thursday. There were used hypodermic syringes, empty drug ampoules and a variety of pills. Among the litter of paper were dozens of phone numbers, some of them of well-known show-business stars and personalities.'

In January 1966 the police arrived. The Centre had been open for less than three months, but in that time Michael Hollingshead had introduced hundreds of people to acid. He took LSD before arriving in court, which made the proceedings even more unreal for him. His jokey replies to cross-examination probably had a lot to do with his stiff sentence: twenty-one months in Wormwood Scrubs for possession of less than an ounce of hashish and a negligible amount of grass. Hollingshead had a plentiful supply of hash and LSD in prison, brought to him by Stanley Owsley and Richard Alpert when they visited the Scrubs. He never gave psychedelics to any of the other inmates, with one exception: the spy George Blake, who was in for forty-four years.

Blake had done five years of his sentence when Hollingshead gave him a tab. Blake spent much of the session ruminating on his chances of being released and concluded that it was not very likely. He was also concerned that he would not be able to handle many more years of incarceration, despite the fact that he had been allowed a carpet, curtains, books and a short-wave radio to 'listen to the Arabic language stations'. A few weeks after his trip he escaped by scaling the wall using a rope ladder thrown over by an accomplice, who had contacted him on the short-wave service of Cairo Radio. Blake was last heard of living in Moscow, working for the Russian Foreign Ministry.

Long Hair

Meanwhile, Hoppy and I pursued our plans to publish an independent literary magazine aimed at the audience that had attended the Albert Hall poetry reading – not just printing poetry, but trying to pull together the various strands of the emerging scene we had observed there. We expected problems. Binn Tivy, who had surreptitiously printed *Darazt* for us at the firm where he worked, had been very worried about the nude photographs of Gala we had published and warned us that any depiction of pubic hair was illegal. Though we had no plans to publish any more nudes, in order to avoid potential censorship problems and to have complete control over what we were publishing, Hoppy decided that Lovebooks should have its own offset litho press. I knew nothing about printing technology, but to Hoppy, a trained reactor physicist, the mastery of a small litho press was not a problem. He found a used one for £100, which he installed in a room of its own in his new flat in Queensway. My only experience with litho was at art college, where we had to grind down great blocks of stone using different grades of sand in order to produce a surface to print from. Hoppy's machine, however, used zinc plates, which he made using a converted kitchen mangle.

After a few single-page experiments, he felt confident enough to print Lovebooks Limited's next publication. This was *Long Hair*, an ambitious eighty-page literary magazine, given its name by Allen Ginsberg and containing 'Ankor Wat', Ginsberg's complete Cambodian journals. I did a line-drawing of Allen for the front cover, based on one of Hoppy's photographs, and Pete Simpson gave us a drawing to go on the back. As the editor, I solicited texts from all the usual suspects: the Beat-oriented British poets Lee Harwood, Brian Patten, Michael Horovitz, Pete Brown and Tom Pickard, and the American Beats and School of New York writers Ted Berrigan, Ron Padgett, Gerard Malanga, Jack Micheline, Tuli Kupferberg, Lawrence Ferlinghetti and others. There was a poem about heroin from saxophonist jazzman Archie Shepp – 'Where the tracks is / the money ain't / it's all in them tracks . . .' – and lots of ads from well-wishers, including the Robert Fraser Gallery. Allen Ginsberg refused payment so we divided his money between the other contributors.

The editorial was jointly written by me and Hoppy:

LONG HAIR is for the POETRY revolution, the PROSE revolution, the JAZZ revolution, the POP revolution, the SEXUAL revolution, the revolution of the mind, free thought and action, and LOVE.

That pretty much summed it up, we thought.

The pages were all printed by the first week of December, and Hoppy laid them all out on a long trestle table. Friends were assembled and we spent a whole evening collating them. Hoppy began 'perfect-binding' them with sticky tape at the spine and handed me a completed copy. I remember the satisfaction we both felt, holding copies in our hands. It looked so fresh with its stark white pages. We had edited, designed, typeset, printed and bound it ourselves, quite independent of the highly unionised and conservative printers and typesetters that other little magazine publishers had to contend with. I remember looking at the huge ear-to-ear grin on Hoppy's face, and then laughing. The edition, apart from the few hand-bound copies, was perfect-bound by a print finisher and, possibly due to our inexperience, was faulty, causing pages to depart unpredictably from the volume. We never did figure out the precise cause.

On 25 November John Dunbar and I flew to Paris to enable John to meet various art dealers – one of whom, Denise Renée, took quite a shine to him – and for me to buy Gaït Frogé's remaining book stock at the Librairie Anglaise at 42 rue de Seine, before she closed at the end of the year. We flew on one of the new Trident jets, checking in at the Cromwell Road Air Terminal and collecting our luggage at the Air France Terminal at Les Invalides, as it was done in those days. Gaït had booked us into the Hôtel de Seine, a few doors up the street from her, and we spent a very pleasant day going through her remaining stock. She seemed a little sad to be closing the shop, and was hopping mad that George Whitman, her arch rival, had just changed the name of his bookshop, the Mistral, to Shakespeare and Company; something she regarded as a blatant attempt to con tourists into thinking that his bookshop had something to do with Sylvia Beach's legendary establishment on the rue de l'Odéon, which had been closed for a quarter-century. 'Why, he will not even stock Olympia Press books! He is too much of a prude. And he takes the name of Sylvia Beach, who took such risks with *Ulysses*!'

Gaït had been the main outlet for Olympia Press and we were able to buy quite a few of the Traveller's Companion series from her, as well as a quantity of Beardsley's *Under the Hill* that Olympia published in a beautiful edition bound in green watered-silk boards with a gilt top edge.

Because of the British customs ban on Olympia Press publications, Gaït sent many of these books to us in plain-paper wrappers, marked as if sent by an individual, and they all got through. However, both John and I experienced problems later. On one occasion John returned from France with six copies of Burroughs' *The Soft Machine*, which were confiscated and burned, and the same thing happened to me in 1968 when they seized eight copies of *The Ticket that Exploded*. The book was already published in Britain, but the philistines at HM Customs and Excise had their own ideas of what the British were allowed to see and read. We could not afford to appeal, so the copies were burned. My request to be allowed to witness the government conducting a good old-fashioned Nazi book-burning was turned down.

At least we didn't have the problems that Ed Sanders was encountering in New York. Ed was busted by an angry sergeant from the 9th Precinct who had gone to the Peace Eye bookstore because a robbery had been reported. There he found hundreds of copies of Ed's *Fuck You/A Magazine of the Arts*, as well as copies of

Long Hair

The Bugger Anthology, *The Marijuana Newsletter* and *The Platonic Blow* by W. H. Auden. He seized them all, including the complete back files of all fourteen issues of the magazine, and hauled Ed off down to the station. The police spent hours 'screaming with glee', as Ed put it, while anxiously looking through the New York Penal Code to find a felony to charge him with. But Ed knew it was a misdemeanour, possession with intent to sell porn, and told them so. Eventually he was set free on $500 bail and the New York Civil Liberties Union provided him with counsel free of charge to fight the case. Ed wrote in his newsletter:

> I am the only person in the history of American obscenity cases who has had his penis examined during station house questioning. At one point an officer who was typing out my personal history asked if I had any tattoos or scars. I said no. About half an hour later my arresting officer, Sergeant Fetta, along with another officer came to the room where I was being questioned. They told me to come with them. Fetta said: 'OK Sanders, get into that room and take off your clothes.' I said, 'What's up?' Fetta said: 'I thought you said you didn't have any tattoos.' Then I noticed he had a copy of *Fuck You/A Magazine of the Arts*, No. 5, Volume 4, in his hand and he was pointing to the Notes on Contributors section where usually there are written funny anecdotes about the contributors. In this particular issue I had stated that 'Ed Sanders . . . has the ankh symbol tattooed on his penis and the first 53 hieroglyphs of Tut-ankh-Amun's Hymn To The Sun Disc on his nuts.' This upset the officers enough that I had to flash my phallus so that they could check it out.

Peter came back from playing concerts in New York with some great books for Indica bought from Bob Wilson at the Phoenix bookstore. He had gone to the Peace Eye, but arrived the day after it had been closed by the police, and there was no one there. One day I met him for lunch, after which we went to visit his partner Gordon Waller, who lived at 15 Baker's Mews, a cottage just off Manchester Square. We went upstairs and found Gordon sitting at a small card table with his girlfriend Sharon Sheeley. It must have been her flat because there were gold records on the wall, awarded for her songwriting (she wrote 'Something Else' for Eddie Cochran, 'Poor

93

Little Fool' for Ricky Nelson and 'Hurry Up' for Ritchie Valens). Sharon was wearing a black negligee and a green eyeshield pulled low over her long straight blonde hair. They were playing poker and it appeared that she was winning. The impression I had was that the game had begun the night before. I was quite moved – after all, this woman had been in the car crash that killed Eddie Cochran.

December was party time. We had a very druggy Christmas Eve get-together at Lennox Gardens with John and Marianne, leaving at 4 am to find that we had locked ourselves out. I tried all the usual stuff with bits of card, but still couldn't open the door and so, still extremely stoned, I went round to the police station on Tottenham Court Road. They hadn't got skeleton keys, claimed that they didn't know how to pick a lock, but would be pleased to come round and kick in the door for us. I thanked them nicely and said I might have to take them up on it. Back at Hanson Street I found two very furtive-looking types at the corner with New Cavendish Street, one of whom happened to have a huge screwdriver with him. I suppose they were burglars. Anyway he easily smashed the lock and let us in.

The next day, Christmas Day, we arrived at about 11 pm at Hoppy's place, where about twenty very stoned people were playing tape recordings of the Queen's Speech and watching a plastic cockroach walk across the ceiling. I don't know why it didn't fall off. I remember looking around and thinking that the whole London scene had really livened up that year.

1965 ended with a huge party at Better Books to celebrate its sale to Hatchards. I had begun to phase myself out of Better Books in November in order to devote more time to Indica. Collins installed a new manager at the end of that month who had just returned from four years' bookselling in South Africa, a country that the rest of us were busy boycotting. I built a model of a train out of Penguin books for the window, to mark Tony Godwin's departure, and Michael Horovitz organised a huge rambling exhibition in the basement. Of the fourteen members of staff, nine of us were leaving on New Year's Eve. One of them, Sue Sárközy, was coming with me to manage Indica Bookshop. I saw Alexander Trocchi, who had returned from Paris still hooked on junk and looking greener than ever, casually walking out with about a dozen books stuffed down his shirt. Tony looked sad and told me he wished he hadn't sold the shop, but he was heading for a new life in New York.

Megalomaniacal Fantasies

On New Year's Day of 1966 I walked over to Better Books to help them clean up. It was a mess and would clearly take days to straighten out. I wandered through the familiar rooms, remembering the extraordinary events of the past year. I strolled through Soho to Indica, let myself in and stood in the gallery, marvelling at the huge white space, a little apprehensive of what we had taken on. It was the beginning of a new season. I had an interview the next day with the *New York Herald Tribune* about the shop, and the previous week *Time-Life* had taken me for an £8 lunch – more than half my weekly wage at Better Books – because *Life* was planning an underground issue and wanted information on the English scene. It seemed good publicity for Indica.

A couple of days into the New Year Paul came over and I showed him a letter from Betsy Klein. She said that on New Year's Eve the Fugs were all round at her place stoned, listening to Beatles records, looking for imperfections. Paul said I should tell her that *Rubber Soul* had fourteen flaws on it, and wondered if they'd noticed the background chant of 'tit, tit, tit, tit . . .' on 'Girl', which was an in-joke for friends. Getting one over on EMI. I asked how he went about writing a pop song and he told me that he and John always gave themselves a three-hour limit, and that so far they had always come up with something. He said they never took drugs when they wrote the words and music, but afterwards, as a reward for writing the song, they would get stoned and decorate the words by colouring in all the letters and doing weird drawings in the margins. On *Rubber Soul* the words were mostly drawn on red paper or the backs of shirt packets, and they played from these at the recording sessions. He said it was not until they got to the studio that they decided how a song would be played, then it was John, Paul and George Martin who worked out the arrangement. When he left,

Paul borrowed my copy of *The Fugs Songbook* to show the others. I replied to Betsy, telling her and adding:

> John Dunbar, Paul and I have been having megalomaniacal fantasies about taking over and changing everything: starting our own TV station, radio station, newspaper and so on. The power of the Beatles. Our second exhibition at Indica will be of John Lennon drawings if he ever finishes them.

Later that week Sue and I were visiting Wimpole Street. 'Paul's acting in a strange way,' Peter told us. 'He won't let anyone into his room. It's all very suspicious.' We went upstairs to Peter's room. Paul's room was next door and Peter knocked on the door. A muffled voice replied. Peter told Paul we were all in his room if he cared to join us. After a while Paul came in looking very Beatlish, even wearing Beatle boots. He had some loop tapes he wanted to play: backwards tapes of drums and guitars made by double-tracking using two tape recorders, varying the tape speeds and superimposing sounds so that some of the time his guitar sounded like flocks of seagulls. It was an experimental area that greatly interested him and occupied much of his time. Some of the results were shortly to appear on the track 'Tomorrow Never Knows'. We asked what he was up to in his room, accusing him of keeping a groupie in there, but he just grinned.

A few weeks later the secret was revealed. Paul arrived at Indica and hauled a heavy package out of the Aston. He had designed wrapping paper for the bookshop and had had a thousand sheets printed. Being Paul (or being the printer), they were printed on the best-quality paper, which made each one virtually an artwork. The design read 'Indica Books and Gallery' with our address, the lines of text forming a cross and a diagonal cross – a Union Jack, in fact – done in large black capital letters on white, each painstakingly hand-lettered. The labour and care he had put into it was amazing, a wonderful surprise gift. He could easily have given a rough design to a printer and had the thing typeset. Peter leaked the fact that Paul designed the wrapping paper to Gloria Stavers at *16 Magazine* and we began to get requests from girls in America, wanting sheets of paper. They usually sent American stamps to cover the postage.

We designed flyers with a map to show how to get to the gallery/

shop; Mason's Yard was quiet, with no traffic, and people would have to make a specific journey to find us. We all sat round my living-room table drawing them. Paul did several designs, one of which was printed. John hired a gallery assistant called Leukie Wink, and organised a wonderful announcement for the art gallery that was printed on limp plastic. It came in several colours and listed all the artists he intended to show or whose work he held on consignment:

> painting & construction exploiting new techniques & ideas; increasing the occurrence of communication contributing to the basic structure of sense data and visual expression; amongst those to be exhibited are:– alviani, dana ashley, groupe de recherche d'art visuel, clive barker, mark boyle, samuel buri, lourdes castro, dietmann, tony morgan, nelson, dei pezzo, david russell, daniel spoerri.

I received a classic business memo from John addressed to us all (misspelling Leukie's name, as he always did):

> . . . Luki has a Miles plan for index system with 4 colour cards . . . See that Plastic scenes get around to GOOD people – but take care as there are not many of them.
>
> Try & get something organised for a SUNDAY PAPER SCENE – Colour supplement, also phone up some of these critic guys & remind them of our existence . . .

He succeeded with the papers and we eventually had a lot of coverage, including a big spread in the *Observer* colour magazine. John continued to act as art critic for *The Scotsman*, introducing its readers to such difficult artists as the Venezuelan collagist Alejandro Otero. There was a very relaxed atmosphere in the Indica gallery compared to the other commercial galleries, which were very straight and intimidating. Even Robert Fraser showed established painters and made it clear that the general public was not welcome to linger. In fact Indica was one of the few places where people could stay to gossip and talk about art, and as a consequence a number of people volunteered their services as unpaid assistants. One frequent visitor was a small, talkative, rather excitable teenage male model called Mark Feld. He was a Londoner with an eye very much fixed on the main chance, who later permed his hair, changed his name to Marc Bolan and did well in the rock world. He was friendly and enthusiastic, genuinely interested in what was going on, and helped to paint the walls of the gallery. Some years later he and his partner, Steve Took, joined us when we took a box at the Albert Hall to see Janis Joplin. I seem to recall that Steve had green hair that evening.

Spontaneous Underground

An American named Steve Stollman arrived in London. His brother, Bernard, owned the ESP record label in New York and had given him the address of Indica. He knew about it through the Fugs, who were on his label. ESP was home to some of the most avant-garde and weird music being put on record, including one group called the Godz whom Bernard had met and signed up on the New York subway without ever having heard them. They were terrible. Steve went looking for similar off-the-wall stuff in Britain. He chose a unique way to do it and started a club. It was his idea that if you provided the space for people to get together and perform, then things would happen spontaneously. He rented the Marquee Club, at 90 Wardour Street, on a Sunday afternoon and charged six shillings and sixpence admission to pay the rental. He made no profit from it. There were no ads, but invitations were sent out to key people consisting of an envelope filled with cut-ups – William Burroughs-style – different in each envelope. There were slivers from Alexander Trocchi's *Sigma Portfolio*, slices of discarded pages from *Long Hair* magazine and a couple of inches cut from a Marvel comic. For the first event there was a mimeo statement, which read:

SPONTANEOUS UNDERGROUND at the Marquee this Sunday January 30th organised by Steve Stollman of ESP Disk with the aid of everybody. Among those taking part will be Donovan / Mose Allison / Graham Bond / Pop / Mime / Kinetic Sculpture / Discotheque / Boutique.

THIS TRIP begins at 4.30 and goes on. Liquor licence applied for. Costume, masque, ethnic space, Edwardian, Victorian and hipness generally . . . face and body makeup – certainly.

This is a spontaneous party, any profit to be held in trust by Louis Diamond, Solicitor, that such spontaneities may continue. Invitation only, donation at door 6/6.

The *Sunday Times* previewed the event:

'An absolutely new kind of rave' claims John Hopkins, who helped to make up the star-spangled invitation list for a massive *soirée*, to be held this evening at the Marquee Club, London . . . The organiser, 23-year-old Steve Stollman, until recently made documentary films in America. Now he wants to make documentary 'happenings' in England. The invited *are* the entertainment . . . Who will be there? Poets, painters, pop singers, hoods, Americans, homosexuals ('because they make up 10 per cent of the population'), 20 clowns, jazz musicians, 'one murderer', sculptors, politicians and some girls who defy description are among those invited. For Stollman their identity is irrelevant because this is underground culture which offers everyone the opportunity to do or say anything without conforming to the restrictions of earthmen . . .

Though the event was not as crowded as Steve possibly expected, it was a great success. After getting up late and reading the Sunday newspapers, people began to drift along to the Marquee dressed in extraordinary combinations of Edwardian and other finery. Among those who showed up were Johnny Byrne, who later co-wrote the book *Groupie* with Jenny Fabian about Jenny's stimulating experiences with rock 'n' roll bands; Roger Jones, Spike Hawkins, whom Pete Brown had discovered living in a hedge, and Lee Harwood. Together this group of poets had produced a series of little mimeographed poetry magazines in the early Sixties with names like *Bean Train* and *Night Train*. One of them, *Horde*, I co-edited.

Johnny Byrne and Spike Hawkins had an act together. They called themselves the Poison Bellows and arrived pushing a wind-up gramophone in an old pram, wearing long overcoats and mufflers and trailing yards and yards of fabric they had found in the street. They set things on fire and performed anti-conjuring tricks using Pete Brown's father's antique collapsible silk top hat. It was a type of typically British slapstick humour that was later developed by the Bonzo Dog Doo-Dah Band, the Alberts and to a certain extent the Scaffold. It had its immediate genesis in *The Goon Show* and reached its peak with *Monty Python's Flying Circus*.

This group of poets and writers had previously been involved with the short-lived Goings On Club, organised by Pete Brown, which was held once a week in a gambling club in nearby Archer Street. By the fifth week so many gamblers had infiltrated back in that the atmosphere became uncomfortable and it closed. There were a number of poetry groups who met in pubs or organised regular evenings. One of them, the resolutely working-class Peanuts group, had entertained Allen Ginsberg the previous summer at Finches pub on Goodge Street – the home of Donovan's 'violent hash smoker'.

The garment district was not far away and many people dragged in great armfuls of fabric offcuts. The thick cardboard tubes that cloth was spooled around made excellent megaphones to sing through, and other people brought scissors, crepe paper and paste. Soon a production line of weird costumes was in progress. Donovan appeared, later in the day, wearing red and black eye make-up: each eye drawn with an Egyptian Eye of Horus. He sat cross-legged on the stage and sang with six sitar players and a conga drummer, but the next day had no memory of the event.

British R&B originator Graham Bond also played, dressed in a buccaneer costume. With his black-magic gestures and much fierce gestalt eye-locking with members of the audience, he tilted and slammed his much-modified Hammond organ around the stage (he was the first musician to build an electronic keyboard and the first to separate the keyboard from the bulky instrument to give himself more room to perform). Though advertised, Mose Allison did not show up.

The 'Spontaneous Underground' immediately became the village pump of the underground. It had something of the atmosphere of the Albert Hall reading, except that it was weekly and there was a lot of pot and acid about. It was like a private club where you knew everyone. The liquor licence never materialised, but it was unnecessary anyway as everyone was already stoned.

The next invite was a promotional insert for ESP Records with a faint two-colour Roneoed message overprinted – barely decipherable. It read:

In memoriam. King Charles. Marquis de Sade. Superman. Supergirl. Ulysses. Charlie Chaplin. All tripping lightly looning phoenician moon mad sailors – in character as IN characters – characterised in costume at the Marquee this Sunday at 5 o clock . . .

The lettering then ran off the page, on both sides of the card. This was probably the evening when a classical pianist calmly played her way through the Bach Preludes and Fugues while Ginger Johnson and his African Drummers pounded out cross-rhythms all around her, highlighting the good bits with trumpet reveilles and concluding by bringing out something called 'the Big Log' which, literally, was a big hollowed-out tree trunk that they beat upon. By this time the stage was barely visible through the clouds of pot smoke. Had the police been on their toes they could have rounded up the whole inchoate London underground scene in one swoop.

Though we always referred to it as Spontaneous Underground, the announcements for the Sunday afternoon events at the Marquee only ever used that name once. Steve Stollman called it the Trip, as in his announcement for the 13 March event:

TRIP bring furniture toy prop paper rug paint balloon jumble costume mask robot candle incense ladder wheel light self all others march 13th 5 pm

That week's line-up featured Robert Wyatt on drums; the illustrator Mal Dean (whose cartoons later enlivened *International Times*) on trumpet and lavatory plunger; Rab Spall on amplified violin; John Surman on soprano saxophone; as well as two conga drummers, several spoons players (played against the thigh – an old London busker's and music-hall instrument) and much shouting. (Many of these people were involved in the early, ever-changing line-ups of the Soft Machine.) Also onstage was a young woman having her long red Rapunzel hair trimmed by a friend, further emphasising the lack of division between audience and performers. This was possibly the first time that Gerry Fitzgerald presented one of his enormous jellies. A large heap of pink jelly became a regular feature of early underground events and someone inevitably stripped off and rolled in it.

AMM

The most memorable Spontaneous Underground occurred some time in June 1966 and featured performances by AMM and the Pink Floyd. AMM was a free-form group at the very forefront of avant-garde experimentalism, and to reinforce the sense of serious scientific investigation they played in white lab-coats. Their line-up consisted of Cornelius Cardew on piano, cello and transistor radio, Lou Gare on tenor saxophone and violin, Eddie Prevost on drums, xylophone and other percussion. Keith Rowe on electric guitar and transistor radio and Lawrence Sheaf on cello, accordion, clarinet and transistor radio. Cardew was professor of composition at the Royal College of Music, had worked with John Cage and David Tudor in Europe and was Cage's leading disciple in Britain; he prepared a version of Cage's *Fontana Mix* for guitar. He spent two years as Karlheinz Stockhausen's assistant, working with him on a massive orchestral work. He later attacked his teacher in a forcefully argued book, *Stockhausen Serves Imperialism*, and took to performing revolutionary Chinese workers' songs, piping out 'We All Love the Three Old Articles of Chairman Mao' in his plummy upper-class accent. At the Spontaneous Underground, AMM used whistles and sirens, tape recorders and electric toys, which were allowed to run loose or to vibrate on a steel tray. There was no division between performers and audience, and all sounds constituted part of the piece being performed, whether they originated in the group or in the audience. There was no melody, no rhythm and no score. Cardew wrote, 'An AMM performance has no beginning or ending. Sounds outside the performance are distinguished from it only by individual sensibility.'

In fact Spontaneous Underground was not a good venue for AMM; the audience was too stoned and out of it. Far better was their weekly sound workshop held in a basement room of the Royal College of Art, where the audience sat on the floor and a musical piece could last for hours. Sue and I took Paul McCartney to one, early in 1966, to hear John Cage's theories of random sound put into practice. At this concert the closest Cardew got to playing the piano was to tap its leg with a small piece of wood. Paul joined in by running a penny along the coils of the old-fashioned steam radiator and, after the intermission, used the penny to carefully tap his pint-glass beer mug. Afterwards, commenting on the performance, he said, 'You don't have to like something to be influenced by it', but he told the organiser Victor Schonfeld, 'It went on too long.' Cage's influence was to show itself in the Beatles' music later in a number of subtle ways.

The Pink Floyd Sound

The Pink Floyd Sound, as they were then called – the name was painted on the bass amplifier – became a fixture at the Spontaneous Underground. Their line-up consisted of Roger Waters on bass, Rick Wright on keyboards. Nick Mason on drums and Syd Barrett on lead guitar. At the June 1966 Spontaneous Underground they had movies projected directly onto the stage and over the group, while red and blue lights pulsated in time to the music. It was hard to make out the features of any of the band because of the continuously moving, changing lights, which rendered them effectively anonymous; an element of the Pink Floyd's show that stayed with them. They rarely allowed their photographs to appear on album sleeves and, even at the height of their fame, could walk around London unrecognised, untroubled by the pressures that confined other rock stars to their limousines and hotel suites.

At this Spontaneous Underground, Syd Barrett paid particular attention to AMM's performance. He was very taken by Keith Rowe's electric guitar-playing technique, which included running steel ball bearings up and down the strings to produce peculiar sounds. Syd used this procedure himself later onstage. It was at this gig that Peter Jenner, their future manager, first saw the band.

One of the frequent visitors to Westbourne Terrace had been a young American record producer called Joe Boyd, who first came to Britain as the tour manager for packages of blues artists. He got to know Alan Beckett, and the jazz critic Ron Atkins, who was also a frequent visitor to Westbourne Terrace and who took a room in Hoppy's new flat on Queensway when he moved. Hoppy, Beckett, Ron Atkins and Joe Boyd, together with Peter Jenner, whom they knew through his activities in the London Free School, formed an independent production company called DNA Productions. Their first venture was an album by AMM called *AMMMUSIC*. Though Joe Boyd managed to get it released by Elektra Records, for whom he was then working, it was not an outstanding commercial success. They next recorded a difficult jazz album by Steve Lacy, which was not released. They quickly realised that they needed some more commercial material to balance the obscure stuff.

Hoppy had a new girlfriend, Kate Heliczer, who had just returned from living in New York, where she had been part of Andy Warhol's Factory scene. She brought with her tapes of the Velvet Underground playing at Warhol's Exploding Plastic Inevitable. This sounded a more commercial proposition and Jenner and Hoppy placed a call to New York, offering to produce the band. But Warhol had pre-empted them and had already done a deal with MGM Records, though their first album had not yet been recorded.

Peter Jenner was a schoolteacher. That evening he was bored with marking examination papers and decided to drop in on the Spontaneous Underground and see how AMM were getting on. When the Pink Floyd Sound took the stage, Peter was intrigued by the strange passages of psychedelic improvisation that occurred in the middle of 'Road Runner' and wondered if this was the commercial group they were looking for. Jenner later said, 'I arrived around ten-thirty and there on stage was this strange band who were playing a mixture of R&B and electronic noises. In between the routine stuff like "Louie Louie" and "Road Runner" they were playing these very weird breaks. It was all very bizarre and just what I was looking for – a far out, electronic, freaky pop group.'

Peter did not approach the Floyd immediately, but after making his decision, tracked them down to their house in Highgate where he told them, 'You'll be bigger than the Beatles!' Roger Waters remembered their cautious response: ' "Yes, well we'll see you when we get back from our hols," because we were all shooting off for some sun on the Continent.'

By this time Syd Barrett was taking acid regularly. There is a famous story describing his first trip, which occurred when he was nineteen. He was in the garden of his friend Bob Gale in Cambridge, along with Storm Thorgeson and Ian 'Imo' Moore. They had some liquid LSD in glass bottles, obtained from John Esam, who was by then living at 101 Cromwell Road in Nigel Gordon's flat. They laid out hundreds of sugar cubes in rows and began putting two drops of acid on each. The acid was highly concentrated and they began absorbing it by licking the sugar granules from their fingers. They became hopelessly confused, giving some cubes a double dose and others none at all. Syd, meanwhile, seized upon three objects, which he sat and stared at for twelve hours: an orange, a plum and a matchbox. The plum became the planet Venus and the orange was Jupiter. Syd travelled between them in outer space. His trip came to an abrupt end when Imo, liking the look of the plum, ate Venus in one bite. 'You should have seen Syd's face. He was in total shock for a few seconds, then he just grinned,' Imo reported. Though he smoked pot and had tried heroin, acid quickly became Syd's drug of choice.

The Pink Floyd's move from R&B into long experimental psychedelic sound-canvases in many ways reflected the listening habits of our little group. The jazz we played was getting further and further out, and there was a widespread interest in electronic and 'modern classical', as we called it. I had a couple of albums by Luciano Berio, who had done a lot of work using nothing but speeded-up, heavily edited tapes of voices, so when a lecture by him was announced for 24 February at the Italian Institute in Belgravia, we went along. Paul was interested in his tape experiments, so he came too. He liked to arrive just as something began, in order not be be harassed, but this time we arrived late and drew attention. The event was sponsored by the cultural division of the Italian Embassy and as soon as Paul stepped through the doors they panicked. 'Please, you will wait there just one minute . . .' Who knows how many people were forced to move by frantic embassy staff, but we entered the room to find that the three front centre seats awaited us. We slunk in and sat down as unobtrusively as possible in the circumstances, embarrassed at disturbing Berio's lecture, aware of all eyes directed towards us.

Shortly, another disturbance occurred as photographers pushed their way through the crowd, throwing open the creaking double doors that led to the corridor and banging the folding metal chairs against each other. Paul was fuming with anger, but sat it out in respect for Berio. The embassy staff now seemed contrite at the outcome of their call to the newspapers. No doubt they thought all publicity was good publicity, but they weren't prepared for the crass behaviour of the tabloids.

Berio presented a tape of his new work featuring Les Swingle Singers, but come the intermission there was another intrusion and more people were moved from their chairs as the cultural attaché showed up and Paul had to pose for photographs shaking hands. Having had his evening spoiled, Paul was sarcastic and non-cooperative. Berio also seemed upset at being manipulated, but did manage to have a few words with Paul at the end of the performance. Even this meeting was photographed. The *Musical Times* carried the photograph captioned, 'Beatle Meets Modern Italian Composer Luciano Berio'. The *Daily Mail*, responsible for all the disruption, ran a picture-spread titled 'What a Beatle Does in the Evenings'.

As we ran for the Mini, pursued by photographers, Paul shouted obscenities at them – 'Blood-suckers! Leeches!' – and observed that he could not go anywhere without them showing up and destroying it: '. . . All you do is destroy things! Why don't you *think* of people, why don't you *create* something?' They kept snapping away.

THE Global moon-edition Long Hair TIMES

Through Betsy Klein I had been asked to become the London correspondent for a new underground newspaper published in New York called the *East Village Other*. It represented the next generation on from the left-wing Jewish intellectuals who had started the *Village Voice* in the Fifties. They had no censorship problems because it was printed on an offset litho press in Chinatown, where the printers couldn't read the boards. They also realised that conventional newspaper layout had been determined by the restrictions of hot-metal letterpress. With offset litho you could print anything; you didn't need to justify the columns – in fact you didn't need to typeset it at all, for handwriting would reproduce just as well if it was dark enough. *EVO*, as the paper was immediately known, was soon filled with an explosion of crazy typefaces and photo-collages, and upside-down writing and cartoons; a visual equivalent of the news items they were printing. *EVO* pioneered the work of underground comic artists Robert Crumb and Spain Rodriguez (inventor of Trashman), which was quickly taken up by other newly started underground papers. I wrote the London column, Simon Vinkenoog was the Amsterdam correspondent and Jean-Jacques Lebel was *EVO*'s man in Paris – the same line-up we later employed in *International Times*. Hoppy and I decided that what we really wanted to do with Lovebooks was to publish a similar paper in Britain. Early in March Hoppy and I sent out a flyer which read:

Please reply to John Hopkins/Miles, THE G.m/e. L-H TIMES, 20 Fitzroy Sq. London W1. England.

Dear

We're on the point of starting a monthly anti-newsletter. Nothing is fixed yet except the intention, the format (8 x 13 horizontal pages carelessly stapled on left edge), and the title of the first issue: 'THE Global moon-edition Long Hair TIMES'.

We're asking for news items of special interest in the following categories:

1. Coming events in APRIL 66 / what just happened yet.

2. Sigmatic / Situationist & other points in time.

3. Global politics / CIA activity.

4. Avant-garde jazz (& this doesn't mean overrecorded hardboppers, either)

5. Free University / Free School / Community Development projects

6. Pot, LSD and other biochemical scenes / fuzz activity / advice

7. Happenings / Non-events

8. Censorship / Love / Funny Things.

and of course anything else.

We hope to print immediate communications from London, New York, Paris. We can print newspaper cuttings, collages, etc, but photos should be screened (cut from mags, newspapers). Our printing press wont carry much ink and if there are large black areas it just wont take it. Better to keep to line until we can afford another press.

Please note, we want news in order to circulate it. The whole thing is a communication idea. Keep it short or it wont get in: there's no editorial staff, just we 2. BUT you might get paid, in copies of the thing itself, to sell, if it ever happens.

Send anything legible, to arrive here before MARCH 20th, 1966 A.D. We send you love, & hope to receive cosmic signals.

THE Global moon-edition Long Hair TIMES got its name accidentally when Hoppy was experimenting with the offset printing press. 'The Times' was cut from *The Times*, and 'Long Hair' clipped from an unused front cover of *Long Hair* magazine. Hoppy added the rest by hand. Since we already had that zinc plate, that became the first page. We ran Ed Sanders' newsletter about his bust; a news item on Tim Leary's recent arrest, an LSD cartoon strip called 'Sugarman'; a letter to me from John Wilcock, editor of *Other Scenes*, about Warhol and the US scene; a letter from 'Bill', a member of the La Jolla Pump House Gang, a group of Californian surfers whom Tom Wolfe later wrote about in the collection of essays of the same name; a drugs column by Hoppy using the 'Bradley Martin' pseudonym that he continued to use in *International Times*; a jazz column by Ron Atkins, *Guardian* jazz critic and one of Hoppy's flatmates; and a back-page competition inserted by Paul McCartney using his backwards-tape pseudonym:

AMAZING COMPETITION – 20 gns PRIZE – AMAZING COMPETITION
Ian Iachimoe, the Polish 'new wave' film director, is offering a prize of 20 guineas to anyone who can supply the missing link in the following script. The dialogue is not needed, just the idea. Here is the outline of the story: a woman (age 35–45) is fanatical about cleanliness. She is amazingly house-proud and obsessional about getting rid of dirt. This carries over in her dress, looks, and so on. SOMETHING HAPPENS to make her *have* to crawl through a great load of dirt, old dustbins, and so on. Good old honest dirt. WHAT IS THIS SOMETHING?

The story continues with the woman's mind being snapped by her experience with dirt. She goes mad and her obsession gets even worse. WHAT IS NEEDED IS THE IDEA. What could cause her to have to become involved with filth. (She is not forced to do it but chooses to do it herself.)

SEND ALL ANSWERS, as many as you like, to Ian Iachimoe – c/o INDICA BOOKS & GALLERY, 6 Mason's Yard, Duke St. – Saint James's. London SW.1. WHI 1424

THIS COMPETITION IS FOR REAL – it seems strange but is real.

Paul was making a lot of home movies at the time and this was obviously the plot of one of them. The thing about the house-proud woman might have been to do with his mother who, being a midwife and nurse, was very clean and tidy. No one remembers if anyone answered the competition or won the prize.

I pasted up the artwork except for the cover, which was already done, Hoppy made the plates, printed it and we all collated and stapled it. It took one day from start to finish, instant non-news. The newsletter was in every way the forerunner of *International Times*. The next day was the start of the annual three-day Easter Campaign for Nuclear Disarmament march from Aldermaston to London. There were only 20,000 people on the march, small compared to the huge ones of the early Sixties. Still, Kate Heliczer, Hoppy, Harry Fainlight, Julie Felix, Sue and I sold about 300 copies. Hoppy and Kate spent more time on it and sold the most. We gave copies to all our friends and contacts: the Rastafarians had a flatbed truck with their banner (complete with Larry's painting of the Egg Marketing Board lion) and one of them was selling copies from the back.

Events were happening so fast that I found it hard to separate them in my head. It was the most frantic period of my life: the phone never stopped ringing, and being in a public place – a bookshop – meant that people were always turning up with schemes and plans that they expected us somehow to realise. I met so many people that they began to blur into each other. It was exhausting, but we were young and had the energy and we loved every minute of it. We seemed to be out every night and up early, heading down to Mason's Yard to write letters and make phone calls before the gallery filled with friends, all ostensibly helping John to mount the first group exhibitions. Early in April I wrote Betsy Klein a report of recent activities:

One Saturday, early in April, there was a scene in Chelsea where the BBC TV bought free acid for everyone and filmed a mass turn on with about 100 people present. The Sunday papers got the story and splashed it all over front pages and the guys at the BBC who made it look like getting the boot. On the film are Hoppy, Steve Stollman, Ewan, Kate Heliczer, Pete-the-Rat and so on. There were a number of police photographers present taking pictures of people all the time. A special ritual for the taking of LSD was invented for the viewing audience by Steve Stollman. It consisted of dressing up as a butterfly and crawling on hands and knees through the bathroom, over the side of the bath while balancing an orange on your head, then, if you could get your head between the bathtaps, while kneeling in the bath, Steve, who was sitting on the toilet, would pop a cube of sugar in your mouth. The BBC were delighted and filmed everything joyfully. The film is on the box in three days time.

At the Sunday night thing at the Marquee the BBC turned up with £3000 worth of strobe lights and gear and filled the place with snow effects, flames and all sorts. It was weird and wonderful. Indica is looking good, books all over the walls, balloons and posters on the noticeboards, the Lovin' Spoonful's 'D'you Believe in Magic' on tape coming up from the basement as the exhibitions get under way. I had an argument with Bill Burroughs yesterday about the Leary thing which he thinks is completely stupid . . .

These were Timothy Leary's presentations at the Village Theater on 2nd Avenue in New York. Tim was re-enacting great moments in the lives of spiritual masters: the enlightenment of Buddha, and so on. Bill objected vociferously, thinking that Leary was possessed with delusions of grandeur. I couldn't really argue, since Bill knew him and I didn't.

Whenever he was in New York, Peter Asher had been seeing Betsy Doster. Now he asked her to come to London and live with him. In America she had constructed a romantic and somewhat inaccurate image of what it would be like. Having never been to England, she naturally assumed that being an old aristocratic family the Ashers would live in some splendour. Descriptions of Wimpole Street would make it sound rather like an Upper East Side town house in New York, only much older. She had not realised that aristocrats do not like things to look new. In fact the more worn-out they are, the better, as long as they were good to start with.

Betsy was clearly surprised at what she found, arriving in the evening, jetlagged from the long flight, and being shown into 'Mrs Asher's Sitting Room', a hopelessly overcrowded room on the second floor where Mrs Asher, Jane, Paul, Clare, Sue and I were gathered having a nice cup of tea. Jane was knitting, an uncommon activity among actresses in America. There was not enough room for everyone to sit, so Jane sat on Paul's lap and Peter perched on the arm of a chair behind Betsy. Seeing how nervous Betsy was, Paul entertained us all with stories of Liverpool: an old man he saw on the upper floor of a bus wearing glasses with no lenses; a man who spoke to an invisible parrot on his shoulder; another man on a bus who simply named every comedian he could think of, pausing to roar with laughter between each name until everyone on the bus was in fits. Unfortunately Paul continually compared his examples with the USA, which he described as being plastic, uniform and standardised, and where even having long hair was regarded as a threat to the stability of the country. Instead of making Betsy feel at home, he made her feel more and more anxious.

Betsy was tall and thin, pretty, with long straight blonde hair and a fringe — 'bangs' as she called it. She was very friendly and did her best to fit in. It took her a while to get used to the household, which still functioned much as a Victorian one, but in the end she managed to wean Peter away from his mother and into a nearby flat on Weymouth Street. Betsy's look of sheer disbelief at seeing how Paul lived, in a tiny attic bedroom, would have been shared by millions of his American fans, though to the English girls who waited outside the house, scratched their names on Dr Asher's brass plaque and wrote messages on the Wimpole Street and New Cavendish Street signs, it would have seemed quite like home.

The Fugs

Early in March I received a copy of *The Village Fugs* at Indica. Just as I was opening the package, Paul dropped by the shop and, seeing the album, naturally wanted to hear it. We had no record player and so, with Paul leading the way, we went next door to the Scotch of St James. After a great deal of banging on the door, the manager appeared. He was shocked to find Paul there and, though he would normally have been delighted to help a Beatle, he seemed disgruntled at Paul's request to listen to an album at this time of day. The club looked seedy, the bare bulbs that lit the place up for cleaning revealing how much of the nightclub atmosphere was created by clever lighting. The DJ's hi-fi was housed in an old carriage, but when the combined out-of-tune voices of the Fugs blared out 'Slum Goddess from the Lower East Side', the manager could not believe his ears. He had been expecting the very latest American soul or R&B. 'What do you want to listen to that filth for?' he asked.

The Fugs provided an example of Paul's retentive memory. One night he arrived at Hanson Street and suggested that we all go immediately to Dollies on Jermyn Street. As usual when Paul arrived at a club, the doorman did a double-take and in no time at all people were moved from the best table so that we might sit down. Though the management usually managed to clear a table while we were checking coats and getting rid of the car, this time we were too quick and arrived at the dance floor in time to see a group of American businessmen complaining as they were manhandled from a table to give us room. As the evening progressed and we sipped our Scotch and Cokes, one of the Americans appeared, weaving drunkenly through the crowd, and demanded to know if Paul was a Beatle. After the usual story about his daughter, he insisted on an autograph. Paul looked momentarily annoyed, then beamed and scribbled something on the proffered napkin. The man stared at it, stared at Paul and staggered away, a puzzled look on his face. Paul leaned across and yelled (the only method of communication in those clubs), 'I signed my name as Tuli Kupferberg! That'll give him something to show the boys back in the States!' Tuli was percussionist with the Fugs.

On a sunny afternoon in late March, Paul stopped by Indica with John Lennon. It was John's first visit. He was looking for a book by someone called 'Nits Ga'. It took me a minute to figure out he was talking about Nietzsche, which was just long enough to make John uptight; he was painfully aware that he had little formal education and was ultra-sensitive to any form of ridicule; he began to rant about university-educated snobs. Paul mollified him by telling John that I had not been to university, that I had an art-college education, just like him. By this time I had found a copy of *The Portable Nietzsche*. (I gave it to him with slight trepidation – the idea of John Lennon getting into *The Will to Power* was slightly worrying.) John was mercurial; by the time he finished reading the announcements on our noticeboard he was in a really friendly mood and was soon chatting happily, remembering Allen Ginsberg's birthday party of the year before with amusement, his paranoia forgotten. He scanned the shelves and soon came upon *The Psychedelic Experience*, Timothy Leary's psychedelic version of the *Tibetan Book of the Dead*. There was an old settee in the middle of the shop and John curled up with the book to read. On page fourteen of Leary's introduction he came upon the line 'Whenever in doubt, turn off your mind, relax, float downstream'. With only slight modification, this became the first line of 'Tomorrow Never Knows', the Beatles' first truly psychedelic song. The track was initially referred to as 'Mark I' and we spent evening after evening playing an acetate of it until it wore out.

At Paul and John's instigation, I sent all four Beatles copies of any new book or magazine that I thought would interest them. 'Just send it along, you know, don't wait to ask us, 'cause we don't know. Just send the bill to the office.' Whenever there was an interesting issue of *Domus* or *Du*, or some good underground material from America, I sent it along. One good example was Ajit Mookerjee's *Tantra Art*. George enjoyed the book so much that he had his Mini-Cooper car painted with Hindu and Buddhist tantric designs taken from it. Unfortunately the book's publisher, Ravi Kumar, saw a photograph of the car in a newspaper and sued George for copyright infringement, though how you can copyright a thousand-year-old image I don't know.

Cavendish Avenue

That March Paul and Jane moved into their new house on Cavendish Avenue. It had been decorated in a low-key manner in keeping with the architecture: in the living room was a small, old-fashioned coke-burning grate in a large open fireplace with a black lacquered coal scuttle standing next to it. The room had dark Victorian leaf-patterned wallpaper and a huge black-and-white television. They had no furniture of their own, so they had been on a buying spree. Most of it was picked up cheap at Coe's auction rooms in the Brompton Road (a favourite of the Ashers): a three-piece suite that they had re-covered in green velvet cost £20, a mahogany antique table £10 and the ornate metal clock on the mantel £7. Paul's biggest extravagance was to buy a Victorian street light for the drive outside.

In the dining room an unframed, slightly-damaged old brown painting of highland sheep hung over the fireplace, but the living-room walls quickly began to fill with modern art, beginning with a René Magritte. On the patio outside stood a set of figures modelled on characters from *Alice in Wonderland*, given to them by Paul's brother Michael.

Paul and Jane's bedroom had a walk-in closet behind the bed, a sunken bath and shower, tiled in blue and white, and a remote control for opening the curtains from the bed. This, like the other James Bond gadgets in the house, quickly broke. The movie screen had to be wound down by hand, and it was rare for both record players to be working at the same time. Even the knobs on the Brenell tape recorders kept coming off.

In the music room at the top of the house the cupboard with the door painted by Pete Simpson now housed an Indian drone instrument called a tubon, a Rickenbacker and a koto. A waist-high chrome Eduardo Paolozzi sculpture called 'Solo' stood beneath a six-foot-high triple portrait of Jane. Paul's cabaret piano, soon to be painted in psychedelic colours by the design team of Binder, Edwards and Vaughan, stood next to the window, giving him a view of the fans gathered round the gates while he played. Paul had now added a Revox A77 and other equipment to his pair of Brenell tape recorders and was able to make quite sophisticated tapes in his room. Now when he wanted to show the other Beatles how one of his songs should go, he was able to play them a fully worked-out tape. One of the first was 'What Goes On'. Using multi-tracking, he played lead guitar, bass and drums, as well as laying down the vocal track to show Ringo how he wanted him to sing it. The Revox could also be used to produce a tremendous echo-chamber effect, and on several occasions we all sat round playing bongos, strumming guitars, while Paul laid down increasingly weird chords on the piano, the massive echo making the whole thing sound terrific. (I remember listening to a similar tape we made at Abbey Road once. With the echo taken away, no one could bear to listen for more than two minutes, it was so awful.)

The house was looked after by Mr and Mrs Kelly, who lived in the basement flat. They had previously been housekeepers to a 'real gentleman' and had their own ideas of how Paul should live. Each day when he set the dining table, Mr Kelly placed a highly polished silver cruet in the centre of the table. Each day, Paul removed it and replaced it with a pair of cheap plastic salt and pepper shakers, spoiling the whole effect of the silver cutlery, gleaming wine glasses and thick linen tablecloth. It was Paul's little protest.

Many of the difficulties faced by Paul and Jane stemmed from her determination to continue her career as an actress. In October 1965, much against Paul's wishes, she had joined the Bristol Old Vic Company, which meant that she spent a lot of time out of London. Jane did not take drugs and was not comfortable when they were used around her, so she did not fit in easily with Paul's druggy entourage. She preferred her own group of – mostly theatrical – friends, and asserted her right to lead her own life. At the Ashers' house there had been little conflict in their lifestyles because they saw their friends separately. Now that they had Cavendish Avenue, their friends sometimes collided.

One amusing instance of this occurred when Jane arranged to entertain a group of actor friends to dinner, unaware that Paul had simultaneously invited Sue and me to meet him at Cavendish Avenue. We were supposed to go on to Abbey Road with John Lennon, who was going to be there as well. Jane's friends, six or seven people, were clearly nervous at having Paul and John hovering in the background, working out small details of one of their songs. Though they tried to concentrate on their own company, their attention kept drifting as John and Paul moved around the room and sometimes joined their table. John was in a difficult mood, unpredictable and snappy. All the same, Jane's guests tried to draw him into the conversation and treat him like any other person. One of the women asked if he knew where an ashtray was. John dropped to his knees beside her and prised open his left nostril, 'Put it here, lady, put it here.' Everyone laughed, but a little nervously because John didn't seem to be joining in the joke. He remained crouching until the woman blushed and Jane, seeing her discomfort, pushed John over with her foot. He rolled over on his back, his feet in the air.

John continued to ignore everyone in the room and roamed around in his dirty white tennis shoes, stopped to stare at the old brown painting of sheep on a Scottish hillside or to play a note or two on the pump organ by the door to the hallway. Jane was thankful when we left; in her original plan we were clearly not supposed to have been there at all.

London Free School

While I was absorbed with getting Indica together with John and Peter, Hoppy had become involved with another new project: the London Free School. Many people on the scene were teachers or academics, many came from a left-wing background in CND or the Labour Party and there was a lot of discussion about education as the key to changing society. This was, in part, what Indica was about: to introduce people to new ideas and the latest developments in art. It was on this same premise – to wise people up – that Hoppy and community activist Rhaunie Laslett began the London Free School in Notting Hill. It was launched with a public meeting at St Peter's

Church Hall on Tuesday, 8 March 1966. The flyer for the meeting, printed on the Lovebooks offset-litho machine in stunning red and black, read, 'The LFS offers you free education through lectures and discussion groups in subjects essential to our daily life and work.' It promised that 'The London Free School is not political, not racial, not intellectual, not religion, not a club. It is open to all.' Areas of study included housing problems, immigration – Notting Hill was then very much a West Indian neighbourhood – race relations, how to start a street nursery, education, law, etc. The main activists were Rhaunie Laslett; Hoppy; photographer Graham Keen – whom I knew from Cheltenham Art College and who was later to become a director of *International Times* – and his girlfriend Jean McNeil; Peter Jenner, who was soon to manage the Pink Floyd; and black community leader Michael de Freitas, later known as Michael X.

Michael had a large basement room at 26 Powis Terrace lying empty – he had previously used it as an illegal gambling club. The rent was paid for eighteen months and he turned it over to the LFS free of charge. There was a billiard table there and local people were encouraged to drop by. Michael himself taught a class in basic English, mostly to elderly Irish people. He also helped improve contacts between the West Indian and white communities by bringing Muhammad Ali, then the heavyweight champion of the world, to visit the fifty children in Rhaunie Laslett's Free School play group.

In the nineteenth century there had been an annual Notting Hill Fair and Pageant, but it had not taken place for over a hundred years. The London Free School decided to revive it and the local council offered a large grant towards its resurrection – but only if the LFS got rid of Michael de Freitas. Michael had a criminal reputation and many of his activities were still on the wrong side of the law. He had been a pimp and an enforcer for the slum landlord Peter Rachman – he would go in with dogs to evict recalcitrant tenants. There was a very hard side to Michael, but these days his heart was (mostly) in the right place, even though he did boast that he once killed a man with a machete.

Hoppy and Rhaunie Laslett were not about to be blackmailed by the council and in July 1966 the fair happened anyway, without the

117

council's help. A Caribbean steel band led a parade of floats and children in fancy dress. There was a real carnival atmosphere, with jazz bands and poetry readings, and about 1,000 West Indians and 1,500 white people filled the streets. The fair continued for a whole week and there were remarkably few arrests, despite a heavy police presence. From this humble beginning, the Notting Hill Carnival has grown to become the largest festival in Europe, attracting more than a million people to the streets of Notting Hill every August Bank Holiday weekend.

Indica Gallery

The first proper show at Indica was the Groupe de Recherche d'Art Visuel, a loose collective of artists working in the area of kinetic art, who were represented by the Denise René Gallery in Paris. John was taught to drive by Taffy, and in June, although he had not yet taken his driving test, he set off for Venice accompanied by Tony Morgan, one of his artists, to represent Indica at the Venice Biennale. He already knew Robert Fraser, but it was in Venice that they became friends. Robert was there in his white suit, silk handkerchief half out of his breast pocket, with a large briefcase filled with drugs. The Americans wanted Robert Rauschenberg to win, but it was the Argentinean Julio le Parc, a founder member of the Groupe de Recherche d'Art Visuel, who received the grand prize for painting. John didn't know he had won until he heard it on the car radio on the way home and Julio was reported to have fainted when he heard the news. Indica was showing the winner of the most prestigious art prize in the world. The phone began to ring, but John was still on the road and no one knew what to tell people.

On John's first day back we were standing in the bookshop when a large man in a tartan jacket approached the door. He burst in and announced, 'I'm a big American collector! Lemme see your Le Parcs!'

John polished his granny glasses. 'I'm a little English art dealer,' he said. 'And the Le Parcs are all downstairs.'

The American bought the biggest that we had. It was only later that we found out that the price list given us by Le Parc was a joke. He did not expect us to sell anything and had put random prices down, ranging from ten pounds to thousands. It was clearly time to be a bit more businesslike. Tony Morgan, who had gone with John to Venice, had a French wife, Geneviève, who knew about such things and she now took over as gallery manager.

The Groupe de Recherche d'Art Visuel show was very popular: it was more like a fairground hall of mirrors than a conventional art show. There were glasses that distorted your vision, balls on elastic, a variety of hand mirrors each of which distorted your features in a different way, and of course light boxes and projections of rays and reflections of light upon polished surfaces.

One of Julio's pieces was 'Passage Accidenté', a set of eight square black boxes, arranged like large stepping stones outside the gallery. Each had a projecting piece of wood on the bottom to make it unstable so that they tipped and moved as you walked over them. They were a favourite of children, and of quite a few adults. One lunchtime we set off for the café to find that they had gone – the dustmen had assumed they were rubbish and thrown them on the back of their cart. John got on the phone, but by the time we located them they were on a refuse barge heading down the Thames. There was no way to intercept them before they finished up under hundreds of tons of London rubbish somewhere down the estuary. At least we were able to get some publicity out of it, and the evening papers had a wonderful time writing about modern art being mistaken for rubbish.

John's new friendship with Robert Fraser meant that we saw quite a bit of him. Robert had one of the most fashionable and hip art galleries in town, where he pioneered the work of Pop artists Peter Blake and Richard Hamilton, Op artists like Bridget Riley and introduced the work of Americans such as Andy Warhol and Claes Oldenburg to the British public. He had a wonderful eye for quality and, though he discovered no unknown artists, he was able to create enough razzmatazz and excitement around his shows that it was as if no one had seen the work before.

Much of the work was sold from his home, a luxurious apartment in Mount Street, Mayfair, filled with antique silver-gilt chairs, a flock of Nicholas Monro's fibreglass sheep, and numerous table lamps and candles, which Robert continually adjusted while pouring drinks and proffering joints. His salon included fellow old Etonians like Christopher Gibbs and Lord Londonderry, whom he mixed with the rock aristocracy of Brian Jones, Keith Richards, Anita Pallenberg and Paul McCartney. Though he came from a wealthy family, Fraser's money all went on a heroin habit, 'rough boys' and an expensive lifestyle: a live-in manservant called Muhammed, fine wines, the best restaurants and drugs of the highest quality. There was rarely any money left to pay his artists, most of whom left him after a while because he did not pay them for the paintings he sold.

He was that archetypal Sixties character, the lovable rogue. He had an utterly cavalier attitude towards money, and simply could not understand why Bridget Riley was so outraged when he left a cab waiting outside her studio while he was inside explaining to her why he could not pay her the money he owed. He constantly borrowed money from his friends and his more wealthy clients and was loath to pay it back, looking startled and angry if anyone dared to mention such an uncool thing. He always hated it when I brought up his outstanding account with Indica, which I frequently did, and which, of course, he never paid. Robert's often stated creed was 'Never apologise and never explain!'

He was, as Christopher Gibbs put it, 'A principals only person, a star fucker.' Robert was never interested in the entourage or the people who actually did the work, it was the famous person or the wealthy person who received the full blast of his charm. He was a crook and a snob, but fascinating and entertaining. We spent many amusing evenings with him nightclubbing, usually with Paul McCartney, during which we would inevitably show up just as a club was closing and Robert would have to bribe our way in, bending double in his skin-tight pink suit to pull huge wads of cash from his trouser pocket to give the doorman.

29 Lennox Gardens

Sue and I often visited John and Marianne at Lennox Gardens, which had become another of the London salons: John's friend Dave Courts, whom he met while hitch-hiking in Greece, was usually there, and Paul often dropped in, as did Robert Fraser, Christopher Gibbs, Shaun Phillips, Terry Southern, Donovan and any number of acquaintances who were passing through town. Mason Hoffenberg, the co-author of *Candy*, stopped by and stayed for six months. Most of the time we talked about music, played records and made cassette tapes of them: Jimmy Reed, Muddy Waters, all the old blues singers. John Mayall would sometimes bring rare 45s from the huge collection of blues records that his father had assembled in Manchester in the Fifties. There was always good music and good dope.

The extraordinary thing about visiting John and Marianne was the extreme contrast in their lifestyles. Marianne had leased the flat and furnished it from Harrods with her rock 'n' roll money. It was on the top floor, with a view out over trees. There was a large living room, which also contained an elegant, highly polished dining table and all the accoutrements of fine living. Sprawled on the floor near the windows and speakers were John's friends, rolling joints, nodding out, or banging on pots and pans, using Marianne's highly polished copper-bottomed saucepans as bongos. The flat divided into the big front room, where John and his friends hung out, and where he sometimes displayed art from Indica, which did not fit in at all well with Marianne's middle-class design scheme, and the rest of the flat which was Marianne's domain.

A good example of the contrast in lifestyles was a story that Marianne told me about John and Dave Courts taking acid in the summer of 1965. Marianne was pregnant with Nicholas and her mother, Eva, Baroness Erisso, was at Lennox Gardens looking after her. Marianne:

> I had had the pre-acid lecture, before they took the acid, which was 'Now, Marianne, David and I are going to take this new drug. And you have to be really nice to us, and not say anything nasty and not *bring me*

121

down!' And I got excited about this, 'Okay, so yes, and whatever I do, I mustn't bring you down! Right!' So off they go and they take it and hours go by, and I'm resting in the bed, and suddenly there's John, gleaming eyed, of course, completely different, and he wants the pillows, so I mustn't bring him down, 'Okay, darling, take the pillows.' Then he takes the eiderdown and then finally the mattress! And so they all ended up in the front room on the mattress lying there, gazing into their heads, seeing colours and things and I was okay with this because I knew I mustn't bring him down. But what really upset me was then my mother walked in with a cup of tea, and she was appalled! I remember the terrible sort of shame, 'You're lying on the springs! Where's the mattress?' I didn't know what to do. What do I say now? 'John's tripping in the front room and I mustn't bring him down.' I had to come up with some reason. I said that John was doing an experiment. It was just incredible, and I ended up feeling jealous and left out.

Dinner at Marianne's could be a harrowing affair. Everything had to go perfectly or else she was distraught. Sometimes the meal took so long to cook that by the time the first course actually appeared, everyone was so stoned that they had long passed the hunger stage and were now just craving munchies. On one occasion, John, Sue and I arrived late for dinner and Marianne was absolutely furious. She had cooked a ham with cloves and as we came up the stairs, she ran out into the street and disappeared. It seemed a shame to waste the food, so we all sat down to eat. Meanwhile, Marianne had gone to Marylebone to tell John's mother how horrible he was. When she got there she felt embarrassed and didn't know what to say. She took a cab straight back and joined us at the table, sliding into her chair as if nothing had happened.

On 10 November 1965 Marianne gave birth to Nicholas at the London Clinic and we went to visit her with John, who seemed a bit bemused by it all. The presence of a baby caused even more of a division in the flat, with John and his druggy friends in the front, and Marianne, her mother, Nicholas and the nanny in the back, separated by a long corridor. There was little contact between the two sides, though I remember on one occasion the Baroness came into the living room and asked if anyone had a cigarette. I offered her a newly opened pack of ten Weights and she took five of them. I couldn't believe it.

Quite early in 1966 Sue and I began to see more and more of Maggie McGivern. She had originally been hired by John and Marianne as a nanny for their son, which immediately led to some uneasy situations. John and Marianne were friendly, liberal people who naturally treated Maggie as an equal. They were also very young to be hiring staff of any kind, so in the evenings there would be an embarrassing situation when they never knew how to tell her that they were entertaining and that she should leave the living room. Maggie was certainly not going to take the hint and leave when there was Paul McCartney sitting on the floor rolling a joint. Soon, to John and Marianne's disapproval, Maggie began showing up at art-gallery openings with Paul. This made things even worse, making it impossible to have Paul to dinner. The situation was further complicated by the fact that John also started an affair with Maggie, turning the household into a three-act farce.

Mac Meda Destruction Co.

I did my best to publicise the bookshop, writing articles for magazines as different as *Isis*, the Oxford University weekly magazine, and *Poetmeat*, a mimeo poetry magazine from Blackburn. Gloria Steinem, with her trademark big hair, came and interviewed us, and Sue and I had our picture in *London Life*. People began to find the shop, but most of the time, though there were plenty of visitors, it was empty of paying customers. I wrote dozens of letters each day, and we sent out a mimeo catalogue of books for sale. The morning mail was always interesting, bringing everything from Fluxboxes from New York to the latest concrete poetry foldout from John Furnival in the Cotswolds. One day I received a decal of a mushroom cloud, with Mac Meda Destruction Co. written underneath it, sent by Bill van Petten, a member of the La Jolla Pump House Gang. That was the name they went by when they sent out announcements for parties. Bill wrote, 'Put this decal in your window and Tom Wolfe will come and see you.' I put it in the window and sure enough, a few weeks later, in through the door came Tom Wolfe in his white suit and shoes with the high collar and tie-pin. He was nonplussed when I told him he was expected. He wrote to Bill: 'All I know is, the Indica Book Shop – scene of London's big avant garde kinetic show – has a large Mac Meda Destruction Co. decal on the front window, right by the door. I will try to get a picture for you . . .' He could not figure out how we knew about the surfers because his book, *The Pump House Gang*, was not yet published and I had forgotten how we came by the sticker until Bill wrote to me again.

John Wilcock had told Bill about the shop, so he wrote me a long newsy letter out of the blue, telling me about the *Los Angeles Free Press* and the gallery scene. In his next letter he sent the decal and explained, 'The Mac Meda Destruction Co. has gone on for some fifteen years now; all manner of dastardly deeds have been credited to it, all apocryphal – perhaps. But if your car breaks down anywhere in Southern California, you have only to call the number listed in the La Jolla telephone book under Mac Meda Destruction Co., and sooner or later someone will show up to help out – or if the car is hopeless – to make a party.' The gang all drove Volkswagens because the sea air rotted out their 'woodies' – wooden-sided stationwagons. Tom Wolfe later wrote that when one of their VWs broke down they were prone to driving around late at night until they found a similar model and exchanging the engine, carefully installing their broken one so that the owner would never know what had happened. It was amazing to be in touch with all the wonderful varieties of the alternative underground scene; this surf and car lifestyle was utterly inconceivable in England.

Our location in Mason's Yard meant that staff of the Arts Council of Great Britain often passed Indica on their way to and from lunch as they were located in nearby St James's Square. Among them were Eric White, the literature director, and his assistant Charles Osborne. They were at first astonished to find a poetry bookshop on their doorstep, as they were supposedly in touch with the literary scene, but they soon became very supportive of our venture. It turned out that the Arts Council was thinking of setting up a centre for the distribution and sale of poetry books, magazines and pamphlets, possibly with enough space for poetry readings, and had already canvassed potential applicants for the job. As this was more or less what Indica was trying to do itself, we applied, then made a joint application with Donald Carroll, a literary agent and publisher who specialised in poetry in translation.

This was when I first became aware of the politics of the Establishment. One of the other applications came from a registered charity, Poets In Public, which I had never heard of. It looked like a jobs-for-the-lads outfit to me. They wanted to set up a 'Poetry Secretariat' and proposed a budget of £6,500. After a great deal of correspondence and a number of meetings, a conference was held at Indica on 7 July, at which it quickly became obvious that there was no common ground between the Indica group, which included Stuart Montgomery and other avant-garde booksellers, and Poets In Public, represented by someone called George Wightman, Trinity College, Cambridge, King's Own Shropshire Light Infantry, managing director of Export Management Consultants Limited. The minutes of the meeting read: 'George Wightman asked why all the money available couldn't go to the Poetry Society. He then accused Indica of being ostensibly commercial and therefore ineligible for Government money, whereas Poets In Public was registered as a charity . . .' Basically, the Poets In Public gang took one look at us and hated us. They were not going to let a bunch of newcomers in on their good thing. The poetry distribution-centre project was quietly dropped, though I remained in touch with Eric White and Charles Osborne, who had tried their best.

Indica Bookshop

It was obvious from the time of our first art opening at Indica that the gallery needed more space. It was also apparent that the bookshop needed to be on a shopping street where it would get some passing trade. Somehow John met Christopher Hill, who had just acquired the lease on Jackson's, a large bookshop at 102 Southampton Row, which specialised in selling school books to convents, most of them in Africa. There was a small amount of general stock left, but the shop had seen better days. Before the war it had been a gathering place for intellectuals and even had its own visitors' book signed by Huxley, Keynes and various other members of the Bloomsbury Group. In June Christopher became a partner of MAD Limited, and we moved the bookshop to Southampton Row. Paul put up the money to enable us to make the move and buy into Chris's lease. Chris lived above the shop at 18 Ormonde Mansions, 106 Southampton Row, in a large flat that he shared with his younger twin brothers, Jeffrey and Alan.

The Hill brothers were brought closer to the scene socially when Maggie McGivern moved in with them. The situation at Lennox Gardens had become untenable and she moved out and took the spare room in Chris Hill's apartment. Breakfast there took place mid-morning and I would sometimes join them as it was a good time to talk with Chris about the shop. The twins often argued with him, constantly questioning his authority, always pushing him. Chris rarely argued back, but just stood blinking, polishing his little glasses. Lisa, a tall silent Swedish woman who also had a room there, would prepare her own food and then leave. Maggie, however, would flop down in her chair to start the day with a cup of coffee and a cigarette. The Hill brothers all kept one furtive eye on Maggie because whenever she leaned back in the chair with her cigarette, her short dressing gown always seemed to fall open, and all three of them would be casting stealthy glances at her pubic hair as they pretended to read the paper or make tea. Maggie had a great sense of fun. She had style and determination. She knew when to wear something stunning to an Indica opening with Paul, and when to be inconspicuous.

The new bookshop was a maze of small rooms comprising 2,700 square feet in all, seven times larger than Mason's Yard. Our first move was to tear down the false ceilings and demolish all the dividing walls, revealing mouldings and ancient gas fittings. New wiring was installed and the walls were lined with wooden bookcases, except in the large back room, which was kept free for posters and for overflow exhibitions from Mason's Yard. The top shelves housed concealed lighting and Melonex was stretched across the room between the tops of the bookcases to make a shimmering silver ceiling, inspired by Andy Warhol's Factory, except that our silver surface would move every time someone opened the door. The Melonex was suggested by Mike Cooper, who wanted to make a neon sign saying 'Indica' for the front window, mounted on a huge block of Melonex-wrapped polystyrene, but the cost would have been enormous and both Peter Asher and I thought the money would be better spent on books. John helped pack the books into cardboard boxes; he couldn't wait to take over the ground floor of Mason's Yard as gallery space.

My old art-college friend Kipps had been working on and off at the gallery, helping to install shows. Now he came to the Southampton Row bookshop where he worked part time, most afternoons, for three or four years. He built the window display unit, a solid wooden structure of three stepped back shelves which he covered in hessian, the trendy covering of the day, so that we looked like a proper bookshop at last. He also designed our new headed notepaper featuring the Mayan flying-saucer figure discovered at Palenque. He had a whimsical style, a mixture of Pop Art and psychedelia, that I really liked.

Peter Asher and I had regular lunches at one of the better Italian restaurants on Southampton Row to discuss the progress of Indica and to explore even grander ideas for a record shop specialising in American imports, possibly in the back half of Indica, and for launching ESP Records in the UK. Peter approached his friend Ian Whitcomb and he was interested in coming in on a record shop; we also made the initial moves to open ESP in Britain. The record shop died in the water, but ESP almost happened. Peter and I started a company, ESP Disc UK, Ltd, and discussions were held with various record companies to distribute the discs. The idea was to launch the company with a Fugs tour. We thought we had a deal with Peter Bates at Polydor UK to release them, but unfortunately the records were seen as too obscure for the British market – even the Fugs – and ultimately we could not find anyone prepared to take them on. Obviously we couldn't distribute them ourselves, so the company folded.

Paul had recently begun listening to the BBC Third Programme and while driving to Liverpool heard a production of *Ubu cocu*. He asked me about Alfred Jarry. As I was a member of the College of 'pataphysics I was pleased at his interest and sent him a copy of Jarry's *Selected Works*. The outcome was that when *Ubu roi* came to the Royal Court Theatre in Sloane Square, we all went to see it. There was some confusion at the box office because the tickets had, as usual, been booked under another name. The problem was that they could not remember what name they had used. The set design at the Royal Court was by David Hockney and the old vaudevillian Max Wall played King Ubu. It was a daring idea to use Wall in this way, casting across traditional theatrical frontiers, and it worked, but I didn't enjoy it as much as Jack Henry Moore's Traverse production. The play was the subject of an intense discussion afterwards at Chi-Chi's, a nightclub located under the *Economist* building on St James's. Jane, naturally, made the most incisive criticisms.

When the drinks bill arrived, Jane was outraged and said so. A round of drinks came to £8, which was almost a week's wages in those days. There was often a slight tension between Paul and Jane over money. Jane was naturally thrifty and, though she had no say over Paul's money, she was horrified when she saw him, as she thought, throwing it away. The rounds of clubs and expensive restaurants must have added up; a whisky and Coke cost about a pound at most places, and eating at Parks on Beauchamp Place was not cheap. Sue and I never saw the drinks bills – Paul always signed an account slip and the bill was sent off to the office. At one club a new waiter asked Paul where he should send it. Paul didn't know any more. 'I've always signed them, somebody somewhere knows what to do with them, somebody somewhere probably pays them.'

The Pink Floyd

Peter Jenner pursued his idea of managing the Pink Floyd and in August he recruited a partner, Andrew King, who had recently left British Airways training and education department and was at a loose end. Nick Mason and Roger Waters secretly believed Jenner and

King to be drug dealers, but none the less, when they returned from their holidays, they agreed to let them become their managers. Andrew had a small inheritance, out of which he spent £1,000 on buying new amplifiers for the band. These were almost immediately stolen and Peter Asher, who knew the group through me, lent them Peter and Gordon's stage gear until they could buy a new set on hire-purchase. True to the spirit of the day, instead of creating a management company like that of Brian Epstein – who took 25 per cent of the Beatles' income before their enormous expenses were deducted, and who therefore made far more than any individual member of the band – Peter and Andrew started a new company called Blackhill Enterprises (named after a cottage in Wales owned by Jenner) and divided the shares into six equal parts. (The papers were finally signed on 31 October 1966.) With Peter now in charge, the Floyd were drawn into the London underground scene. He immediately booked them into the London Free School at All Saints' Hall, Powis Gardens, Notting Hill. There were about twenty people when they first played, the second week saw about 100 people, then 300, 400 and from then on you couldn't get in.

The band had evolved its own version of psychedelic rock without having heard any of the San Francisco groups, though there was some input from Los Angeles. Syd spent the summer of 1966 listening to Love's eponymous debut album and *Fifth Dimension* by the Byrds. He was introduced to the former by Peter Jenner, who tried to hum to him the guitar hook from Love's version of Burt Bacharach's 'My Little Red Book'. Syd played it back on the guitar, but it came out sounding quite different. He used it as the main set of chord changes in 'Interstellar Overdrive', probably the most emblematic of the Floyd's early work. Peter and Syd used to spend a great deal of time smoking pot and taking acid together; the rest of the group confined themselves to a very occasional toke on a joint. Despite this, Nick Mason didn't feel that Syd was ever a fully paid-up member of the underground scene. 'I don't think Syd was a man of the times. He didn't slot in with the intellectual likes of John Hopkins and Joe Boyd, Miles, Pete Jenner, the London Free School people. Probably being middle-class we could talk our way through, make ourselves sound as though we were part of it . . . But Syd was a great figurehead. He was part of acid culture.'

The Pink Floyd played the London Free School Sound/Light Workshop throughout the autumn to packed houses, and it was here that they developed their first light-show. An American couple called Joel and Toni Brown arrived from Millbrook bringing with them a light-show they had developed while living in Timothy Leary's psychedelic community. They set up a projector for their water-slides and began throwing strange images over the group. Though not as mind-blowing as the descriptions people had heard of Californian light-shows, it none the less encouraged Peter Jenner to build one of his own for the group. Together with his wife Sumi and Andrew King, he mounted a number of domestic spots on a piece of board and lashed up several bits of coloured perspex in front of them. The lights were turned on and off by ordinary household light switches. This rudimentary arrangement was soon made more sophisticated by a seventeen-year-old called Joey Gannon who hung out at the lighting workshop of Hornsey College of Art. Joey became the Floyd's first lighting director. In a 1966 interview Joey explained, 'I design the slides, basing them on my idea of the music. The lights work rhythmically – I just wave my hand over the micro switches and the different colours flash. In San Francisco the lights were provided by entirely separate light-show artists who were used by all the groups; the groups didn't have their own integrated show like the Floyd.'

Syd's then flatmates, Peter Wynne-Wilson and his girlfriend Susie Gawler-Wright, joined in and developed a method of playing with lights with a keyboard. Wilson worked in a West End theatre and was able to salvage theatrical lighting equipment that was being discarded. The projectors grew from 500 watts to 1000 watts, projecting intense spots on the band. By late autumn 1966 the three of them had developed the trademark pulsating liquid slides that were to characterise most of the London psychedelic light-shows: coloured inks were expanded between plates of glass by heating them with a blowtorch, then cooled with a hair-dryer. These were a featured part of the act, as a flyer for the 14 October show at the London Free School showed:

Announcing Pop Dance featuring London's farthest out group, The Pink Floyd in Interstellar Overdrive, Stoned Alone, Astronomy Domini (an astral chant) & other numbers from their space-age book. Also Light projection Slides, Liquid Movies . . .

Nick Mason said later, 'There were elements of the underground that we did tune into. The main one was mixed media. We may not have been into acid but we certainly understood the idea of a Happening. We supplied the music while people did creative dance, painted their faces, or bathed in the giant jelly. If it had been thirty years earlier Rick would have come up out of the floor in front of the cinema screen playing the organ.'

International Times

Hoppy and I had not given up on the idea of starting a newspaper to cater to the new underground scene. We had many late-night conversations, but it was obvious that even if we got a paper started, neither Hoppy nor I had the time to edit it. We set about making Lovebooks Limited into a bigger operation. We already had a third director in our accountant Michael Henshaw. Michael also acted for Arnold Wesker's Centre 42 arts organisation and had a number of writers and playwrights on his books. At my suggestion we brought in Jim Haynes, who was then in London directing a season of Traverse Theatre plays at the Jeanetta Cochrane Theatre with Jack Henry Moore. Jim was interested in the idea of a *Village Voice*-type newspaper, but insisted that Jack should be a director as well. They were very much a double-act. Jim had thousands of contacts, mostly in the arts and publishing; he knew everyone from Samuel Beckett to Norman Mailer. Through him we hoped to get some good editorial content as well as to attract financing.

International Times, or *IT* as it became, was named at a meeting held at a flat over a butcher's shop in Shepherd Market, in the shadow of the recently built Mayfair Hilton. Jim Haynes, Jack Henry Moore, Michael Henshaw, John, Hoppy, Sue and I were there. Jim had brought along an impressive American lady called Bubu LeJeane because he thought she might give us some money. Bubu was the last Va-Va-Voom girl. She was from New Orleans, had big hair, and the polished wooden floorboards creaked and shook when she stamped across them. She was in competition with Marion Javits for the position of premier patron of the theatre on Broadway. Bubu bubbled and gurgled as the search for a name became more and more tedious. 'Let's call it IT!' she shrieked. This seemed a good idea; it could stand for anything: Intergalactic Troublemakers, Interminable Tripping, International Times. This is my memory of the meeting; there are conflicting claims over the naming of the paper. In Jonathon Green's *Days in the Life*, Jim Haynes thinks Jack Henry Moore named it, whereas Sue told Jonathon that she named it. I know it was not me.

At Hoppy's suggestion we approached the Scottish dramatist Tom McGrath to edit the paper. We wanted someone with journalistic experience, and until recently Tom had been working as editor of the weekly newspaper *Peace News*. He had used Hoppy's photographs in the paper. Jim agreed to the idea as it had been Tom who first introduced him to Jack Henry Moore in Dublin some years before. Tom was staying in Adrian Mitchell's holiday cottage in Wales when a telegram arrived bearing a brief message: 'Phone Hoppy.' Tom agreed to take the job, but would only do it providing he was paid £25 a week – a huge amount for those days (the staff were to receive £10 a week). It turned out that this was in order to pay for a heroin habit that Hoppy and I were unaware of.

Before the paper was launched, Tom and I went to the Kardomah café on Southampton Row to sit with all the county ladies up in town for shopping and discuss ideas for the paper, sipping watery cappuccinos from glass cups. This became a regular weekly event to discuss the editorial content of the next issue. We talked a lot about Charles Olson, whom we both admired, and about Andrei Voznesensky. I had recorded a spoken-word album with him and had spent some time talking with him when Allen Ginsberg stayed with us, so Tom was very interested to know what he was like. Tom was also very keen on Burroughs, and agreed with me that we should try to get William to write for us regularly. Allen was of course another mutual interest. We had both heard his voice for the first time reading from 'Howl' on the BBC Third Programme *Art & Anti-Art* series. We seemed to have very similar tastes in poetry: we both liked Robert Creeley, Ed Dorn and Michael McClure. It seemed to me that Tom would do a great job of editing the paper. His sense of humour appeared to be spot-on: when he laughed his whole face screwed up in amusement, his nose pinched at the nostrils, his eyes reduced to two slits, his balding pate shining.

Indica's new premises at 102 Southampton Row included a large basement, divided into one very large space and a smaller room which could be locked. I used the smaller room as my office. There were also a number of little rooms in the back, which could only be reached from the street door to the block of flats above. Sue and I very much liked Chris Hill's flat above the shop at number 106, and when a similar flat became vacant on the top floor of 100 Southampton Row that summer, we took it. There was a large room suitable for a studio for Sue, who wanted to take up painting again – she had gone to Goldsmiths College after Cheltenham Art School – several bedrooms, an office for me with a direct phone line from Indica, and a pleasant kitchen with a view out to the east over the rooftops.

Michael X and Howard Parker, known as 'H', Jimi Hendrix's roadie, used to stay up all night taking acid in our kitchen, seated one each end of the glass dining table. Michael said that he couldn't trip among members of the West Indian community, that they just couldn't see the attraction and were not sympathetic, whereas he felt perfectly secure in our flat. We used to go off to bed and leave them to it. In the morning they'd still be there, nodding and grinning.

It was a great location: our front windows looked out over the dome of the British Museum, one block to the west, and a little further on the tower cranes were hoisting into place the Y-shaped units of Richard Seifert's Centre Point, an imitation Mies van der Rohe high-rise, complete with a road-bridge leading nowhere, which was to cause planning blight all down Charing Cross Road for the next two decades.

International Times needed an office, and the obvious place was the basement of Indica, which was not being used except for the small room I had taken. The rent was paid in copies of the paper. *IT* started on a £500 loan to Jim from Victor Herbert, an American who had made millions from Bernie Cornfeld's IOS insurance business. (He pulled out before it went spectacularly tail up.) We couldn't afford any office equipment, so at first Tom McGrath used my typewriter, which was obviously inconvenient, then Jim received an ancient portable donated by Sonia Orwell, which had supposedly been used by George himself. (Jim roomed at her Gloucester Place basement when he first moved to London.) Tom was joined by David Zane Mairowitz as assistant editor, Hoppy was in charge of production, Roger Whelan organised distribution, which was mainly through street sellers, and the few ads we ran were obtained by Suzanne Kahn. The first issue was ready to go just as soon as Victor Herbert's cheque cleared.

IT Launch at the Roundhouse

Flyers were sent out – the usual communication method in London in the days before everyone had a telephone – announcing the launch of *IT*, which was described as being 'in the same spirit to London that newspapers like the *Village Voice*, *East Village Other* and *Los Angeles Free Press* are to their communities; however, since no equivalent European newspapers yet exist, IT will be international in its coverage.' The verso of the flyer announced an All Night Rave featuring the Soft Machine, the Pink Floyd and steel bands:

STRIP?????HAPPENINGS//////TRIP//////MOVIES
Bring your own poison & flowers & gas-filled balloons & submarine & rocket ship & candy & striped boxes & ladders & paint & flutes & ladders & locomotives & madness & autumn & blowlamps &
POP / OP / COSTUME / MASQUE / FANTASY / LOON / BLOWOUT / DRAG BALL
SURPRISE FOR THE SHORTEST/BAREST COSTUME.

Binn Tivy – who had printed *Darazt* for us – hand-set the tickets on thick white shiny card and they went on sale at Indica, Better Books and other sympathetic outlets. The launch party was held at the Roundhouse on Chalk Farm on 11 October 1966. The Roundhouse was originally built to house the winding gear and machinery to pull trains up the steep hill from Euston Station. When steam engines improved, it became engine-shed 1B. After the war, Gilbey's built a huge circular platform inside to store vats of gin, but by 1966 it had stood empty for more than fifteen years. Arnold Wesker had acquired it for his workers' arts organisation Centre 42, but had not yet raised the money to do it up. Michael Henshaw, who was a director of Centre 42, already had the keys. When he asked Wesker if *IT* could have a party there to launch the paper, he agreed, thinking it would be something along the lines of a book launch or cocktail party. He had never attempted any fund-raising events there himself, even though it was the obvious place to do so. It was incredibly filthy, with jagged stumps of iron sticking up out of the floor, which was itself covered by a thick crust of grime, with huge muddy patches making walking hazardous.

The main entrance was, of course, from the railway tracks, but there was no way that British Rail would allow thousands of people to walk half a mile up the tracks to an abandoned building. The bands drove up this way with their equipment, and Alexander Trocchi and a group of friends tried to get in the same way without paying, but were refused admission. The only other entrance was a very long, narrow set of steps leading down to the road. Only with great difficulty could two people squeeze past each other, so once you were in, you couldn't get out again. There was about an hour's wait to get in.

There were only two lavatories for 2,000 people, which soon overflowed, flooding that part of the building. The doors were taken off and some old crates were broken up to provide duckboards for the huge lines of people trying to reach them. There were few complaints, however, except about the cold; it was October and there was no heat.

Hoppy had a big tray of sugar cubes on the wall by the entrance, which people gobbled down as they handed in their tickets, thinking it was acid. Some people, of course, brought their own. David Mairowitz helped on the door, repeatedly slapping his forehead and yelling, 'Awww, man!' over and over as more and more exotically dressed people swarmed up the narrow staircase and into the psychedelic light-show which filled the dome of the Roundhouse with coloured blobs and patterns. Dutch couple Simon and Marijke had a fortune-telling tent, from which billowed great gusts of incense. Marianne Faithfull, in a nun's habit that did not quite cover her bottom, won the prize for the 'shortest/barest'. Half-naked people danced furiously to keep warm. Paul McCartney wandered around dressed as an Arab to avoid recognition. Michelangelo Antonioni and Monica Vitti looked stunning and drew considerable attention. People wore silver-foil headdresses and masks, refraction lenses in the middle of their foreheads, eighteenth-century military uniforms, rubber bondage wear, and glitter dust. Acrid clouds of hash and pot smoke drifted around the room. Sue and I just walked around hand-in-hand, staring in amazement at it all, watching the underground be born.

Gerry Fitzgerald had made a huge jelly for the event using a bathtub as the mould, but Syd Barrett and the Pink Floyd's roadie, Po, accidentally destroyed it by removing a key piece of wood that was holding the whole structure in place, and gallons of jelly splashed all over their King's Road clothes. There was still plenty left for people to roll in. Another attraction was a Fifties Cadillac painted in psychedelic colours by Binder, Edwards and Vaughan, which had previously been exhibited at the Robert Fraser Gallery.

There was an all-night film show organised by the concrete poet Bob Cobbing, one of the original organisers of the London Film-maker's Co-op, and featuring underground favourites such as Kenneth Anger's *Inauguration of the Pleasure Dome* and Antony Balch and William Burroughs' *Cut Ups* and *Towers Open Fire*. Bob was a man of many parts; he had worked with me at Better Books and became manager shortly after I left. He was the publisher of the Writers Forum series of poetry books; he published Allen Ginsberg's *The Change*, which Allen read from at the Albert Hall; and he also organised art shows under the collective title of Group H. (I exhibited in one of them somewhere in North London.)

And there was music.

The Australian poet Daevid Allen, then twenty-one, already had a long history of beatnik activity, performing at the Domaine Poétique in Paris with William Burroughs and Brion Gysin and recording with Terry Riley. He was an early experimenter on the acid scene: Robert Wyatt, Daevid Allen and Gilly Smyth (poet and occasional vocalist with Soft Machine) first took acid with John Esam at Allen's place in Deya, Majorca, in 1964. Soft Machine was formed in 1966 when they were joined by Mike Ratledge, who took the band's name from the novel by Burroughs. Their line-up was always very flexible and Mal Dean, Rab Spall and other modern jazz musicians often sat in with them. They played at both the Spontaneous Underground and, as support to the Pink Floyd, at the London Free School, which was why they were invited to play at the launch party for *IT*. The line-up that night consisted of Daevid Allen, Kevin Ayers, Mike Ratledge and Robert Wyatt.

Daevid Allen wrote, 'That was our first gig as a quartet. Yoko Ono came on stage and created a giant happening by getting everybody to touch each other in the dark, right in the middle of the set. We also had a motorcycle brought onto stage and would put a microphone against the cylinder head for a good noise.' (They also gave young women rides around the outer rim of the Roundhouse on it, bumping through the dirt and debris, raising clouds of dust.)

The other group was, naturally, the Pink Floyd. Their set was reported in *International Times*: 'The Pink Floyd, psychedelic pop group, did weird things to the feel of the event with their scary feedback sounds, slide projections playing on their skin (drops of paint ran riot on the slides to produce outer-space/prehistoric textures on the skin), spotlights flashing in time with the drums.' It was the first time most of the people in the audience had seen a light-show and many stood staring open-mouthed as the organic bubbles of lights expanded and contracted like breeding amoeba. They did an inspired version of 'Interstellar Overdrive', with the sympathetic audience urging them to explore dangerous territory and go as far out as they could. The Roundhouse only had the electrical power supply of an ordinary domestic house – it was wired as a warehouse – and as an unintentional but dramatic climax to their act, the Floyd blew out the fuses, plunging the building into darkness. When I pushed my way through to pay them, both groups were surrounded by newly made fans. The Soft Machine received £12 10s and the Pink Floyd got £15 because they had a light-show to pay for.

The poet Kenneth Rexroth, visiting from San Francisco, mistook the Soft Machine for an audience jam session and obviously left before the Pink Floyd came on. He was terrified by the whole event and reported in his column in the *San Francisco Examiner.*

> The bands didn't show, so there was a large pickup band of assorted instruments on a small central platform. Sometimes they were making rhythmic sounds, sometimes not. The place is literally an old round-house, with the doors for the locomotives all boarded up and the tracks and turntable gone, but still with a dirt floor (or was it just very dirty?). The only lights were three spotlights. The single entrance and exit was through a little wooden door about three feet wide, up a narrow wooden stair, turning two corners, and along an aisle about two and a half feet wide made by nailing down a long table. Eventually about 3,500 people crowded past this series of inflammable obstacles. I felt exactly like I was on the Titanic. Far be it for me to holler copper, but I was dumbfounded that the police and fire authorities permitted even a dozen people to congregate in such a trap. Mary and I left as early as we politely could.

The police and fire authorities, of course, knew nothing about it, but there were fire exits through the huge doors onto the railway tracks, and Stuart Montgomery, a fully qualified medical doctor, was in attendance. The London *Sunday Times* reviewed the event (the first national press for the Pink Floyd) with less concern for their own safety:

> At the launching of the new magazine IT the other night a pop group called the Pink Floyd played throbbing music while a series of bizarre coloured shapes flashed on a huge screen behind them. Someone had made a mountain of jelly and another person had parked his motor-bike in the middle of the room. All apparently very psychedelic . . .
>
> The group's bass guitarist, Roger Waters, [said] 'It's totally anarchistic. But it's co-operative anarchy if you see what I mean. It's definitely a complete realisation of the aims of psychedelia. But if you take LSD what you experience depends entirely on who you are. Our music may give you the screaming horrors or throw you into screaming ecstasy. Mostly it's the latter. We find our audiences stop dancing now. We tend to get them standing there totally grooved with their mouths open.' Hmm.

More *International Times*

IT unintentionally broke a lot of conventions. We used unjustified type; whereas newspapers always set their copy in columns, we didn't mind a ragged right-hand margin. Not long after, the *Observer* began to do the same in some sections of the paper. But the most shocking thing was the format. We were a tabloid dealing with serious issues, whereas the convention in Britain was that intellectual newspapers were always broadsheet. This reversal irritated many people, quite unreasonably; it just didn't seem *right* to them. As there were only six offset-litho machines in the country capable of printing a newspaper, *IT* had to use old-fashioned hot metal, just like every other newspaper, which made the layout and graphics pretty boring. As every graphic and photograph had to have a copper plate made for it, there was no room for spontaneity and the plates printed in a terrible grey smudge.

Aside from that, the first issue, published on 14 October 1966, was in many respects a fairly conventional arts magazine: we printed a poem by Adrian Mitchell called 'Make and Break', written for the Royal Shakespeare Company's production of *US*, and a review by Charles Marowitz of the same play. There was a long report on the Warsaw International Festival of Music, complete with a portrait of Penderecki; there was a review of Bob Cobbing's latest Group H exhibition and two contrasting views of the recent Destruction in Art Symposium, one of them by Yoko Ono's husband Tony Cox, as well as a review of 'She', the ninety-foot-long woman built by Nikki de Saint Phalle, Jean Tinguely and Olof Ultvedt in the Stockholm Museum of Modern Art. Jean-Jacques Lebel contributed an obituary of his friend André Breton, who had just died, and an exhibition of Yoko Ono's Instructions paintings at Indica Gallery was announced for 9–22 November: 'viewers of the show will be requested to participate in the actual making of the paintings . . .' The announcement was written in the stuffy formal journalism of the day: 'Also on exhibit and on sale for the first time in this country will be Bag Wear, a style of clothing that completely envelopes the body, covering head to foot – said to be the next step after the topless look.

Miss Ono has used the bag wear for her concerts in this country . . .'
It could have been written in 1956.

But there were also elements that could only be found in an
underground newspaper: 'The IT Girl' pin-up by Hoppy; a cartoon
by Mal Dean, who also designed the logo for the editorial page; a
strip cartoon by Jeff Nuttall; Simon Vinkenoog contributed a long
article on Provo, the Amsterdam-based group that used spectacular
happenings and street demonstrations to bring points of social or
political conflict to the attention of the public; and a report on Tim
Leary's spiritual stage show from Bubu in New York. Peter Asher
wrote a pop column under the name 'Millionaire' and shamelessly
promoted his latest single, and Jack Henry Moore, under the name
'Elizabeth', contributed a festive column – homosexuality was still
illegal at this point. But none of this would have caused opprobrium;
it was the straightforward, uncritical style of Hoppy's Bradley Martin
column on recreational drugs that incensed people: 'Greece. The
price of hashish in the archipelago is reported at £23 an ounce.'
Fleet Street was outraged and so were some powerful members of
the Establishment. There was also a report on LSD, which had been
made illegal in Britain the previous month.

There were free announcements in the 'What's Happening'
column at the back: the London Free School was presenting a pop
dance at All Saints' Hall with the Pink Floyd Mix Media Show, on
14 October and again on 21 October. Roland Kirk was at Ronnie
Scott's, Bert Jansch at St Pancras Town Hall, and Long John Baldry
at Les Cousins Folk Club on Dean Street. The paper noted that
Karma was now open. This was Simon Posthuma and Marijke
Koger's shop at 28 Gosfield Street in the West End, which I visited
often. It was a tiny space – now a sandwich bar – selling Moroccan
fabrics and objects, highly coloured clothes of their own design,
psychedelic posters by Marijke called 'Love' and 'Dylan', and a row
of esoteric books on commission from Indica – which naturally we
never got paid for. It was a prototype New Age shop, with incense
burning and Indian ragas playing quietly in the background. Simon
and Marijke were soon to join up with two others, Josie and Barry,
and call themselves The Fool. Karma was a dry run for the Apple
Boutique.

Surrogate Americans

Tom McGrath did an exceptional job in getting the paper off the ground. Certainly his *IT* was closer to my idea of the paper than that of later editors. Though he was sympathetic to it, he had a healthy suspicion of the West Coast psychedelic scene and resisted any whole-hearted move in that direction. Under Tom's editorship the paper remained international, not just Anglo-American. He wrote:

> Some Americans write to say that International Times has not gone far enough: they point to the psychedelic newspapers exploding in various parts of the States in a riot of Buddhas, Mandalas, LSD-scene news, and all those other groovy images psychedelic drugs have blown out of the human consciousness. Admit, they are groovy images. But this time and place of operations, London, 1967, is not ready for a completely flipped-out 'newspaper'. To begin with, there is the hard fact that many of IT's closest friends are, to say the least, wary of what they put down as 'the acid-scene.' And that's our friends . . .

Tom was referring to Alex Gross, our Berlin correspondent, who, along with several of the other Americans involved with *IT*, thought we should emulate the US underground papers. To Alex we were very staid and British, terribly *reasonable* about everything, but that was the point. *IT* was a British underground newspaper for British readers, not an imitation American one. For all their criticisms of how low-key and polite we were, we could have countered that the American papers were crude, brash and insensitive and would have done well to become more like us. But even in hip circles, Americans virtually always believed that the rest of the world should be like them – the British were the same when they had an Empire – so there was no point in engaging in protracted arguments. I was personally hoping for the best of both. In fact *IT* did become very similar to the American papers, but not for several years.

The second issue of *IT* ran into copyright trouble by printing some of Ezra Pound's unpublished wartime broadcasts on Radio Rome. It was a moot point whether enemy propaganda is covered by copyright, particularly as Faber & Faber had no intention of ever actually publishing it, but they owned the copyright on Pound's other work and claimed the rights. At the same time, Sue approached their publicity department, thinking they might like to advertise. 'Your Mr Pound and our Mr Pound are two different people,' she was told. Not wishing to antagonise Faber, we refrained from publishing any further Pound extracts. Bill Levy, whose idea it was, published *Certain Radio Speeches* himself in Rotterdam in 1975 in a small edition of 250 copies. This was followed by *Ezra Pound Speaking* from the Greenwood Press three years later, so thanks to Bill's pioneering work the forbidden texts are finally out in the open and Faber's Mr Pound and *IT*'s Mr Pound turn out to be the same person.

The second issue also ran two other previously unpublished texts: the Living Theatre's *Frankenstein* and William Burroughs' film-script *Towers Open Fire*; these with the blessings of the authors. The third issue continued to mix important texts by contemporary thinkers with underground news and gossip from around the world. The major articles were by avant-garde American composer Morton Feldman, an article on American war crimes in Vietnam by Bertrand Russell, and William Burroughs' powerful 'The Invisible Generation'.

In issue three we started our campaign for London to be a twenty-four-hour city – a hopeless task of course, since even thirty-five years later everything still closes before midnight unless you are rich enough to join an expensive club and take a taxi home afterwards. We also continued our 'Censorshit' column, begun in the second issue, one of the few editorial platforms that everyone on the paper felt strongly about. The usual guardians of public morality, this time in the shape of right-wing MP Sir Cyril Black, president of the London Baptist Association and long-term participant in the Billy Graham Evangelistic Association's crusades, had brought a private prosecution against Hubert Selby's novel *Last Exit to Brooklyn* and the police had raided the warehouse of John Calder and seized all the copies in stock, intending to destroy them unless Calder and Boyars could show that they were not obscene.

Meanwhile customs and excise officers carefully tore out the pages containing an article on the Berkeley Sexual Freedom League from every copy of the November 1966 issue of *Playboy* that entered the country, despite the fact that there were no pictures in the article. The very idea offended their puritan minds.

Marijke Koger did the mastheads in issue four, which came out on 28 November. Despite the constraints of letterpress, *IT* was turning psychedelic. It was an interview in this issue with black American comedian Dick Gregory that got the paper busted, though it took the police three months to respond. Gregory was in London to film a TV special for BBC2 and to appear on the Eamonn Andrews show. He became heated at one point during the interview and shouted: 'A hundred years we worried about what white folks think. I say fuck white folks. One hundred years of worrying about that bastard and he ain't got off my back. I say fuck him up his ass. I got five black kids and I couldn't give a fuck what a white man thought of them from now until the day I die . . . Five white kids burn their draft cards and in two weeks' time we got an anti-draft burning bill. But we can't get an anti-lynching bill in a hundred years. So this man just told me that he thinks more of a piece of cardboard than he do of my five black babies . . .'

Later in the interview Gregory affirmed, 'I'm thoroughly non-violent, passive to the extent that I am a vegetarian. I don't believe anything should be killed . . . I wouldn't kill anybody.' It was perhaps naive of us to print such an interview verbatim, but it was our policy to run interviews as straight transcripts, not to edit or censor the interviewee's words – this was one of the many ways in which we differed from Fleet Street. Someone, rumoured to be Cyril Black, reported *IT* to the police.

John and Yoko

From 31 August until 30 September 1966 London hosted the Destruction In Art Symposium (DIAS), organised by Gustav Metzger and John Sharkey. I was one of the twelve-man honorary committee, along with Bob Cobbing, Dom Sylvester Houedard, Jim

Haynes, Mario Amaya, Enrico Baj, Wolf Vostell and others – all male. More than twenty artists came to Britain specifically to take part, and twenty-seven more sent work over for exhibition. Each day there were events, film-shows, lectures, happenings. Wolf Vostell dug a hole in Better Books basement and struck water. The hole was so large that Westminster Council insisted that they get planning permission before they were permitted to fill it in again. Otto Muhl skinned a lamb and covered everyone with blood, and Ralph Ortiz, a tall Puerto Rican artist, chopped Jay Landesman's piano to pieces on the staircase of his home in Duncan Terrace. Al Hanson – whose grandson, Beck, later became a famous pop-star – spent time hanging out at Indica bookshop, making it his unofficial headquarters. Mario Amaya, the editor of *Art and Artists*, paid for Yoko Ono to attend, and she arrived with her husband, the annoyingly loud Tony Cox, and their baby, Kyoko.

John Dunbar offered Yoko an exhibition at the gallery and her high-pitched giggle was often to be heard around the bookshop and art gallery in the weeks leading up to her show. I remember one interesting conversation with her about Surrealism and the Fluxus Group and the role of labels and titles in creating meaning. She was a founder member of Fluxus and, as I had stocked Fluxus publications and boxes back in Better Books days, I was already very familiar with her work. She had performed with John Cage, George Maciunis, George Brecht and the other happenings-artists in New York and had many interesting stories to tell about the downtown New York art scene.

We had to take down Yoko's 'baby sitter wanted' ad from the bookshop noticeboard after two customers complained that they had babysat until the early hours for her and had not been paid. I liked Yoko but, as with many artists, she was concerned solely with herself and her art. Other people were there to further her aims. As John Lennon later remarked, 'To Yoko men are just assistants.'

Yoko's 'Unfinished Paintings and Objects' show at Indica was due to open to the public on 9 November, so two days before Sue and I went over to the gallery to help with the hanging and preparations for the *vernissage*, the private party for potential buyers, which John was throwing on the day before the show opened. Yoko and Tony Cox were there, along with John Dunbar and Geneviève Morgan, the gallery manager. Yoko had also invited Tony McAulay, a student at Liverpool College of Art and Design, to help with the work. Tony Cox was on his best behaviour, not wanting to cause a fuss. A few days before John had had to eject him from the gallery for frightening the customers. The British were not then attuned to the anti-social American habit of exercising in public. Feeling a little stiff from building stands for Yoko's work, Tony began flapping his arms to loosen up. This strenuous activity made him hyperventilate and he began shrieking at the top of his voice, while continuing to hug himself and then spread his arms wide, like an owl about to take off.

Late in the evening, with the show more or less ready for the next day's opening party, John Lennon arrived in his chauffeur-driven Mini-Cooper, having been invited to drop in by John Dunbar. Lennon and Dunbar were seeing a lot of each other at this point, mostly to take drugs, so it was not unusual to see John at the gallery. He recalled his first meeting with Yoko in a long interview with Jann Wenner:

> I got there the night before it opened. I went in – she didn't know who I was or anything – I was wandering around, there was a couple of artsy type students that had been helping lying around there in the gallery, and I was looking at it and I was astounded. There was an apple on sale there for 200 quid, I thought it was fantastic – I got the humour in her work immediately . . .

John Dunbar introduced him to Yoko and she handed him one of her instruction cards, which said 'Breathe' on it. John panted like a dog. The work that most impressed Lennon was 'Ceiling Painting', a piece made earlier that year for Yoko's *Blue Room Event* in New York in which one entire room was painted white, with a few white furnishings on the walls and a painting on the ceiling. For the London show she added a white ladder. The piece was installed just inside the door, where it would receive the maximum amount of light from the window. The painting appeared to be a blank canvas, with just one word written on it in tiny letters. The viewer climbed the ladder in order to reach a large magnifying glass hanging on a chain next to the canvas. With this it was possible to read the word. Lennon climbed the ladder, and balancing at the top, peered through his little round glasses, and through the larger round glass, at the word. He was pleased to find that it said 'Yes'.

Yoko later claimed that she did not know who the Beatles were at that time, but she had been to visit Paul McCartney the previous week, trying to get him to donate an original song manuscript to John Cage's collection of modern music scores. Paul said he wanted to hang on to his manuscripts, but that John might give her one. As soon as Lennon came into Indica, Yoko took his arm. They got on well; John was obviously impressed with her, and she was very taken with him. When it was time for Lennon to leave, Yoko tried to get into his car, forcefully demanding that John take her with him.

All the objects in the show were either white or transparent, with one exception: 'Add Colour Painting', where the viewer was allowed to add one colour to the painting. Paints and brushes were provided. 'Apple' consisted of an apple on a transparent perspex stand; the catalogue featured a photograph of John Dunbar eating it. The apple was replaced daily. The show also contained a 1964 piece called 'Pointedness' consisting of a small sphere on a perspex stand. The most popular piece with the public was an all-white chess set 'for playing as long as you can remember where all your pieces are'. It was arranged on a white table with two white chairs. Actress Sharon Tate and film director Roman Polanski visited the show several times, once late at night after they had been to the Scotch of St James's, to play long games of white chess. Sharon Tate was dressed in white on their second visit, perhaps to co-ordinate with the exhibition, and looked stunning. But they did not buy the work.

Freak Out

There was another significant meeting around this time. Suzy Creamcheese arrived from Los Angeles and got rooms at the White House, a short-let apartment hotel just by Great Portland Street tube station. Hoppy met her on the day the first issue of *IT* was published, 14 October. She telephoned the printers, looking for Donovan, but by the end of the day she was with Hoppy back at the White House.

Suzy Creamcheese was a generic name that Frank Zappa gave to the group of Jewish girls, fans of the Mothers of Invention, who hung out at Ratner's Dairy Restaurant on Fairfax. The girls did publicity for the band, danced at the front of their gigs to get the crowds going, and performed other, unspecified services. The Suzy on the *Freak Out* record was Pamela Zarubica, who also moved to London, but the one Hoppy was to marry was Susan Zeiger, whose father owned the Zeiger ballrooms where the Mothers often performed. Suzy was loud and filled with energy, always laughing, smiling and dancing. She looked the epitome of the tabloid hippie chick with her long blonde hair, bare feet and very short dresses.

As well as sending books to the Beatles, I sometimes included any new albums I thought they might like to hear, among them John Cage's *25 Years Retrospective* boxed set, *Freak Out* by the Mothers of Invention, which we imported months before it was released in Britain, and some of the more challenging ESP jazz albums, such as Sun Ra and his Solar Arkestra. Paul had already heard *Freak Out* at my place a number of times, and one day, not long after I sent him his own copy, he said, 'We're getting ready to do a *Freak Out* of our own. Not the same as Zappa, of course. We've got our own way of doing it.' The Mothers' *Freak Out* didn't influence him much, if at all, musically in the making of *Sgt Pepper*, but the idea of treating a pop album as a complete unit, rather than as a series of singles, appealed to him very much, and Zappa was the first to do it.

Dr Benway

That December William Burroughs made one of his regular visits to the Southampton Row shop. Bill was then in his early fifties, but with his three-piece suits and ties, his hat and overcoat, he looked much older. In the early Sixties he wore a chesterfield, with a velvet collar, making him look like a Victorian prime minister. As he was no longer on junk, his face had filled out somewhat, but it was still bony. Surrounded by five or six people, most of whom he did not know, his lips pursed like a guppy, a nervous tic that betrayed how uncomfortable he felt. He had come to see the new poster half-issue of *International Times*, number 5.5, which featured one of his texts, 'The Invisible Generation', and a cut-out word machine designed by Michael English. William thought that the silver-on-white silk-screen printing made the text unreadable, which it did, and we promised we would do the reprint in gold, which would show up better. After studying it for a while William said, 'Well, go on then. Cut it up.' We quickly found him a pair of scissors and he cut up one of the posters and assembled one of the word machines. You turned several wheels with words on them, which lined up in random order. It didn't really work very well, but William didn't seem too bothered. He liked *IT* and used it to run a number of his think pieces, knowing that they would be taken up through the underground press syndicate – of which *IT* was a member – and reprinted in the *Los Angeles Free Press*, the *East Village Other*, the *Georgia Straight* and other underground papers across the world. It was the revolutionary aspect of the underground that he was attracted to; flower-power never meant much to him. 'The only way I'd like to give a flower to a cop,' he said, 'is in a flower pot from a high window.'

Bill had pinned a sign on the bookshop noticeboard some weeks before offering free Scientology auditing sessions to anyone who wanted them in order to improve his own auditing technique – even giving his home address and telephone number, which I thought was very trusting of him as he usually wanted that kept very much a secret. I was tempted to give it a try myself. Much as I despised Scientology, the idea of having Burroughs audit me was an intriguing one. He told me that he had a number of responses to his notice and was pleased with the results.

'Well, a merry Christmas everyone,' he said, raising his hat. He looked as implacable and unfriendly as ever, with no trace of a smile or feeling of goodwill upon his visage. When he left, those assembled discussed whether he had been joking. It was typical with Bill that even the most mundane, polite utterance was examined for hidden meaning, instead of being taken at face value. Perhaps it was a Sixties thing, when every line of Bob Dylan's amphetamine babble was examined microscopically and Beatles records were even played backwards to look for secret messages. Bill was revered as a guru, in much the same way as Ginsberg and Kerouac had looked up to him as an elder statesman and teacher back in the Forties and Fifties. His every utterance was regarded with the greatest respect, something which, I suspect, paralysed him with self-consciousness and was in part responsible for his icy public demeanour.

UFO

The pressure of bringing out *IT* every two weeks led to immediate financial difficulties. We organised a couple of events: an underground film festival and a fund-raising jumble sale at the Roundhouse, called the Uncommon Market, but neither provided the long-term cash flow needed. The concerts at All Saints' Hall had been a great success and solved many of the London Free School's financial problems; in fact Joe Boyd had suggested to Hoppy that they take it to the West End. Hoppy decided that this could be the answer to *IT*'s problems; if the *IT* staff ran it, it would at least cover their wages. Joe found an Irish dance hall called the Blarney Club in the basement of the Berkeley Cinema at 31 Tottenham Court Road and did a deal with the owner, Mr Gannon, to rent the place for £15 each Friday night. With Joe as the musical director, and Hoppy doing everything else, the UFO Club was born. They originally planned to try two evenings, one either side of Christmas on 23 and 30 December, and if that worked, to continue it as a regular event.

The Pink Floyd and the Soft Machine were the house bands, but there were a number of other acts who appeared regularly. The most popular was the Crazy World of Arthur Brown, whom Joe Boyd discovered doing a cabaret act in a nightclub. He was an amazing dancer with a tall skeletal frame, a skull face accentuated by face paint and a thin beard. He did what was known in music hall as 'Egyptian Dancing', a jerky sideways movement with all his limbs at right-angles, and frequently wore a long robe or dress. When the people sitting out on the staircase heard his group begin the introduction to

'Fire', Arthur's theme tune, they scrambled inside to watch him make his entrance with his headdress in flames.

Tomorrow was formed early in 1967 when the In-Crowd – Keith West on vocals, Steve Howe on guitar and John Wood on bass – added Twink on drums. The sight of Twink wriggling along the top of the Marshall stacks like a snake, while at the same time reaching down and playing his drums, quickly endeared them to the UFO audience. Twink was one of them.

Another regular group at UFO was the free-form jazz outfit the Giant Sun Trolley, which was assembled by Dave Tomlin. When Tomlin was busted, drummer Glen Sweeney – distinctive in his goatee and shaved head – joined another free-jazz group at UFO called Hydrogen Jukebox, a group of musicians that eventually transmuted into the Third Ear Band.

There were two key records at UFO, guaranteed to get the crowd dancing: 'My White Bicycle' by Tomorrow and 'Granny Takes a Trip' by the Purple Gang. The Purple Gang were produced by Joe Boyd and played UFO only once before their masked leader, Peter 'Lucifer' Walker, disbanded the group in order to become initiated as a Warlock.

Though, in the public memory, UFO and the London underground scene are somehow twinned with San Francisco, there was in reality very little connection between the two. For starters, none of the San Francisco bands released records until July 1967, long after UFO had passed its peak. Of those, though everyone liked Grace Slick's voice, the Jefferson Airplane's first album was good but not earth-shattering and the Grateful Dead's first album, released at the same time, gave no indication of the band's live performance. Warner Brothers had somehow managed to make them sound like a good-time jug band, and furthermore it was difficult for the ultra fashion-conscious London underground to take Jerry Garcia seriously when he wore those terrible jumpers. Of course, people talked about the bands and the light-shows, but no one had actually seen or heard any of them.

Los Angeles was a different matter. We very much liked what was happening there: the Byrds, Love, the Doors, Frank Zappa and the Mothers of Invention were all played constantly. If London was twinned with anywhere it was LA. The other record constantly on people's turntables was the first Velvet Underground album, with Warhol's peel-off banana cover. They dressed in black, they were from New York. They always meant more in London than any of the San Francisco groups. And then there was Dylan, and his was definitely not a San Francisco sensibility.

Though the majority of the audience sat on the floor to watch the bands, UFO featured many forms of dancing: at the front, as near as possible to the band, were the leapers, as they were known by the staff. They leaped high in the air, arms outstretched, bouncing on or off the beat with a look of sheer abandon and bliss on their upturned blurred faces, which often featured a refractive lens or at least a gummed Christmas star in the centre of the forehead. They favoured caftans and bells, bare feet and incense, which they sometimes wore, lighted, in their hair. They were the real flower children and most people felt protective towards them as it was rather obvious that some of them were unable to look after themselves.

Then there was the art-school-dance-goes-on-for-ever style, best described as boots-stuck-to-the-floorboards, in which considerable effort is spent in apparently trying to get one's feet unstuck from the floor and, on finally detaching one, finding that the other has become attached, and so on. The country cousins affected the old-fashioned shit-kicking, hog-hollerin' style, stomping heavily on the polished dance floor with clod-hoppers (usually made by 'Tuf'). Then there were the super-cool King's Road heiresses gliding about making barely perceptible arm and head movements.

One man came every week and stood on the same chair next to the wall every time, slowly gyrating his body and flapping his arms to an internal rhythm not immediately connected to what was happening onstage. Another, a Soho hustler, brought his dog with him each week and turned quite nasty when animal-loving hippies suggested that the exceptional heat and noise levels of UFO might be detrimental to its health.

The club consisted of a large polished wooden dance floor complete with a mirror ball and a smaller area to the side where Mr Gannon had the food concession (there was no alcohol). There was a low stage, a backstage area and a small office used to talk people down from bad trips. As public transport – with the exception of a few night buses – stopped running at midnight, UFO was designed from the very beginning to run all night, or at least until the tube trains started up again at 6 am. It officially opened at 10.30 pm, and by 5 am there were people huddled together asleep on the floor in the corners while psychedelic lights flickered over them.

The area furthest from the stage was used for non-musical activities. Bob Cobbing showed films and each week there were poetry readings, jugglers and David Mairowitz acting out the latest part of his interminable dramatic production *The Flight of the Erogenius*. In the early days the music was almost incidental, the club being more important as a social event. It was the village pump. At UFO people met Manfred, a fat German acid dealer who sometimes gave away as many as 400 trips a night – but sold many more. People would order frilly shirts and velvet trousers from Michael Rainey of Hung On You or from John Pearce of Granny Takes a Trip. Craig Sams would lecture on macrobiotics to anyone who bought one of his rice rissoles at the food counter, and many friendships were made. The early audiences came from Notting Hill, Camden Town and Chelsea and many of them already knew each other from the LFS or various other *IT*-related activities. People arranged to sell each other gigantic quantities of dope, musicians found each other and arranged gigs, and record-company A&R men and producers found rock bands. Pete Townshend liked Arthur Brown so much that he signed him to Track and produced his first record, 'Fire'.

Pete was a regular and had become closely involved with the underground scene. His girlfriend, Karen Astley, was featured on the very first UFO poster: a monochrome close-up of her face with the words 'Nite Tripper' painted across it by Michael English. Pete would always pay £20 to get in, instead of the usual ten shillings, knowing that the money went to *IT*. UFO was far removed from his 'mod' image, which associated him with sharp clothes, amphetamines, scooters and fighting. In reality he was into tripping, studying spiritual texts and, when at UFO, wearing 'hippie' clothes. Pete Townshend:

> I remember being in the UFO Club with my girlfriend, dancing under the influence of acid. My girlfriend used to go out with no knickers and no bra on, in a dress that looked like it had been made out of a cake wrapper, and I remember a bunch of mod boys, still doing leapers, going

up to her, and literally touching her up while she was dancing and she didn't know that they were doing it. I was just totally lost: she's there going off into the world of Roger Waters and his impenetrable leer, and there's my young lads coming down to see what's happening: 'Fuckin' hell, there's Pete Townshend, and he's wearing a dress.'

The young mods were a street gang called the Firm, named after the Krays' gang but no competition, who behaved very badly at first, providing the only disruptive element at UFO, which had no security at all. However, someone quickly gave them some LSD and they fitted right in. Two of them, Peter Shertser and Boss Goodman, went on to careers in the music industry, Goodman as a promoter at Dingwall's Dance Hall and Shertser through his blues label Red Lightning.

It was hot and airless at UFO and people escaped the heat by sitting on the wide staircase, wiping away the sweat and watching the new arrivals. Sometimes the stairs were almost impassable for the hundreds of people sitting on them. People wore colourful costumes, and sometimes wore nothing at all. I remember one telephone call from the local police. 'We've got one of yours up at the station. Perhaps you'd like to send someone to fetch him. And you might as well bring his clothes while you're about it.' The Tottenham Court Road police station had seen a naked person flash past their window, hair on end, mouth wide open and eyes in a state of nova. 'Yeah, he's ours. We've found his clothes. Someone'll be up in a minute.'

A curious old man wearing a paper crown hung around the doorway at the top of the UFO stairs, surreptitiously tape recording the conversations of the police who were there on duty, though it was quite obvious that they were being kind to him and playing along with the fantasy. It was also unlikely that it was a real tape recorder. He talked in a halting, disjointed way, very friendly and loving towards all the young people but very paranoid about the police. Most of the time he talked enthusiastically about flying saucers, something the hippies loved to go on about, so he often had a circle of indulgent friends listening to his bizarre theories and explaining equally bizarre theories of their own. Everyone made of UFO what they wanted.

The lights were operated from a central control tower erected each week from scaffolding and planks. From here announcements were made, poetry was read and Jack Henry Moore played records in between the groups. The gantry also housed a film projector, as Dave Curtis from the London Filmmakers' Co-operative programmed at least one major feature each UFO – a Monroe movie perhaps, along with experimental shorts and anything he felt like bringing along. Most of the platform was taken up with light-show equipment and their operators. All of the walls of the club had a light-show, not just the stage, and there were often different operators playing with different walls. The main club light-show was controlled by Mark Boyle, one of Indica's artists, who had been putting on light-shows as art events since 1963. His art shows had themes such as bodily fluids: a show which utilised saliva, blood, semen and urine and for which he had even managed to raise a bit of green bile. Boyle was regarded as the father of the English light-show and his work with liquid slides was much copied. Whenever the Floyd played they had their own show, run by Peter Wynne-Wilson and Joey Gannon, geared totally to their music. In one corner of the room Jack Bracelin's Five Acre Lights played all night: that was where the psychedelic nudists hung out.

Jack Bracelin had taken over the Floyd's light-show at the London Free School when Joel and Toni Brown returned to the States, and he had developed his own show, which he called Five Acre Lights. It was named after the five-acre nudist colony he ran in Watford, about an hour from London. The nudists lived in caravans scattered around the site in a sea of mud. There was a battered wooden hut, a relic of a wartime airfield, used as the community centre, where the nudists – who were mostly physical education teachers from local schools – sat watching the 'trip machine'; a slowly revolving disc set in the ceiling, onto which thin strips of Melonex – mirror-coated plastic sheet – were attached, which reached down to the floor. Hoppy, Sue and I drove out there once to see what was happening. The ice cracked on top of each mud puddle as we walked to the hut. It was freezing cold and the nudists all wore overcoats and wellingtons as they huddled round a one-bar electric fire. There was nothing to drink. The Pink Floyd played there on 5 November 1966 – Guy Fawkes Night – stopping off on their way home from a concert at Wilton Hall, Bletchley, to see the bonfire and fireworks. It was a scene as far removed from my life as the psychedelic surfers at La Jolla, but wonderful none the less. British psychedelia was characterised by these strange offshoots: parallel developments by people in other communities, united only in their common interest in psychedelics.

Jack Bracelin also ran Happening 44, a weekly rock club at a strip club at 44 Gerrard Street in Soho. It was here that Joe Boyd first saw the Fairport Convention play, a group that he later managed and produced. It also became a frequent venue for Mickey Farren's group, the Social Deviants.

The Arts Council of Great Britain

One thing that was achieved from the abortive attempt to set up a poetry distribution centre was that Eric White and Charles Osborne of the Literature Panel of the Arts Council were now aware that there were two distinct poetry communities in Britain: the Establishment, centred around the Poetry Society, received all the Arts Council money and produced what to me seemed dull, uninspired verse published in a series of dull, uninspired, heavily subsidised magazines. They were an older generation of poets: Keith Harrison, Charles Causley, George Macbeth, Peter Redgrove, Jon Silkin and of course G. B. H. Wightman, who so objected to Indica. The new generation was the loose group of poets united by a series of mimeographed magazines, underground events and readings, and Michael Horovitz's *New Departures* travelling show. These included Roger McGough, Adrian Henri, Libby Houston, Brian Patten, Lee Harwood, Adrian Mitchell, Pete Brown and Tom Pickard. These poets received no government money and their magazines were not subsidised by the Arts Council. Eric White wanted to change this and invited me to join the Literature Panel as a junior member in order to shift the balance and present the opposing case. This looked a good idea and accordingly, on 29 January 1967, an Arts Council press release named me and Ben Ridler as the two junior members of the panel for 1967. I had in fact already attended a meeting of the panel, held on 4 January.

But I had not reckoned with Lord Goodman, chairman of the Arts Council, who, unknown to me, had it in for *IT* and was not averse to using his power to push through his own agenda. Goodman believed in High Art, and had been enormously disappointed by Jim Haynes' decision to leave the critically successful Jeanetta Cochrane Theatre – in which Goodman had played an important role in providing funds – to start an experimental theatre, the Arts Lab, in a derelict slum building in Covent Garden. Jim wrote in his autobiography, *Thanks For Coming!*:

> When *IT* was born, my name on the masthead, I impetuously sent him [Goodman] the first issue in the post saying 'Look what I founded,' and expecting to get a 'good for you' message back. But what I got was a message saying 'Come and see me immediately'. Lord Goodman didn't like the paper at all. He thought it was explicitly pro-drug . . . he could see no difference between hashish and heroin. I think he may have had personal reasons for being so against all drugs and believed that *IT* and the Arts Lab were hand-in-glove leading the youth of Britain into heroin abuse.

Goodman's hatred of drugs stemmed from his experiences with one of his wards, Mikey Portman, heir to the Portman Estates, whose finances were under Goodman's control. Mikey was a spoiled brat with a penchant for black boyfriends, who alternated between cures for alcoholism and heroin addiction. He had an unhealthy obsession with William Burroughs, presenting himself on Bill's doorstep when he was seventeen and imitating him in manner, speech and tastes. He lived briefly with Bill and Ian Sommerville in Tangier in 1961, and for a while Goodman blamed Mikey's heroin addiction directly on Burroughs, an opinion he later revised when he represented Burroughs as his lawyer. But all drugs were anathema to Goodman and he made sure that no one and no organisation associated with the underground, including the Arts Lab, received a penny of Arts Council money.

I received a letter from Nigel Abercrombie, the secretary-general, saying:

Further consideration has however now been given to the fact of your association with *International Times*. Some of the views and principles regularly advanced in that paper are, in our view, unhappily incompatible with the responsibilities of members of the Arts Council advisory panels, and I am instructed to say, with much regret, that the earlier decision upon your appointment has been rescinded.

I naturally wrote to Goodman, pointing out that I was not the editor of the paper, only on the editorial board, and that I could not be judged personally to hold the views and principles advanced in *IT*, which were, in any case, frequently incompatible, any more than he could personally be expected to admire everything that the Arts Council subsidised or published. But I knew it was a losing game. Lord Goodman would do anything in his power to stop us; he didn't even have the courtesy to reply to my letter.

When news of my 'sacking' got out there was a bit of a fuss and Brigid Brophy resigned from the Literature Panel, saying, in a letter to *The Times*: 'Mr Miles is indisputedly competent to give advice about one of the arts to a council whose sole purpose is to promote the arts. The public do not finance the Arts Council to pursue an ideological programme or to supplement the police and the courts.' Lord Goodman told *The Times* that my dismissal was the unanimous decision of the entire council, with the exception of Brigid Brophy. As Eric White, who appointed me, and many of the other council members knew all about *IT*, I can only assume that Goodman used his usual bullying tactics on them, or was lying – probably both. To cap it all, Goodman had the nerve to refer to Paul McCartney's attendance at a Berio concert in his introduction to that year's Arts Council Annual Report as proof that the Arts Council's policies were reaching out to young people.

I didn't give up completely. Using my personal contacts, I wrote an application for a bursary for Spike Hawkins, one of the most interesting of the new poets. It was, of course, turned down, and when the Arts Council literature grants were announced in the autumn, the money all went to the usual group of Establishment figures, with no support for the young or the experimental. *The London Magazine* received thousands of pounds as a matter of course and the only people doing interesting work in Britain received nothing; there were no grants for experimental, innovative magazines like *POTH*, *Poetmeat* or Brian Patten's *Underdog*. In the end, as a protest against the cronyism in the Arts Council, we held a book-burning outside their offices to protest against the fact that only the old guard ever got grant money and that creative young poets never saw any. We burned some subsidised Poetry Society books, three or four of them, knowing that the political overtones were enormous. There were twelve of us altogether, including Stuart Montgomery and Spike Hawkins, gathered on a nice sunny day in St James's Square outside the Arts Council building, while curtains twitched and a few worried-looking functionaries watched from a distance. Naturally it freaked them out, and all the newspapers came up with the predictable 'Nazism on the rise again' headlines. But when customs seized half a dozen copies of the first edition of Burroughs' *The Ticket that Exploded*, which John Dunbar was bringing from Paris, and burned them (even though the book was in print in Britain), the same newspapers were not interested. There are book-burnings and book-burnings.

It's All Trying to Create Magic

One evening just after Christmas 1966 I was telling Paul about *IT*'s terrible finances when he suggested that I should interview him, reasoning that if *IT* ran pop interviews, we could get record-company advertising. Aside from reviews of the Pink Floyd, and a news item about Little Richard, *IT* had not really covered rock 'n' roll in the first five issues; its music coverage had been almost entirely of jazz and modern classical music. I had never interviewed anyone before and it did not occur to me to prepare any questions. I just went round to Paul's house in St John's Wood and recorded a conversation with him. Before I turned on my cassette machine Paul played me an acetate of 'Strawberry Fields' and 'Penny Lane', which the Beatles had just recorded. Mrs Kelly brought us some tea and biscuits and we smoked a joint. The interview was interesting because it showed the frame of mind that Paul was in just as he was about to embark upon the *Sgt Pepper* recording sessions. He talked about random events in music and seeing the potential in just one note – as in the giant piano chord that occurs at the end of 'Day in the Life', but said he wanted to bring his audience with him. He did not want to leave any Beatles fans behind by being too avant-garde. The interview was published in issue six, on 16 January 1967, and got picked up by the Underground Press Syndicate all around the world. For me it was the beginning of a career in journalism and writing that continues to this day.

Hapshash and the Coloured Coat

Though information spread quickly throughout the underground by word of mouth, we still needed posters to advertise the UFO Club. Hoppy's friend Michael English designed the first – 'Nite Tripper' – poster. Michael had studied at Ealing College of Art and was inspired by the work of the then-current Pop artists. His follow-up was a double-size poster in Day-Glo pink: no image this time, just the information written in blobby Pop Art lettering.

Joe Boyd also had a friend who wanted to design posters, Nigel Waymouth, so in the spirit of the times Hoppy and Joe decided to introduce the two artists and see if they wanted to work as a team. Their first work together was a poster called 'UFO Festival', a pair of giant lips – similar to those later appropriated by the Rolling Stones – inspired by Man Ray's painting 'Observatory Time – The Lovers' of giant lips floating above a landscape, but painted using the polished Pop Art technique of Tom Wesselmann. These giant Day-Glo pink lips looked wonderful on the walls of building sites all over London, particularly when four or six were fly-posted together on a hoarding.

This was the first time that Michael and Nigel used the name Hapshash and the Coloured Coat for their combined activities. The name arose after an evening at my flat when we looked through books on Egyptian antiquities, including Barbara Mertz's *Temples, Tombs and Hieroglyphs* and the E. A. Wallis Budge translation of the

Egyptian Book of the Dead and I told them the story of Queen Hatshepsut's journey to the Land of Punt. When Michael and Nigel got together the next day, they could not remember the pronunciation of Hatshepsut and spelled it Hapshash instead – the 'hash' part could, of course, have been deliberate. Following the Egyptian theme, Joe Boyd set up a company called Osiris Visions Limited to market their posters commercially as they were being torn down, not in acts of vandalism, but by people who wanted to put them on their own walls at home.

One quarter of Osiris was owned by Lovebooks Limited. In September 1967 another company, Effective Communications Arts Limited (ECAL), was created to distribute the posters. This was owned by Lovebooks Limited, with Osiris taking a 25 per cent share. ECAL was also technically the distributor of *IT*, though this was mostly done by street sellers who collected bundles directly from the office.

The early UFO posters were printed in small quantities just for fly-posting and were not designed to be sold. With the exception of the first one, they were 40 × 30 inches and silk-screened. When it was decided to run on enough to sell as well, the size was cut to 20 × 30 inches, but they were still silk-screened. Stories had reached London about rainbow printing being used in California in magazines like the *San Francisco Oracle*, though no one had actually seen an example. Michael and Nigel set out to create their own rainbow printing and when it was applied to actual silk-screen printing – instead of offset – the results were fantastic. They quickly developed techniques that allowed them to run one screen with a fade from silver to gold and another fading from green to yellow. This was a very expensive, labour-intensive technique and cost a great deal more than offset litho, but there was no way that the intensity of colour could be reproduced by any other means. At first the UFO posters were sold at five shillings each through *IT*, which had a mail-order service for back issues. Then someone did a costing and realised that the silk-screen process was so expensive that we were losing money. It was decided to set the price higher and sell fewer copies, and the price was raised to seven shillings and sixpence. To me, the series of images produced by Hapshash and the Coloured

OZ

Coat throughout the summer of 1967 were among the most innovative and exciting graphic works of the post-war period.

Osiris began to produce posters for record companies and boutiques, as well as for other venues such as Brian Epstein's Saville Theatre, for which they did a series of four posters covering the period from August to October. Hapshash couldn't keep up, so other artists began to be used: Michael McInnerney, a friend of Pete Townshend's (who later did the sleeve for *Tommy*), and Martin Sharp, an Australian artist working as the designer for *OZ*.

OZ

By 1966 the news of Swinging London had reached Australia, prompting a large number of Australians to travel halfway round the world to investigate. There had always been a large Australian enclave in London, but the newcomers were a different generation, middle-class and well educated, and they quickly moved into the media and arts community: Richard Neville, Martin Sharp, Germaine Greer, Robert Whitaker, Marsha Rowe, Louise Ferrier, Jenny Kee and others, all of whom were involved in the start-up of an English edition of *OZ*, a satirical magazine that Neville had been publishing in Sydney. Richard's sister Jill, the novelist, already lived in London and Martin Sharp was staying with her when Richard arrived in London via the hippie trail in September 1966. Richard quickly connected with his old girlfriend Louise Ferrier and made plans to get a London *OZ* off the ground. Martin Sharp moved in with Bob Whitaker, who was then the more-or-less official photographer for the Beatles: he took the notorious 'Meat' cover, which Capitol Records withdrew from sale after complaints from the American public.

Martin was a regular at the Speakeasy, one of the new late-night clubs which opened to cater to the rock aristocracy and their followers. There he met Eric Clapton, whose new group Cream had made its first appearance in July 1966. Martin announced that he'd

161

written a song, and read aloud from a scrap of paper. 'That's great,' said Eric, 'I've just written some music.' The music and lyrics were combined to make 'Tales of Brave Ulysses', which featured on Cream's second album *Disraeli Gears*, for which Martin also designed a full-blown psychedelic cover with some of his innovative collages on the back. (He once came into Indica and bought an expensive book of Van Gogh's paintings. To my horror he immediately began tearing out the pages. It was his book, of course, and I knew that he was intending to use them for his collages, but I hate to see books mistreated. He tore out the pages he wanted and tossed the mutilated book in the wastebin.)

Martin Sharp also designed the sleeve for Cream's third album, *Wheels of Fire*, which is a good example of his fully developed psychedelic period. The sleeve of the American edition was printed in black on silver paper, and was regarded as the correct copy to have in underground circles. (Imports were only available at that time at One Stop Records, a very expensive store on South Molton Street.) The UK edition was a muddy grey colour. Martin's posters and designs were more American-influenced and closer to 'psychedelic art' than Hapshash and the Coloured Coat. His most memorable work is probably his enormous exploding Jimi Hendrix, which at one time could be found in virtually every student pad in London. His influence, however, came through his work as the designer of *OZ* magazine, in particular the two issues that were composed entirely of his graphic work.

Martin and Eric Clapton got on so well that they decided to get a flat together, and moved into the Pheasantry at 152 King's Road, Chelsea, a wonderfully eccentric block of artists' studios, surrounded by a private garden and entered through a large stone archway on the King's Road. (The original building is still standing, but property developers have built hideous modern apartments all over its walled garden.) There was a great deal of acid around the Pheasantry, and it was easy to get spiked. The effect on Eric was dramatic: he grew his hair and had it permed into an immense Afro. He took to buying ruffled shirts and velvet trousers from Hung On You and Granny Takes a Trip, and painted his guitar in psychedelic paisley patterns.

In Sydney, Richard Neville had been publishing *OZ* since 1963. It was badly designed and had the feel of a public-school satirical magazine, but none the less it managed to annoy the highly puritanical Australian establishment enough for Richard to find himself in court. Without really planning to, Richard found himself preparing to publish an English edition of *OZ*, despite having only arrived in Britain a few months before. The first issue came out in February 1967 and included a take-off of the London underground scene, which the *OZ* gang regarded with a certain disdain: Indica, *IT*, Ginsberg (whose name *OZ* always misspelled) and the Beats were used as the subjects of a satirical photo-collage. The first few issues were very self-conscious imitations of *Private Eye*, the model of Australian *OZ*, but even by the second issue it was obvious from the cartoons that Martin Sharp, at least, had taken acid. Martin's cartoon-collage style occupied even more of the third issue and, even though Sharp could not spell psychedelic – 'pschyedelic' he called it – his bit of the magazine showed him to be an underground convert. *OZ* was completely psychedelicised by its fourth issue, which came complete with a foldout Hapshash and the Coloured Coat cover printed in gold ink. From then on, *OZ* was *the* magazine for hippies: the whole of issue five was one gigantic foldout poster collage of a pair of identical teenage twin girls naked in a field of flowers, called 'Plant a Flower Child'. The editorial content had much in common with *IT*. The difference was that *IT* was a newspaper and carried a lot of underground and community news, whereas *OZ* was a monthly and was almost entirely given over to essays and full-colour graphics. The two were complementary and many people, myself included, wrote for both.

One evening in February 1967 George Martin and his wife, Judy, were invited to dinner at Paul and Jane's house along with Sue and me. We hadn't realised that it was a dinner invitation and hadn't dressed up, but George and his wife made up for all of us. Judy wore a very Sixties dress with panels of different materials, including one with zebra stripes, if my memory is correct. I had first observed Paul and George Martin relating to each other in the recording studio in 1965, and it seemed to me that their relationship had changed; a new element had been added. There was an obvious mutual respect and friendship from working together for years, but now it seemed to me that George was relating to Paul more as an adult than as one of the

Fabs, perhaps because Paul had finally 'settled down' with a house and a beautiful woman, even if they were not married. However, it was still more like the relationship of a father to a grown-up son than man-to-man. There were still differences of age and class: Judy spoke with the same modulated cut-glass tones as the Queen of England, and George, with his hair slicked back, looked as if his Fleet Air Arm uniform was still waiting in his closet.

The age gap was evident after dinner when Paul mischievously played *Bells* by saxophonist Albert Ayler, one of the most extreme examples of the 'screams from the ghetto' style of free jazz. George sat through it politely with little more than a raise of his eyebrows, but then fell into the trap laid by Paul and confessed that he didn't regard it as music. This was an excuse for Paul to launch into a discussion of 'What is music?' and 'With so much going on in one note to listen to, the possibilities are endless . . .' Paul had a wicked gleam in his eye as he threw each new idea – random sound, John Cage, free jazz, electronic music, Stockhausen – at poor George, who each time had to defend his position as teacher and producer.

Judy looked left out and Jane, with impeccable timing, changed the conversation to Gilbert and Sullivan in such a skilful way that Paul was not aware of what she was doing. She had been watching him closely for about three minutes, waiting for a suitable moment. I caught her eye afterwards and she had to smile. Paul did seem bent on proving to George Martin that he was now ahead of him musically, and that the Beatles had indeed grown up and were now doing their own thing: *Sgt Pepper*.

George seemed very worried about the album, though that may have been because of the cost rather than its musical content. It was certainly the most expensive rock album being made at that time and it finally clocked up more than 400 hours of studio time, much of it at night rates, so he might have been getting some static from EMI.

Neil Aspinall came into Indica one day, presumably sent by Paul or John, as he had not been there before. He gave me a list of photographs he was looking for: Yogis, the Marquis de Sade, Hitler, Nietzsche, Lenny Bruce, Lord Buckley, Aleister Crowley, Dylan Thomas, James Joyce, Oscar Wilde, William Burroughs, Robert Peel, Stockhausen, Aldous Huxley, H. G. Wells, Einstein, Carl Jung,

Beardsley, Alfred Jarry, Tom Mix, Johnny Weissmuller, Magritte, Tyrone Power, Karl Marx, Richmal Crompton, Dick Barton, Tommy Hanley, Albert Stubbins, Fred Astaire. I was able to help him with a few of them, such as Burroughs and Jarry, and suggested that Neil try the National Portrait Gallery. Dick Barton would prove a problem, I thought, as he was a fictional character from a BBC radio series, *Dick Barton Special Agent*.

Neil looked alert and resourceful as ever, which was more than I did. We had all been to the Bag O' Nails the previous night after a session at Abbey Road. The Beatles had been working on 'Lucy In the Sky With Diamonds', a song that John had brought in. Though nothing final had been laid down, they felt they had it in their heads. It was already 3 am in the studio, but everyone was still feeling fresh. Neil Aspinall and Mal Evans brought round the Austin Princess and we were soon in Kingly Street, standing outside the Bag O' Nails. The staff beamed with joy as soon as they saw who it was. There were quite a few people still there, including Jimi Hendrix, who sat at the end of the room to the left of the stage, surrounded by his usual entourage of slender blonde girls. Music was playing full blast and, with our arrival, the dancing picked up. We all ordered steak, chips and peas, with whisky and Cokes. When the food arrived Neil produced a small torch and inspected it, turning the steak over, taking care not to splash himself or anyone with the gravy or to lose any peas. He insisted on value for money and looked a bit peeved when Paul teased him about it. We sat to the right of the empty stage, in the furthest of the three alcoves, next to the dance floor. 'Watch that girl there,' said Paul, indicating a girl in a tiny red dress with long blonde hair. Sure enough, she manoeuvred her partner, who looked like a young city gent, to a place on the small dance floor where she was close to our table. Positioning herself so that her partner had his back to us most of the time, she began to dance with great abandon, raising her hands above her head, clasping them together and twisting her hips so that her dress rode up to show her panties. She thrust her pelvis towards Paul three or four times, giving him a pleading look. 'I knew she was going to do that,' he said after she had given up and danced away. 'I can spot them.'

Pilcher's Progress

On 12 February the drug squad, acting on a tip-off from the *News of the World*, raided a weekend party at Redlands, Keith Richards' country house. The paper had been tipped off by an American known as Dave 'Acid King' Schneidermann, whom Keith vaguely remembered meeting the previous year in New York. Schneidermann appeared in England bringing with him some dynamite White Lightning acid, and suggested a party to try it out. Keith invited Mick Jagger and Marianne Faithfull, antique dealer Christopher Gibbs (who wore Pakistani national dress), photographer Michael Cooper, Robert Fraser, who arrived with his manservant Muhammad, and others. When the police burst in Robert took off across the lawn where he was rugby-tackled by a policewoman who found twenty jacks of heroin on him. The police took away all the bars of hotel soap in the house and a bottle of Ambre Solaire suntan lotion, but ignored the cocaine, presumably not knowing what it was. The press made a great deal of fuss about the fact that Marianne was wearing nothing but a fur rug, which she had wrapped around herself after taking a bath. Mick Jagger had four amphetamine tablets on him, legally obtained over the counter in Italy where one did not need a prescription. Apart from Robert's heroin, the only drugs found on the premises were two types of hash and a bag of grass, all in Schneidermann's pockets. But the police seemed to know who he was, and pointedly ignored his aluminium flight case, filled with a pharmacopoeia of drugs. After the raid, Schneidermann was allowed to leave Britain with no charges brought against him. Because of the grass, Richards was told that he would be charged for allowing his premises to be used for taking drugs.

The *News of the World* predictably denied that they had set up the bust, but Max Zwemmer – in charge of 'operations' at *IT* – and I arranged to meet one of their reporters in a Fleet Street pub, and he told us 'off the record' that the newspaper had a 'man in the Stones camp'. Using the *News of the World*'s own methods, I secretly taped the conversation with a Philips cassette recorder hidden in my bag. The paper had accused Jagger of taking acid at a Moody Blues party and he had, probably unwisely, issued a libel writ against them. The bust was the paper's revenge. On 10 May 1967 Mick, Keith and Robert appeared in court at Chichester in West Sussex, and were remanded on bail.

The bust seemed to precipitate a wave of police activity. Sergeant Pilcher of the Metropolitan Police Drug Squad – John Lennon's 'Semolina Pilchard' – was a zealot with a particular hatred of rock 'n' roll stars and the underground: first he busted Donovan, whose arrest was unlikely to incite the public, and though it is possible that Pilcher had originally targeted the Stones because he saw them as an easy source of bribes, now that the police had Jagger and Richards he went for a complete set of the leading Stones by raiding Brian Jones' flat in London and arresting him for possession of pot. He was to get John Lennon and George Harrison before he himself went to jail for eighteen months after being extradited from Australia to stand trial for perjury; one of many bent cops who went down during the series of police corruption trials in the early Seventies.

In March the police turned their attention to *IT*. On 9 March twelve plain-clothes CID officers entered Indica with a warrant for the seizure of *International Times*, which was still operating from Indica's basement. The warrant was issued under the Obscene Publications Act and was designed to allow police to seize the contents of pornographic bookshops. The Porn Squad had with them Sergeants Pilcher and Philips from the Drug Squad. Pilcher spent more time trying to body-search Christine Erin, my secretary, than he did looking in ashtrays, though he did that as well. 'We're looking for weed,' he said. The Porn Squad stripped the office clean of all files, correspondence, back issues of *IT*, the editor's address book and even the pile of London phone books. It was a classic piece of police-state intimidation, the sort of action that occurred in South Africa or Indonesia: there is no way you can run a newspaper without your lists of advertisers, your accounts of who owes money, your subscription lists or the copy that was intended for the next issue. Tom McGrath was told that if he published another issue – issue ten – they might come and seize that too. Britain has no written constitution, there is no enshrined freedom of the press, and the police were able to do anything they wanted.

The MP Tom Driberg was one of the few Members of Parliament

friendly towards us. I first met him when he visited Allen Ginsberg at Hanson Street in 1965 and had met him on occasion since then, once to discuss an article about his friend Aleister Crowley. Driberg told us that the raid was prompted by Lord Goodman who, knowing that Roy Jenkins, the Home Secretary, would not sanction such obvious police bullying, had gone over his head straight to the Director of Public Prosecutions. Goodman hated *IT* and it would have been typical of him to use his powerful position to close down the paper. We were never able to find out who ordered the raid, or what the legal grounds for it were. The use of a 'seizure' warrant was apparently rare, which suggests that someone, somewhere, thought about it a bit before Pilcher and his mates were set loose.

After emptying the basement, the Porn Squad spent an hour searching Indica. 'You won't have much left by the time we've finished,' they chuckled happily. 'Just look for pictures,' the police were told, but of course there weren't any, and in the end they could only find such obscene classics as *Naked Lunch* by Burroughs; Kenneth Patchen's *Memoirs of a Shy Pornographer*; *Mainline to the Heart*, a book of poems by Clive Matson; a cartoon book about dope-smoking written in Dutch; and a bundle of back issues of *IT*. Naturally no receipts were given for anything. They took all the back issues of *IT* that we had for sale, tore down posters advertising *IT*'s Uncommon Market benefit and even took the 'You Can Get IT Here' poster from the shop door. It took a large police lorry to transfer everything to New Scotland Yard.

The idea of raiding Indica for dirty books was laughable when just a few hundred yards away in Soho there were literally dozens of porn shops selling the real hard-core stuff. I offered to show the police their location, but they declined. Of course they already knew where they were – they went there each month to collect their bribes. In the 1976 police corruption trials, John Mason, who owned porn shops in Soho, told the court that his payments to the Porn Squad had risen from £60 in 1953 to £1,000 a month by 1971. One detective superintendent was paid £10 a week to advise on which articles and pictures to publish in Mason's magazines.

The day after the bust, articles and news items intended for the next issue of *IT* were read aloud by David Mairowitz at the UFO Club, with the illustrations projected on a screen; in this way

publication went ahead as planned, but using a different format. If
the Establishment wanted to kill off the underground they succeeded, because they made it come above ground where it was a lot
more dangerous. This was achieved in a solemn ceremony, reported
in *IT* when issue ten finally hit the stands:

> On Saturday London saw the Death and Resurrection of *International
> Times* as performed by the inmates of the Central Line, under the
> direction of John Hopkins. Harry Fainlight, a London poet who LIVES
> out all that is meant by that word POET, volunteered to die in the role of
> *International Times*. He was put in a red coffin at the Cenotaph,
> Whitehall. A ceremony took place [and] the coffin was carried into the
> bowels of London via the portals of Westminster underground station
> where a rebirth journey took place. Music and dancing accompanied the
> coffin on the tube train. The police arrived and ordered the cortege to
> leave the train. They did – but caught another. After four hours, the
> resurrection at Notting Hill was followed by a march down Portobello
> Road market. Two arrests.

Unfortunately one of those arrested was Harry Fainlight. The
police had erected a barricade near Ladbroke Grove, which brought
the march to a halt. The demonstration was never intended as a
confrontation and the marchers began giving the police flowers.
Things seemed to be going well when suddenly the corpse of *IT* –
Harry – leaped up out of its coffin and started throwing punches at
the nearest policeman. Harry was only a skinny fellow and it did not
take the police long to push him into a Black Maria. As the coffin
was now empty, the march broke up.

The Sunday tabloids predictably missed the point: SACRILEGE AT
THE CENOTAPH screamed the *Sunday Mirror*, but the ceremony was
not intended as an insult to the dead of two world wars – it was a
tribute to them; that they died in the cause of freedom and saved
Britain from becoming a police state under the Nazis. Fleet Street
was not concerned that a newspaper had just been closed down by
the police, with no charges brought against it, and most did not even
report it. We didn't expect any support and received none – we
were by definition an underground newspaper and not an Establishment one.

One positive result of the death and resurrection ceremony was the introduction of Mick Farren to *IT*. Mick's father had been shot down over Germany during the war and he believed passionately in what the *IT* event at the Cenotaph was about. He joined the *IT* staff and some time later became editor. I had seen him around the shop, but now we became friends. He represented a different London scene from the one I knew. He was living in the East End, he went to pubs, and he appeared to me to be a bit of a Teddy boy. For him, the underground was a logical extension of the original rock 'n' roll rebellion. He cared passionately about Elvis Presley, Gene Vincent and all the original rockers, and quite rightly thought they should belong in the pantheon along with Buckminster Fuller, William Burroughs and Jack Kerouac. He saw the Hell's Angels and mods and rockers as a part of the same energetic thrust to change society as the Beat Generation or Che Guevara; something I had not considered before. Sue and I visited his flat and met Joy, his wife. I remember a huge James Dean poster taking up most of one wall and the fact that there was no front door to the building ('the police have kicked it in so often that the landlord doesn't bother to have it fixed now'.) We walked around the streets of the East End and Mick showed us several Jack the Ripper sites in dark alleys.

We had been publishing *IT* every two weeks, and the staff had expanded in order to provide enough news, reviews and articles for it. But our lack of operating capital meant that the paper had cash-flow problems almost from the first issue. Though happy to participate in collective decision-making as far as editorial content went, the staff immediately reverted to the old bosses-and-workers syndrome as soon as they felt their wages were threatened. Tom McGrath in particular insisted on regarding the editorial board – the directors of the company – as the bosses, responsible for providing money, and ideally keeping our opinions about everything else to ourselves, even though he himself was a director. He could not see beyond the fact that *International Times* was published by a company – Lovebooks Limited. Unfortunately, if one made the slightest suggestion of any kind of commercial activity, Tom bristled, even though we were only trying to get him his £25 a week.

We offered to make all of the staff directors, if that would enable them to see the financial situation clearly and take some of the responsibility, but they didn't want that. As far as Hoppy, myself and the other directors were concerned, our aims were the same as theirs. We were not receiving any income from the paper at all; I was not paid for my articles and interviews. The company was there to provide limited liability in the case of unpayable bills – otherwise, the editor and staff would have been liable. No one expected the paper ever to make a profit, that was not the idea, but neither did we want to go personally bankrupt for it as the result of unpaid bills or a law suit. There were harsh words spoken.

Allen Ginsberg sent us $200, Charles Olson signed a royalty cheque over to us, and Panna Grady, the American heiress who brought Olson to Britain, gave us a cheque. Unfortunately she asked Alexander Trocchi to deliver it. He held on to it, no doubt hoping to find some way to endorse it over to himself. We were eventually able to prise it loose from his junkie fingers by pretending that half of it was a loan from Sigma, but the incident provoked such jealousy in Alex that he immediately wrote to Panna demanding, 'Give your money to AT not IT.' Panna, of course, showed us the letter. At least Alex didn't put Lyn, his wife, on the streets again, as he had done in the past in order to get money for junk.

We could not survive on handouts, however. We really did need to get our finances in order. After the police raid we naturally expected to be engaged in an expensive trial, making our financial needs even greater. It would be months before we knew whether or not a prosecution would proceed; in the meantime we were left on tenterhooks.

The Family Dog

Chet Helms, the manager of the Avalon ballroom in San Francisco, arrived in Britain in the spring of 1967. Chet was a rail-thin, six-foot four-inch Texan with long blond hair to his armpits, a full chest-covering beard and shining eyeglasses. He was larger than life and I liked him a lot. Chet ran the Family Dog, a loose community of musicians, light-show operators, couples and children that operated from the Avalon. Chet described it as 'Religious – a weekly communal, cathartic, ecstatic expression', fuelled very much by acid.

Love, the Charlatans, Great Society with Grace Slick, Captain Beefheart, the Grateful Dead, Big Brother and the Holding Company, the 13th Floor Elevators and Quicksilver Messenger Service had all played the Avalon, which was always regarded as the cooler of the two San Francisco venues. Bill Graham ran the Fillmore strictly as a business; he warned bands that he wouldn't book them if they played the Avalon, but he couldn't stop them going there after their Fillmore gig to jam. Chet was more interested in the vibe; as long as the Avalon brought in operating costs, he was happy. Bill Graham went on to become a millionaire promoter; Chet opened an art gallery.

Tom McGrath was very wary of Chet, though I think the problems were largely cultural – similar to my initial inability to reconcile Frank Zappa's endless talk about 'product' with his uncompromising dedication to his music and his message. The American underground culture operated in a commercial environment, whereas in those days British culture did not. There was little in the way of entrepreneurial activity on the cultural front: no independent record labels, no independent recording studios, few small avant-garde art galleries, off-Broadway-style experimental theatres, little poetry magazines, radical bookshops and the like.

For Chet, it seemed quite natural to market posters and handbills to pay the running costs of the Avalon, whereas the British non-Establishment culture tended to look around for grants and rich benefactors. That was how the arts were funded in Britain. The Americans thought they could change the world, the sky was the limit; in England the horizon was very low indeed – if we kept our heads down, with a bit of luck the authorities wouldn't see us. This was why I enjoyed having so many Americans involved with *IT* – they didn't have the 'mustn't grumble' mentality.

There was some talk of forming a co-operative that the Family Dog would finance. It seemed an idea worth exploring, but Tom McGrath was adamantly against it. Tom devoted a lot of space to his own experiments with drugs in his editorials, including one written on acid, but though he virtually spelled out that he was a junkie, we still didn't get the message: 'I have taken heroin ad nauseam. Some of my friends have died in the course of their addiction; others have kicked. Some are still using and unhappy. Some are still using and happy . . . Last piece of advice: don't turn on. Heroin is a beautiful kick but it's insidious. It gets inside you and fills you with longing – for more heroin. That can get to be a drag.'

After editing twelve issues Tom suddenly disappeared without a trace, taking the newspaper's only typewriter with him. He told no one he was going, and it was not for many months that we discovered he had returned to Scotland.

Sgt Pepper

One evening Sue and I arrived at Abbey Road and encountered George Harrison running down the corridor, wearing his *Sgt Pepper* outfit, which had just been delivered. He stopped, did a neat pirouette, scarf flowing, and left in a trail of incense and hash smoke. I hadn't realised that the *Sgt Pepper* theme was going to be taken so far. The costumes looked great. A few days later, on 30 March, we went with Paul to Chelsea Manor Studios, Michael Cooper's studio in Flood Street, to see the cover shoot.

Peter Blake, who designed the set, was busy arranging the potted plants, which were wilting under the powerful floodlights. Adam, Michael Cooper's toddler, crawled around, picking at the flowers. Several extremely efficient women in neat aprons appeared carrying the four *Sgt Pepper* outfits that the group were to wear and the four Beatles were shepherded off to change. We examined the models from Madame Tussaud's; they looked completely unlike the Beatles, there was no resemblance at all. Joints were passed around. Robert Fraser was being immensely important, even though he really had nothing to do. Then suddenly the Beatles entered in their uniforms and everyone was drawn to them like iron filings to a magnet. It was a huge joke and everyone found the uniforms incredibly amusing, except the Beatles themselves, who didn't seem to think it was *that* funny.

They all wore their MBEs to give the uniforms an authentic touch and there was a huge box of additional trinkets for them to choose from. They had all brought things to add to the set and Paul had filled the boot of the Aston with old instruments. A Rolling Stones sweater was added, at Robert Fraser's suggestion, as a way of showing support for the Stones after their drug busts.

The original idea was that the album would have a centrefold painted by the Fool, but the artwork that Simon and Marijka turned in was the wrong size and very crudely painted. Robert Fraser was instrumental in persuading the Beatles that a photograph would be much better because the painting was 'just bad art!' The Fool's pink wave pattern for the inner sleeve was retained. The double page, foldout portrait was taken as soon as a series of front cover shots was finished. The idea of the portrait was to communicate love, and they all stared intently at the camera for minute after minute, trying to beam as much love as possible into its lens as Michael fired off rolls of film, just like David Hemmings in *Blow Up*, and his assistant scurried up with new cameras.

To me, *Sgt Pepper* was very much Paul's album. John had almost retired from the group by then. By the time they started *Sgt Pepper* he had taken so much acid that he felt burned out. John always did a thorough job and he approached the task of demolishing his ego with typical vigour. Now he felt empty. His marriage to Cynthia was on the rocks, but he did not want to walk out and do to his son what his own father had to him, so he stayed at home and took more and more drugs, rarely going to London except for recording sessions. He told me later, 'I was still in a real big depression in *Pepper* and I know Paul wasn't at that time. He was feeling full of confidence, but I wasn't. I was going through murder.'

Paul's home movies were filled with what he called 'random', and he was always intrigued by how well virtually any set of visual images always fitted to music: the brain just imposed the connections. He made quite a few movies, Marianne Faithfull appeared in one of the more memorable, and Jane was a regular. Many evenings were spent with a group of us sitting in his living room, very stoned, watching his latest films. The screen was supposed to come down from the top of the built-in bookcase, but it had not been constructed correctly and always jammed.

Paul began subtly to introduce into his work with the Beatles some of the ideas he had gathered the previous year. John Cage's work with random sound certainly informed the central section of 'A Day In the Life'. It was Paul's idea to record twenty-four bars containing nothing but Mal Evans counting, signalling the end with an alarm clock, then using a full orchestra like a single instrument, rising from their lowest to highest notes to fill the space.

One evening during the *Sgt Pepper* sessions at Abbey Road, the Beatles were distracted by a *Time-Life* reporting team. As far as the photographer was concerned, it was a huge honour to be chosen for *Time*'s cover, but the Beatles couldn't have cared less. However, they did agree to pose and went off to the huge Studio One, to stand around in appropriate poses while 'A Day In the Life' thundered through the speakers normally used for symphony orchestras. But the photographers also wanted more intimate shots. Back in Studio Two, Ringo was sitting by the wall in a corner made from sound baffles, where the provisions for the evening were laid out: a crate of Cokes, a huge tray of Smarties, Mars Bars and assorted sweets. He was eating a plate of Heinz baked beans on toast, made for him by Mal Evans, and drinking a cup of tea. The American photographer – very short hair, shiny pink face, as if he had stepped from a Fifties movie – came up to him:

'My God, man, you can't eat that!' he gasped.

'Why not?' demanded Ringo, looking insulted. 'Is there something wrong with it?'

The American backed away, 'It's just that, well, I expected you boys to be eating caviar and everything . . .' He began to get flustered.

'Did you?' asked Ringo, ending the conversation.

The Rolling Stones did a lot of their recording in America, where the studios were much better equipped than in Britain, but for some reason the Beatles stayed at Abbey Road – possibly because they had unlimited recording time. Apart from the low fidelity of the recordings, this also had its down side in waiting around, as George Martin and his team endlessly doubled up backing tracks in order to free up a track for a vocal or guitar solo. Even *Sgt Pepper*, made in 1967, was recorded on only a four-track machine. Eight-track machines had been in use in the USA since 1958, but EMI was loath to spend money and Abbey Road remained a museum of antiquated equipment.

I remember one session in late March when the Beatles arrived and wanted to get straight to work. The engineers had already spent hours synchronising two tape recorders in Studio One to record the evening's session and wanted to take a break first. These were the days before groups and recording engineers became part of the same team. The Beatles got on well with Glyn Johns, but they were pretty stroppy with all of the other engineers. The Beatles – mostly John – tried to pull rank, but were immediately reminded of the union rules. The engineers had the legal right to take a certain amount of break time, which they now did, informing John to the minute when they would be returning. While they were away the Beatles began messing about in the control room and, although they didn't touch much, managed to mess up the planned synching operation. The engineers were vocal in their displeasure. Lennon argued back, but they knew him too well to get caught in a slanging match with him. The group left the control room and the engineers contented themselves with exasperated looks and muttered curses of 'Fucking pampered kids' and 'If it weren't for George [Martin] saying we were to always pander to them, they are always right . . .'

'Come on, get on with it!' Lennon yelled up from the studio. 'We're the fucking Beatles, you know, not some green kids you can push around!'

'You won't do a fucking thing till we tell you,' shouted back one of the engineers over the intercom, 'and that'll be when we've got the tape on and run a tone and taken your levels.' The engineers were used to having their own way, but so were the Beatles.

John, in particular, liked to have his every wish fulfilled. He only had to say, 'Apples, Mal' at 3 am, and Mal Evans would drive to the wholesale fruit-and-vegetable market at Covent Garden and return with a box of fresh Golden Delicious. I once overheard John mutter, 'Socks, Mal' and an hour later Mal appeared in the studio with a dozen different pairs of brightly coloured socks. John then spent a delighted quarter of an hour in a corner, trying them on. Where Mal found them in the middle of the night is a mystery, but roadies have an astonishing fund of knowledge. Food was relatively easy, for there was a café near St John's Wood station where Mal got take-away meals for the group, and there were late-night fish-and-chip shops and Chinese take-aways that he knew. Ringo was partial to a fry-up and Mal had his own electric ring and frying pan to cook up beans and fried eggs for him. There was a small canteen at Abbey Road, but EMI worked normal office hours, and it was always closed by the time the Beatles started work. It was exceptional that they were permitted to work at night at all and must have involved some tricky negotiations with the union.

One evening George Harrison and I walked down to the canteen to get some cold Cokes from the machine. To George's fury the canteen had a padlock on the door. Complaining bitterly that EMI was making millions of pounds from the Beatles each year, but couldn't even see its way to leaving the canteen door open for them, George found a heavy object and smashed the lock off the door. The Coke machine was well stocked. 'They'll know who did it,' he said, 'and they'll probably charge us for it.'

It was Mal's job to roll the joints, which he usually did hidden from George Martin's view behind the sound baffles surrounding Ringo's kit. There was a room containing the air-conditioning plant for the entire building, where the Beatles would sometimes sneak away for a smoke, but usually it was done discreetly as they worked; the studio was so large that the musicians seemed quite small and distant when viewed from the control booth upstairs where Martin and the tape ops were ensconced. Years later, in a television documentary about the making of *Sgt Pepper*, George Martin asked Paul, 'Do you know what caused *Pepper*?'

Paul replied, 'In one word, George, drugs. Pot.'

Martin protested, 'No, no. You weren't on it all the time.'

'Yes, we were, George. *Sgt Pepper* was a drug album.'

By this he meant pot. Robert Fraser came to some of the *Sgt Pepper* sessions, usually bringing drugs with him. From his top pocket he would produce a laboratory testtube filled with speedballs: cocaine and heroin mixed. The Beatles didn't touch it, but some of their entourage were happy to indulge. The band liked to smoke pot while recording because it enabled them to focus more clearly on the music, but the Beatles had a policy of no cocaine, no LSD or anything that would blur their senses. Even alcohol was frowned upon because they found that it made them lazy and not want to try one more take to get something right.

There were drinks for friends, however. When it looked like the recording sessions were going to continue for months, Mal Evans established a little commissary of his own where he dispensed soft drinks, alcohol, Wagon Wheels, Penguin bars and other snacks. The usual arrangement was that visitors sat near to whichever Beatle had invited them, usually in folding chairs against the wall, so that they would not get in the way. Visitors were seated in the studio and only got to visit the control room when the musicians themselves gathered there to hear a playback or a mix. We sat and watched, for hours at a time. In fact there was not much to see. Recording sessions are almost as time-consuming as film-making. Much of the time was taken up by tuning up, setting up microphones, taking levels and technical procedures which these days can be done at the flick of a switch. Playing back a track in the studio then required patching in cables on the patchboard, like an old-fashioned telephone switchboard. An inordinate amount of time was spent adjusting headphone levels, which again had to be done from the control room.

One evening Sue and I arrived to be greeted once more by George running down the corridor towards us: 'Oh you should have been here the other night, we recorded a really great number, all about a girl leaving home. It really says . . . it!' He waved his hands in the air expressively. 'It says it in a way which they can listen to, you know, the mums and dads up in Wigan and Manchester, and you never know, it might get through to a few of 'em.' His eyes were twinkling. It was surprising to see George so excited about a song, as he had appeared bored during the previous few sessions we'd been to. He jumped onto the low drum platform, strumming his guitar. 'Live at EMI!' he yelled, and delivered a heavy chord. The Beatles were all pleased about 'She's Leaving Home', which I thought definitely captured the emptiness of middle-class family life. One of Paul's best.

That evening they were putting on the animal noises that John wanted to use at the end of 'Good Morning, Good Morning'. After playing around with dog barks and the sounds of a hunt, Paul suggested putting on a tone that only dogs could hear. The idea was

Allen Ginsberg's 39th birthday party.
Left to right: Allen Ginsberg, Miles, Sue Miles (*John Hopkins*)

Allen Ginsberg and Ian Sommerville, 1965 (*John Hopkins*)

(*Above*) Hoppy, 1965

(*Above right*) Gala Mitchell

(*Right*) Alan Beckett (*John Hopkins*)

Paul McCartney's drawing
for an Indica handbill

Building Indica Gallery.
Left to right: Miles, John Dunbar,
Marianne Faithfull, Peter Asher,
Paul McCartney (*Graham Keen)*

Playing shops with Peter and Jane Asher (*Graham Keen*)

A party at Indica. In the foreground, left to right: Miles, Pete Simpson, Maggie, Paul McCartney, Kate Wallhead. Behind Paul is Binn Tivy. At the end of the table Christie Johnson and Sue Miles. Behind them stands Chris Hill (*John Hopkins*)

Paul McCartney and Miles
with Luciano Berio at the
Italian Institute, 1965

William Burroughs
in Duke Street,
St James's, 1969 (*Miles*)

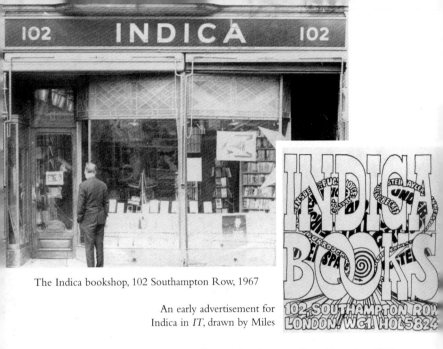

The Indica bookshop, 102 Southampton Row, 1967

An early advertisement for
Indica in *IT*, drawn by Miles

(*Below*) *International Times* staff at 102 Southampton Row, December 1966.
Back row left to right: V.I.Lenin, Miles, Peter Stansill, Sue Miles, Roger Whelan, David Z.
Mairowitz. Middle row: Jeff Nuttall, Jim Haynes, Tom McGrath, Christine Uren.
Front: Jack Henry Moore, John Hopkins (*Adam Ritchie*)

Shooting the sleeve for *Sgt Pepper*, Michael Cooper's studio, 1967.
Left to right: Miles, Sue Miles, George Harrison, John Lennon, Mal Evans, Robert Fraser,
Paul McCartney, Ringo Starr, Michael Cooper. Adam Cooper on floor (*Apple*)

Betsy Klein and Charles Olson, Gloucester, Massachusetts, 1969 (*Miles*)

Harry Smith at the Hotel Chelsea, 1969 (*Miles*)

Allen Ginsberg's Poetry Farm at Cherry Valley, New York. Back row, left to right: Peter Orlovsky, Denise Felieu (holding Don't Bite Me), Julius Orlovsky, Gordon Ball. Front row: Allen Ginsberg, Bonnie Bremser with Georgia Bremser on her lap, Ray Bremser, Gregory Corso

to have dogs all across the country raising their heads and howling when this particular track came on. All the Beatles thought this would be very amusing and they asked George Martin to do it. There was a lot of discussion about frequencies that animals could hear and humans could not. George was not sure that a 22,000-hertz tone would be reproduced by most record players and proved to be very knowledgeable on the subject of frequencies. He said that women could hear up to 20,000 hertz, whereas men rarely heard above 18,000 hertz and told us that, as one grew older, the upper registers fell away so that you could no longer hear bat squeaks, for instance. He found a signal generator and we all took turns – Sue and I included – at testing how high a frequency we could hear. We indicated when the sound disappeared and George told us our reading. I could only hear to 17,000 hertz, but Ringo's score was even lower than mine.

On 21 April everyone in the studio recorded the run-on spiral for the album, about two seconds' worth of sound. It was a triple session – three three-hour sessions – which ended around 4 am. The Beatles stood around two microphones muttering, singing snatches of songs and yelling for what seemed like hours, with the rest of us standing round them, joining in. Mal carried in cases of Coke and bottles of Scotch. Ringo was out of it. 'I'm so stoned,' he said, 'I think I'm going to fall over!' As he slowly toppled, Mal caught him and popped him neatly in a chair without a murmur. In the control room no one seemed to notice. A loop was made from the tape of the muttering and was mixed, but not without some altercation between John and the tape operator.

The engineers were bored by sitting up all night watching the Beatles become more and more stoned in the huge recording studio, so they did dubs and caught up on work-sheets, while George Martin did test mixes and cut acetates for the group to take home with them. To me, as an occasional visitor, the project seemed to be moving at snail's pace. Six or eight hours' work produced two or three minutes of usable tape. But out of the apparent chaos, and the hours of sitting around, *Sgt Pepper* was slowly born and, even in the making, everyone knew this was going to be the greatest rock album ever made.

★

One afternoon that April I arrived at Cavendish Avenue and found Paul in a meeting with Brian Epstein. They invited me to make myself at home and I watched them at work. Brian obviously adored Paul and it was always interesting to see them together. He touched Paul at any time that it might seem natural, laying his hand on Paul's arm to make a point or placing a casual hand on his shoulder as they left a room. I often noticed a certain admiring look, a slightly moist eye. He sat next to Paul on the big settee beneath a pair of René Magritte paintings and an alternative, unused, painted drum skin from the *Sgt Pepper* sleeve. Brian was dressed in his usual impeccable Savile Row suit, hair neatly parted, though longish and with long sideboards. He seemed relaxed, happy and completely unlike the usual hyper businessmen of the pop world.

Sgt Pepper had not yet been released, but already Paul was explaining to Brian at length his plan for the *Magical Mystery Tour* movie. Every few seconds Brian would make a note on a scrap of paper. Paul drew the whole plan out as a diagram, a cosmic plan with time and action and motion. Brian could translate this, as he could all Beatles commands, into a specific timetable of booked studios, rehearsal halls, rented equipment, tea for forty-five people and everything else they needed, without the Beatles even knowing what degree of organisation was required to satisfy their often obscure and demanding requests. Brian was on Paul's wavelength and treated him as the most organised Beatle, who could in turn translate management needs back to the other three. It was the last time I saw Brian.

Sue and I were at a Jimi Hendrix concert at the Saville Theatre on 27 August when someone came onstage and announced that Brian Epstein had died. There was an audible gasp from the audience. In the spirit of the times, the show carried on, with Jimi giving a particularly emotional performance.

14-Hour Technicolor Dream

Even before the paper was busted, Hoppy and several other *IT* staff had been working on organising a monster fund-raising event. With an expensive obscenity case in the offing, planning was suddenly intensified. In the end the event was billed as the 14-Hour Technicolor Dream: a 'giant benefit against fuzz action', as the *Melody Maker* ad read. Alexis Korner, Alex Harvey, the Cat, Creation, Charlie Brown's Clowns, the Crazy World of Arthur Brown, the Pink Floyd, the Soft Machine, Graham Bond Organisation, the Flies, Champion Jack Dupree, Gary Farr, Ginger Johnson's Drums, Jacob's Ladder Construction Co., the Move, Denny Laine, Noel Murphy, 117, the Sun Trolley, the Poetry Band, the Purple Gang, the Pretty Things, Poison Bellows, Sam Gopal, the Social Deviants and the Stalkers all agreed to donate their services, as did Yoko Ono and poets Christopher Logue, Michael Horovitz and Alexander Trocchi. Hoppy took time off from *IT* to work full time on the project, assisted by Dave Housen and dozens of part-time helpers, including his tumultuous new girlfriend, Suzy Creamcheese. Suzy did what she did best, causing chaos and, in doing so, publicised the benefit.

Michael McInnerney designed a beautiful poster for the event – printed in rainbow ink, no two alike – and at dusk on 29 April rockets burst over the London skyline, like a bat-signal telling the freaks to come out.

Alexandra Palace – Ally Pally, as it is always known – stands high on a hill in North London overlooking the city, a huge Victorian pleasure palace of metal and glass set in the middle of a park. London's first television transmitter was mounted on one of its towers because of its prominent position. In the early Sixties it was used as the venue for all-night jazz raves, which is probably why Hoppy came to think of it.

On that April night the impression inside was of a giant cathedral: a vast space filled with light. A fairground helter-skelter stood at one end, rented for the night, offering free rides to anyone prepared to climb the steps to the top, and there was a fibre-glass igloo for smoking banana skins – that month's hippie craze – which were handed out by a smiling Suzy Creamcheese. The space was so big that there was a stage at each end, with poetry or folk singing on one, and rock on the other. White sheeting had been stretched over the upper part of the two long iron arcades which divided the aisles from the main space to provide screens for the light-shows, and there was a long light-board of the sort used on buildings to spell out news and advertisements. In the centre stood the biggest sound and lighting gantry erected in Britain during that era, where, from a platform high above the floor, Hoppy and his crew ran the event. The only hitch in the proceedings came at midnight when people started climbing up the scaffolding. We had no insurance, so the music had to be stopped to get them down.

Mick Farren's Social Deviants opened the show, followed by a procession of something like forty groups – no one kept a record of who actually played there. The Flies were best described as a proto-punk band. They had gathered round the stage at UFO and yelled, 'Sell out! Sell out!' when the Pink Floyd signed a recording contract with EMI. Now the lead singer of the Flies unzipped his crushed-velvet loon pants and pissed over the audience, something even Johnny Rotten did not dare to do a decade later.

The Beatles had completed *Sgt Pepper* one week before. John Lennon and John Dunbar were tripping at Kenwood, John's mansion in Weybridge, when they saw a news clip about Ally Pally on the nine o'clock news. John's chauffeur Terry was summoned and they set off for North London. Both Johns had known about the event, but had forgotten about it. John Dunbar said later that he had never before seen so many old friends gathered together in one place; for many of us it was like a school reunion. John Lennon looked a little out of it, but seemed to be enjoying himself. One of the events he watched was a happening organised by Yoko Ono in which members of the audience were invited to cut off a girl's clothes, a small piece at a time, using a pair of amplified scissors. On previous occasions this event had been marked by the hesitancy and self-consciousness of the audience, but at Ally Pally it was not long before the girl was naked. John and Yoko had already met at Indica Gallery and Yoko was very keen to get together with him, but John had so far not responded to her stream of postcards and letters.

182

Ten thousand people came to the 14-Hour Technicolor Dream, which, though it only half filled the building, was the largest underground gathering London had experienced to date, and was surpassed only by the 1969 Stones in the Park free concert in Hyde Park, with its audience of half a million. The Ally Pally was like an enormously enlarged UFO Club and felt very familiar and comfortable. This was partly due to the line-up of UFO regulars: Arthur Brown, who gave an inspired performance, doing his very best to transform himself into the God of Hellfire; and the Soft Machine dressed up specially for the occasion: Daevid Allen in a miner's helmet, Mike Ratledge in his Dr Strange cape, Kevin Ayers with rouged cheeks and wide-brimmed hat, and Robert Wyatt with a short-back and sides. The Pink Floyd arrived around 3.30 am, having played a gig in Holland that evening and returned on the ferry. They were tired and exhausted and both manager Pete Jenner and Syd Barrett were tripping. The band went on just as the first fingers of dawn entered through the enormous rose window of Alexandra Palace; the throbbing bass line of 'Interstellar Overdrive' galvanising the crowd. Their music was eerie, solemn and calming. After a whole night of frolicking and festivities and too much acid came the celebration of the dawn. Throughout the hall people held hands with their neighbours. The Floyd were weary and probably did not play so well, but at that moment they were superb. They gave voice to the feelings of the crowd. Syd's eyes blazed as his notes soared up into the strengthening light and the dawn was reflected in his famous mirror-disc Telecaster, the light dancing on the crowd. Then came the rebirth of energy, another day, and with the sun a burst of dancing and enthusiasm.

The concert over, Hoppy and Suzy stood at the door shaking hands with everyone as they left – hundreds and hundreds of them. Some hippies had made a fifty-foot-long joint from photographic backdrop paper, filled with leaves and flowers, and were running around in the park with it. Quite a few mods had turned up, intent on causing trouble, but had been spiked with acid before anything could happen. Now they had finished their trips they reverted to their old selves and found amusement in kicking the hippies' joint to pieces.

The event should have made money, but virtually all the ticket receipts were stolen. *IT* made enough to pay its debts and even get ahead a little, though the hall never did get paid for. Michael Henshaw received bills and letters for years afterwards. The subsequent issue of *IT* carried a long list of names of people who had taken tickets to sell and not yet paid for them. It was the apogee of underground activity.

The first new venue to cash in on the hippie scene was the Electric Garden in King Street, Covent Garden, which opened on 24 May. Organised by Jay Landesman and described as a mixed-media club, it had two stages, a separate film room and a restaurant. They announced that they intended to present performance artists like Yoko Ono, the Living Theater and John Latham. The opening night featured the Crazy World of Arthur Brown, Tomorrow and Yoko Ono. It sounded like a welcome addition to the scene; however, when owners Jess Reid, Brian and Paul Waldman saw what performance art was, they didn't like it; nor did Peter Dale, the club's designer. Yoko was in the middle of a performance piece, tied to a chair with white bandages, screaming her head off. As *IT* put it: '[The] Waldman brothers didn't want to interrupt the prevailing mood (heavy drinking). Peter Dale to Tony Cox: "You're not going to perform that shit here."' Her microphone was turned off and a tape of loud music switched on instead. Jay Landesman, who was being paid £200 a week as artistic director, continued the story in his autobiography:

> I encouraged Yoko to continue screaming. 'Good background music. You've got the place jumping at last,' I said enthusiastically. Her husband Tony Cox rushed to the tape deck to cut the blasting music. He was grabbed by the manager and bouncers, dragged to a corner and thrown on the floor, and was about to be pummelled when I arrived. I told Cox to announce to the audience what had happened. 'This club is run by gangsters,' he hollered into the mike. 'Will somebody call the fuzz.'

Yoko remained tied to a chair, still screaming, helpless in the middle of her piece. The police arrived, Yoko was untied, a fierce argument ensued and the performers eventually left, unpaid, followed by most of the audience and the light-show operator. It was an unpleasant forewarning of what the commercialisation of the underground was going to be like.

New management was introduced in the form of Dave Housen, co-organiser with Hoppy of the 14-Hour Technicolor Dream, and Neil Winterbottom, from Dandy Fashions on the King's Road. The name was changed to Middle Earth, and the Waldman brothers and company stayed out of sight. Though initially plagued by gangs of mods looking for trouble, by visits from uniformed police and an edgy suspicious atmosphere, the club eventually developed a regular clientele and a genuine atmosphere of its own. Middle Earth recognised UFO membership cards, hired the same bands, poets and performers, and did everything it could to re-create the UFO atmosphere – but some things cannot be repeated.

UFO itself was still going from strength to strength at this point: there was an evening late in May when Procol Harum and Soft Machine were on the bill. Procol Harum played their first and third gigs at UFO; by their second appearance 'A Whiter Shade of Pale' had already reached number one. Paul had brought along an acetate of the song 'Sgt Pepper's Lonely Hearts Club Band' and gave the audience an advance preview. That evening Mark Boyle and his team were presenting a light-show entitled 'Earth, Air, Fire and Water', projected onto a white screen before and after the music. Soft Machine's Mike Ratledge asked Mark if he would project his lights directly onto the group, which he did. At one point Ratledge hit a long discord and held it. Boyle quickly poured some acid on a piece of perforated zinc in front of the projector and, as Mike held the discord, the acid melted the zinc into terrible distorted shapes, which were projected all over the band. At the end of their set they were joined on stage by Jimi Hendrix for a jam session. That was a good UFO.

Scandinavian Love

One afternoon a huge Swedish hippie, wearing a grubby Afghan coat and long tangled blond hair and brandishing a gnarled stick, leaped straight through our plate-glass window, sending shards of glass flying throughout the shop. 'Books should be free!' he yelled, scooping up an armful of books and magazines and departing through the jagged remains of the window. He ran off down Southampton Row, shrieking. Pedestrians cowered against the wall to let him past. I didn't follow him. My assistant Ann Shepherd sighed and got out the broom. An editor from Grove Press who was visiting couldn't believe it. 'I've never seen anything like that in all my years in New York!' he exclaimed.

'Ah yes, swinging London's pretty exciting,' I told him.

Ann was very organised and all the hippies were scared of her as she shooed them out of the way. A sharp word from her would send them scuttling down the stairs to *IT*. Unfortunately nothing could stop them from stealing books. The other assistant was Nick Kimberley. He was passionate about poetry and produced a couple of issues of a little magazine, *Big Venus*, while he was there. They coped brilliantly, given the constant lack of money and the pressures on them from the stream of visitors looking for the underground scene. Most bookshop work consists of dusting the books, putting them in order, noticing what is missing – sold or stolen – and reordering if it is a stock item. Most booksellers can hold a stock of about ten thousand titles in their heads, though they would not be able to recite them out loud. There were daily visits to the bank and weekly visits to Michael Henshaw's office; his staff dealt with the paperwork and sent off the cheques. They paid the monthly accounts, apportioning money between those publishers whose books were essential stock items, fending off others and juggling whatever remained between the landlord, the GPO and the London Electricity Board. I dreaded the monthly meetings because there was never enough money to go round.

Ann and Nick usually dealt with the publishers' reps, who often held very peculiar ideas about what would suit us. We specialised in poetry, and made up for our lack of capital by acting as a showcase for certain publishers such as Fulcrum Press, displaying their full range of titles in return for holding the stock on sale-or-return, which was a rarity in those days. We carried a lot of imports, mostly the American small-press books and magazines that I first stocked at Better Books. This entailed a lot of correspondence, but was generally worth it. We also imported hundreds of copies of Timothy Leary's *The Psychedelic Experience* and the *Psychedelic Reader*, sold scores of George Andrews and Simon Vinkenoog's *The Book of Grass* – in fact, anything about drugs. Our most saleable titles were published by City Light Books, New Directions, Grove Press, Peter Owen and John Calder, and our most popular authors, aside from Leary and company, were William Burroughs, Paul Bowles, Tolkien, Wilhelm Reich – when we could get him – Robert Anton Wilson, Herman Hesse, Buckminster Fuller, and the authors of the *Tibetan Book of the Dead* and the *I Ching*. I issued a sporadic rare-book catalogue of Beat Generation first editions, selling mostly to American university libraries, which were just beginning to collect in that area. We struggled along.

Kinfauns

After the success of my taped conversation with Paul, I approached George Harrison. He and Patti came over and we discussed eastern religion for an hour or so before going off to Parkes restaurant for dinner. It was the first long, serious discussion I'd had with George and we got on well. He sent a telegram to say how much he loved the interview when it appeared in the 19 May issue of *IT* and invited us to spend a day at Kinfauns, their house in Weybridge. The Beatles' Austin Princess came to collect us. This limo was famous in its own right from *A Hard Day's Night* and it was fun to ride in it, but I always found it strange to be in a situation where the chauffeur was asking if he could smoke, as my father had been a chauffeur before the war. The driver wanted to know how long we would be. George said airily, 'Oh, come back at midnight. It'll probably be one or two.' At Weybridge the only other guests were Barry Finch and Josie, his Dutch girlfriend, members of the Fool. The house was very American, all on one floor with a large living room and a fireplace that had been painted – rather crudely, I thought, and probably rather expensively – by Simon and Marijke. The house was a strange mixture of hand-made North African fabrics, crude West Coast psychedelia and Ken Partridge – 'interior designer to the stars' – in full Sixties mode. The grey silk bedroom walls, hung from floor to ceiling with closely spaced strings of pearls, looked like his. George was busy painting the outside of the house with a random abstract pattern which we all added to. That afternoon I painted a Buddha's footprint six feet high in silver and green on the garage door. George had already moved onto the roof and presumably eventually covered the whole place. The swimming pool had a wall, about eight feet high, with one of John Lennon's drawings picked out in white mosaic on a blue tile background. As we worked in the spring sunshine, heads could sometimes be seen peeping over the high wall that surrounded the property. George had unfortunately bought a house that backed onto a girls' school.

The house was filled with objects brought back from India: small tables, carvings, statues and musical instruments, and the smell of incense and sandalwood permeated the entire space. The Beatles had spent £3,000 in one shop during a brief stopover in New Delhi on their way back from the Far East the year before. Paul had a basement room filled with Indian objects from that particular shopping spree. George and Patti's living room had as a feature a very large hookah with what looked like about an ounce of finely sieved grass in it. It made a splendid centrepiece.

Patti cooked us a fine meal – 'completely vegetarian' George explained, since, being a Hindu, he could not take another creature's life. Sue looked at Patti, who smiled knowingly back. They both knew that there were minced shrimps in the Pilau rice. There was a movie screen in the living room with a movie projector in a small annexe. Visiting a cinema was a potential security problem, so the Beatles watched films at home, renting them from the same companies that supplied cinemas. It was the only way in the days before videos. Patti, being the more cultured, chose the films and that night we saw Jean Renoir's *Grande Illusion*. The food, conversation and large quantities of grass put us all to sleep, and only the rustling of the leader of the film flipping through the projector awoke us.

Intimidation

As there was no way the police could justify holding such documents as *IT*'s financial records, Michael Henshaw and I visited Scotland Yard to collect them. In a huge basement, like an underground car park only with a higher ceiling, were a series of locked cages. In one of them the entire contents of the *IT* office had been dumped on the floor in a heap and looked as though they had been walked over. A sullen, bored policeman unlocked it for us, then watched us in case we tried to sneak a London phone book out. After some time we were able to find the various items we were looking for, including the editor's address book, and left. We both breathed a sigh of relief when we got into the fresh air; it was as if we had been released from prison.

On 9 June Scotland Yard informed us that the DPP was not going to bring charges against the paper and arranged to return all the seized material. When their lorry arrived, they refused to unload it because there were photographers present and, after calling the Yard, they departed again. The materials were finally returned a few days later, more than three months after they had been seized. Patchen's *Memoirs of a Shy Pornographer* and John Calder's edition of *Naked Lunch* were covered in grubby fingerprints, so I assume a policeman had actually read them. I hope he enjoyed them: 'Why this is great stuff! The Sarge was all wrong about Burroughs – where can I get some more of this?' A friend at the British Library, just around the corner, suggested that in the event of another raid, we should make a run for it with any suspect books to the shelter of the British Museum forecourt, because the British Library premises are exempt from the laws of obscenity and libel. Fortunately I never had cause to take up this option, though it would have been interesting to try it out.

No business could survive with all its accounts and paperwork impounded, but fortunately *IT* was not a business in the conventional sense: any money coming in paid the printer and (sometimes) the staff and that was all. Naturally, after being deprived of all our office records, and then having them returned all jumbled up, our business affairs were in an ever more sorry state.

Meanwhile we were given another reminder that the Establishment had its evil eye on us. When Tom McGrath made his unannounced departure, Jack Henry Moore stood in as editor while we decided what to do. He edited four issues, but then left on a trip to the States which he could not cancel. While he was there, his passport came up for renewal. He applied for a new one, but when he went to pick it up he was told to report to a certain address in Manhattan. It was an anonymous-looking apartment building with nothing on it to indicate that it was government property. He went to the apartment, feeling uneasy. He was shown into an office and asked to sit down by a polite young man. On the desk was a pile of *International Times*, a complete set as far as Jack could tell. The polite young man asked him, 'Do you intend to continue working for this newspaper, Mr Moore?'

Jack said he did.

The polite young man said, 'Here is your passport, Mr Moore.' It was a fairly crude, but effective, attempt at intimidation. They were letting Jack know that they had their eye on him.

Hoppy Sent to the Scrubs

On 30 December 1966 the Drug Squad had arrived at Hoppy's flat at 115 Queensway and arrested him and his four flatmates for possession of marijuana. At the time it did not look really serious, but when the case reached court on 1 June, the next year, Hoppy was sentenced to nine months in Wormwood Scrubs. His flatmates and girlfriend had been cleared in the magistrates' court, but Hoppy had elected to go for trial by jury. Instead of kowtowing to the court, Hoppy lectured the judge that pot was harmless and that the law should be changed. Judge A. Gordon Friend found him guilty and told him, 'I have just heard what your views are on the possession of cannabis and the smoking of it. This is not a matter I can overlook. You are a pest to society.'

An emergency meeting of Hoppy's friends was called the next day in the back room of the Indica Bookshop. There were dozens of people present, the first time that the King's Road and the West End scenes had assembled anywhere other than at UFO, but no one had any constructive ideas except Steve Abrams, founder of the drugs-research organisation SOMA. Steve was a tall American, originally from Beverly Hills but now in possession of a perfect Oxford accent. He was enormously knowledgeable about drugs and the laws pertaining to them. He told the meeting that on 7 April that year, Home Secretary Roy Jenkins had appointed Baroness Wootton of Abinger to head a sub-committee of the Advisory Committee on Drug Dependence looking into hallucinogens. Abrams thought that the best way to get the law changed was to influence the deliberations of this committee. In order to bring the whole issue of soft drugs and the law into the public debate, he proposed running a full-page advertisement in *The Times*. Since Steve was prepared to organise this, the idea was unanimously approved. The matter of paying for the advertisement, however, was not solved. I called Paul McCartney and arranged to take Steve over to meet him the next day.

Steve met me at the bookshop and we took a cab to Cavendish Avenue. The French windows in the living room were wide open and a slight breeze stirred the warm air in the room. Psychedelic posters lined the hallway and the drum head with 'Sgt Pepper' written on it was on the wall over the settee. An Indian sarod leaned drunkenly in the middle of the carpet where Paul had left it. Steve was well prepared and had the idea very thoroughly worked out in his head. He told Paul the names of some important people he thought would sign the advertisement. Paul said the Beatles would pay for the ad and that he would arrange for all of the Beatles and

Brian Epstein to put their names to it. As we left the living room, Paul gave Steve a copy of *Sgt Pepper* from a big pile on a table by the door. Steve later wrote, 'Unless my memory is playing tricks on me, McCartney thrust a copy of *Sgt Pepper* into my hands and said, "Listen to this through headphones on acid."'

Jack Henry Moore managed to insert a front-page box about Hoppy's case just as *IT*'s issue fourteen went to press. A half-issue, 14.5, came out shortly afterwards devoted mostly to Hoppy's bust, followed by a three-quarter issue, 14.75, which was a poster drawn by Sue of a flower springing from a box with the slogan 'Free Hoppy'. The copy pinned up at Indica Books was signed by John Lennon, Peter Asher, Robert Fraser and Michael Cooper, among others.

The jailing of Hoppy filled me with rage. I realised how impotent we were in the face of the Establishment. First, we had a corrupt police force, and now a vicious judiciary. I was also saddened. Hoppy and I had been through so much together: the *Darazt* anthology, *Long Hair* magazine, our spoken-word album, then the endless meetings and hassles over *International Times*. Without Hoppy the scene would not have happened at all, at least, not in the form it took; he was a constant source of ideas and immediate solutions to problems. We were the best of friends. I had shared a flat with him, he was one of the kindest men on earth, and now he was locked away by a bunch of life-hating shits.

He was not the only one, of course. Every week *IT* received news of about ten arrests for pot; many of those taken were friends. In one raid, when the police found nothing and had, unusually, forgotten to bring any with them, they told the shaken hippies, 'We intend to close down the Roundhouse and everything it stands for!' Theirs was a moral battle, not one based on the law. It was us against them.

The Maharishi

In June the Beatles began to use Kingsway studios in Covent Garden, a new studio that we hadn't visited before. Sue and I were uncertain that we even had the right address until, walking through the underground car park to the only entrance that was open at that time of night, we came across John's huge white psychedelic-painted Rolls. I had with me a pile of fresh copies of *International Times* to give out. The Beatles were working on an orchestral arrangement of one of the songs for *Magical Mystery Tour*, and George Martin was there with some horn players. This was the first time I discussed anything political with John, who took issue with something in *IT*. First he complained to Paul, who was sitting next to him, and stabbed at the paper with his finger. John always associated Paul with *IT*. Paul neatly side-stepped John's wrath by simply indicating Sue and me with his finger, the way a doorman directs you to the cloakroom. John was very stoned and illogical. His arguments just didn't make any sense. He often attacked ideas vehemently and then a few hours later you would overhear him arguing for them as if they were his own. In *Sgt Pepper* days Paul and I often discussed random sound, in the John Cage sense, but John would hear nothing of it and sometimes grew quite ardent in his opposition.

This time we had a long talk about the Maharishi whom John and George were becoming very interested in. I said that I had written to Allen Ginsberg to ask him what the Maharishi's reputation was. Allen had lived in India for several years and had made a point of meeting as many holy men as he could. His reply stated that the Maharishi received most of his support from right-wing Indian politicians and his teaching was regarded as a vulgar commercialisation of the traditional methods. I added my two cents' worth by criticising the Maharishi's policy of demanding a tithe of one week's wages from his followers, whereas the traditional teachings are free to anyone who asks. At this Lennon scoffed at me. 'Ain't no ethnic bastard gonna get no golden castles outta me,' he exclaimed. And as for 'vulgar commercialisation', 'What's wrong with commercialisation?' he asked. 'We're the most commercial band on earth!' He had me there.

Some Time in New York

Early in June a nervous, arrogant young man offered his assistance in distributing *IT*. Nigel Samuel was skinny, with high cheekbones, long lank hair and an incredibly disdainful expression on his long thin face, rather like that of Dame Edith Sitwell. It did not take us long to notice that he was piling the bundles into the back of an Aston Martin. His throwaway remarks suggested that he knew quite a lot about newspaper publishing, so I took him out for coffee. He was the son of Howard Samuel, a member of what Nigel described as 'the northern Jewish property-developer mafia who came down to London when Labour got in'. He told me that when he reached his thirteenth birthday his father took him on a trip to Switzerland. There he introduced Nigel to the madame of a brothel, and explained to him how to choose and smoke a cigar. Having done his duty, his father then drowned himself in Lake Geneva, leaving Nigel alone in a luxury hotel. His father's lawyer Lord Goodman became his guardian, and as Nigel grew up an elaborate series of trust funds began to kick in.

His inheritance included an important book collection, and one day Nigel took me along to see it. It was in a bank vault at Coutts. A man in a black tailcoat took us to the basement and unlocked a series of barred iron gates. In a small room deep below the Strand were hundreds of leather-bound books, loosely piled in cardboard boxes: Caxton's first illustrated book, a handwritten short story by Napoleon, a Shakespeare first folio. Amazing objects, stored away in the dark because they were too valuable to have at home. Rather than cherishing them, Nigel felt oppressed by them: they weighed him down, and were the hand of his father controlling him from beyond the grave. He would have liked to sell them, but they appreciated faster than stocks and his financial advisers had advised him to keep them.

Nigel's heart was in the right place, even if his logic was sometimes tortuous. His knowledge of the inside workings of the

194

Labour Party was of great interest. His other guardians included Jennie Lee and George Brown, both in the Cabinet. Goodman was of course Harold Wilson's private lawyer. Nigel regaled us with tales of corruption in high places and we never doubted that his stories were true and that he really did know these people. His connections were verified rather spectacularly when he was driving drunk at 80 mph down Park Lane at two in the morning in his Aston and hit a police car, causing severe damage. He made one phone call to Lord Goodman and did not even appear in court. We were impressed.

As we got to know each other, I lent Nigel a pile of copies of *East Village Other*, as well as a few other American underground papers. A week later Nigel decided that he and I should visit New York to get to know the people at the *East Village Other* and improve relations between the American underground newspapers and *International Times*. I arranged for us to stay with Ken Weaver and Betsy Klein; I had not yet met Ken, but I knew Betsy from her visit to London in 1965 and we had been in correspondence ever since. They lived at 719 East 9th Street between Avenues C and D; in those days a very insalubrious neighbourhood, though Nigel and I didn't know it. It was my first trip to America and my first flight in a VC 10: BOAC stewards in white jackets passed around typewritten index cards, giving the height and speed of the plane and details of our flight path as if we were on a luxury liner. Nigel brought with him handwritten letters of credit from Coutts, bankers to the Queen. This was wonderfully like travelling with Byron, except that the New York banks had no idea what they were. We eventually found somewhere on Wall Street where, in an ornate office, we were given tea, and Nigel received a fat envelope of banknotes from a thrilled functionary who seemed under the illusion that Nigel was some sort of royalty.

Nigel wore green suede Beatle boots, crushed-velvet loon pants and a long green suede overcoat that reached the ground, though he didn't need it in the June weather. On our first morning there, Nigel and I woke early because of jetlag and went out to explore and get breakfast. We passed the stolen Cadillac that Ken had pointed out the night before, parked in front of their building. Its tyres and wheels were already missing, including the spare, and in the course of our stay the seats and the mirrors went, the chrome was peeled off, then every part of the engine that could be carried away. The remains were used by the kids as a trampoline. Nigel and I smiled – New York was measuring up to be everything we had expected.

Nigel was fond of a drink and we had only walked half a block before he insisted that we go to an extremely seedy-looking Puerto Rican bar on the corner of Avenue C, basically an empty room with one or two tables by the door and a bar at the far end. Nigel marched in, with me following rather reluctantly. He slapped the counter and ordered a whisky. Though it was very early, there were already a few customers who all seemed shocked at this strange apparition. The bartender explained something in rapid-fire Spanish, gesticulating and raising his eyebrows. One of the customers eventually translated for us: they only had beer, they were not licensed for liquor. Nigel was not convinced and threw a banknote on the counter saying, 'Well, go and buy some then', and, seeing their hesitation, added, 'And be quick about it, I'm thirsty!' Astonishingly they did just that, and after a couple of whiskies, with beer chasers, Nigel was ready to face New York. That evening Ken explained that this was one tough bar we'd been in, someone had been murdered there only three weeks before. They must have thought Nigel was some kind of English mafioso to behave like that in there.

My first impression of Ken was one of immense size: huge cowboy boots, massive jeans, large muscular torso, a full black beard and long hair piled up on his shoulders. Though he was over six feet tall, the formidable aspect of the man was partly a pose, for he had a sensitive nature and kept his violent side well in check around his friends. One threatening look from Ken was usually enough. He was the drummer with the Fugs. As a child he played drums for the El Campo, Texas, high-school marching band, which meant that he was more qualified as a musician than the other permanent members: poets Ed Sanders and Tuli Kupferberg. All three wrote songs, and Ken's were among the most popular: 'I Couldn't Get High' and 'Slum Goddess' being audience favourites. The Fugs were a controversial band as far as college authorities were concerned and they often ran into opprobrium: one college turned off their power supply forty-five minutes into an LSD-driven version of 'River of Shit' and another actually threw them off campus.

A lasting image from that visit is of Ken lying sprawled on the folded mattress that did as a settee in front of the television, reading the El Campo newspaper – to which he subscribed – chuckling over stories of lost cows and minor road accidents, commenting lewdly on marriages and divorces, while working his way through six-pack after six-pack. As he finished each beer, he would crush the can in his fist and toss it into the corner to join its mates. On the wall behind him was a life-sized drawing of Trashman, the underground comic figure from *EVO* drawn by his friend Spain Rodriguez, who lived in the building.

That afternoon we walked over to the *East Village Other* offices. Though in its early days *IT* had some of the intellectual seriousness of the *Village Voice*, we were more closely modelled on *EVO*, with its underground comics, its open advocacy of pot and LSD use, and its role as a mouthpiece for youth culture. *EVO* was housed in offices above the Village Theater on 2nd Avenue. This was before Bill Graham changed the venue's name to the Fillmore East. One wall was covered with a huge black-and-white mural of life-sized characters drawn by Robert Crumb, Spain Rodriguez and Gilbert Shelton. The vast office above the auditorium made *IT*'s cramped premises look pathetic, but the staff were all very complimentary about *IT* and we basked in their praise.

EVO was founded by Walter Bowart and the poet Allen Katzman, who also acted as editor. Walter was a big friendly fellow from Omaha, Nebraska, who had studied journalism at the University of Oklahoma, which meant he actually knew something about running a newspaper. He was tall, muscular, healthy and straight-looking. Nigel and I were used to underground types having long hair and freaky clothes and it came as a big surprise to find that most of the staff of *EVO* looked straight, even if their habits were not. Walter explained that this was to avoid drawing attention to themselves, to evade being beaten up or arrested. He took us to the Saint Adrian Company, a bar in the Mercer Street Arts complex, on the Broadway side of the building where, amazingly, *EVO* had a bar account. The idea of *IT* having a running tab at a London pub was so improbable that we quickly realised that the American under-ground scene was very different from ours.

Walter took us to visit the Hell's Angels who controlled a section of East 2nd Street. The legend was that they had snipers on the roof and the police had not set foot on the block for two years. A row of stripped-down Harley Davidsons parked at a forty-five-degree angle to the kerb indicated their buildings. The choppers looked very vulnerable among the burned-out cars and heaps of uncollected garbage, but no one in their right mind would have tampered with them. I was not convinced of the advisability of this visit, but the Angels liked *EVO* because it supported pot smokers – they had several front pages from *EVO* crudely framed on the wall of their clubhouse – and they liked Walter, who took their views seriously. To my surprise they were courteous and welcoming, offering us beers and joints.

When the beer ran out, a group of Angels took us to their favourite local bar. Nigel could charm anyone and, as he had no fear, the bikers loved him. At one point they threatened to kidnap him, insisting that he must live with them and be their mascot. They had grim expressions on their faces and made it sound like a serious threat. Then they crowded around him, shoulder to shoulder, a circle of chapter colours sewn on dirty denim jackets, isolating him from Walter and me as if protecting the king on the field of battle. Nigel was unmoved, raised his eyes in exasperation and called for more drinks all round. The majority of people hated the bikers or were scared of them. Never before had a stranger showed up and bought them drinks. After a few more beers, I was alarmed to see Nigel setting off for a ride on the back of a Harley, his long green coat trailing behind him, as an enormous biker wearing a First World War German helmet gunned the motor, then roared off in a cloud of blue smoke. We were assured of Nigel's safety, and he returned to Ken's place, unscathed, six hours later.

I visited Allen Ginsberg, who lived one block away on East 10th, between C and D. I had not seen him for two years, ever since he stayed with me in London, but we had maintained a constant correspondence. So much had happened during his 1965 visit that we felt like old friends. We caught up on the gossip, and Allen gave me some books. The tremendous cacophony of radios, Spanish music, bongos, traffic and car horns from the nearby intersection made conversation difficult. I had not previously met Peter Orlovsky, Allen's lover for the previous twelve years, who was sitting on the floor beneath the open window wearing a pair of shorts and nothing else. It was a very hot day and to my surprise, Peter, who had been drinking from a glass container of orange juice, suddenly upended it and poured it over his head and torso. Any momentary cooling effect was immediately offset by the uncomfortable stickiness. Allen sighed. Peter was on methedrine and the day before had been out cleaning the street with a toothbrush and dishwashing liquid, watched suspiciously by the Puerto Rican boys perched on the stoop.

Betsy Klein worked at the Psychedelicatessen on Tompkins Square, the world's first 'head shop', where one could buy a selection of hash pipes and oversized rolling papers, psychedelic posters and UV lights to make them glow in the dark. On her day off she took me to Macy's to buy the latest records. I was astonished at the size of the record department; Britain in those days had no megastores. Macy's had about 1,000 copies of *Sgt Pepper* piled in waist-high stacks, surrounded by the Jefferson Airplane's *Psychedelic Pillow* and the Grateful Dead's first album, which had just been released. It turned out that the Dead were playing their first-ever New York gigs, and Ken, who knew some of the band, took Nigel, me and Betsy to see them play the Cheetah. The darkness of the entrance to the basement was broken up by polka-dot blobs and points of light emanating from below, which bubbled up the stairs, over the threshold and into the street. I had never seen anything like it – so this was a famous West Coast psychedelic light-show. As we approached, Ken gave a shout and broke into a run. Standing outside the club was Pigpen, keyboard player with the band, in his full Hell's Angels regalia. He and Ken embraced, and as there were a lot of tourists around enjoying the early evening sunlight, they French-kissed, thrusting their tongues down each other's throat, grunting and yelping with delight as Midwestern couples shielded their children's eyes, looked the other way and hurriedly crossed the street.

Ken also took us to see Frank Zappa and the Mothers of Invention, who had rented the Garrick Theater on Bleeker Street in

Greenwich Village for the summer season. Zappa was standing in the street outside, wearing skin-tight flower-patterned trousers that bulged suggestively. He was turning in slow circles, barking the show and occasionally signing autographs. The presentation was quite theatrical: the stage was in complete darkness except for the little red lights on the amplifiers, then a drum roll made itself heard above the noise of the audience and, as it grew, Zappa was silhouetted against a backlit stage curtain, standing beside a large gong. I thought he might bang it, like the man in the J. Arthur Rank movies, but not so, which was something of an anticlimax. The set was less organised, in the sense of musical precision, than I was expecting, although all the famous hand-signals were in use and worked very effectively. The group would get stuck into an extended rock-out, apparently totally improvised, when Frank would give an imperceptible hand-signal – crook his little finger or jerk his elbow – and the music would change completely from, say 4/4 to 7/8. During the set, which included 'Brown Shoes Don't Make It' and, of course, 'Call Any Vegetable', a groupie allowed herself to be dragged onstage and pawed while other members of the group performed ritual acts with vegetables. The Mothers threw some of the vegetables at the audience and, while not being felt up, the girl busied herself playing tambourine or sweeping up the squashed fruit and veg with a broom.

Zappa was very intrigued with the English music scene and asked a lot of questions that I could not answer. He was interested to hear about *International Times* as he used the Los Angeles underground papers as his main form of advertising and regularly published a Mothers newsletter in the *Los Angeles Free Press*. When the Mothers toured Britain not long afterwards, they used *IT* to publicise their new album, *Absolutely Free*.

Walter Bowart was married to Peggy Hitchcock, an heir to the 'Mellon Millions', a fortune made in the Pittsburgh steel industry. Her younger brother Billy gave financial support to Timothy Leary and had also loaned him one of his properties, a sixty-four-room mansion outside Millbrook in upstate New York, two hours' drive from the city. Allen Ginsberg was insistent that I should meet Tim, and Walter agreed. Within a few days of arriving in New York,

Nigel and I, in the company of Walter, Ken and Betsy, found ourselves in a shiny late-model cherry-red Buick on our first American super-highway. We travelled north on the Taconic State Parkway with Betsy at the wheel, a stubby brass pipe clenched firmly between her teeth, puffing on a large smouldering block of hash. She took care to stay within the speed limit. 'San Francisco (Flowers in Your Hair)' was alternating on the radio with 'White Rabbit'.

We made a right at Highway 44 and by this time the grass and hash had done their work and everyone felt hungry. We pulled up at a white clapboard store in Millbrook. The locals regarded us with open hostility, but with bad grace allowed us to buy sweets, cigarettes and beer. We had parked outside a watchmaker's shop and as soon as he saw us he pointedly locked his door. Long hair, beards and women's legs were not allowed in this stuffy little town. It was the first time I had experienced this kind of hostility and I was shocked. In England, back in the early Sixties, one could expect a good-natured jeer at long hair, but this was 1967. I suddenly realised what all the hippies were talking about when they told their horror stories about the 'straights'. A sour-faced citizen glared in horror at Betsy's mini-skirt and Walter decided that we had better leave quickly before the citizens of Millbrook got uptight and called in the cops. After a few false starts Walter found the road leading to Leary's house.

'STOP!' bellowed Ken.

Adrenaline hit everyone's cannabis-sensitised bloodstream, and Betsy screeched to a halt on the grass verge. 'I thought I saw a little woodchuck back there beside the road,' said Ken, scratching his massive Tolstoy beard thoughtfully.

The main entrance to the estate, an imposing gatehouse complete with a portcullis, was closed, but further round the walls was an unmarked gate. The road curved through pines and past a lake, said to have been dug by 3,000 Italian labourers. We rounded another curve and the house and its gardens appeared at the end of a mile-long avenue lined with maples. It was like a house in a dream: a huge white Victorian gothic extravaganza, with twin turrets and dozens of staring windows. A pair of gigantic stylised Tibetan Buddhist eyes painted on the wall stared out across the formal lawns, and prayer flags fluttered from the roof as on a Nepalese temple. On the balcony to the left of the main house hung a huge bell. We parked with all the other cars on the gravel next to the kitchen entrance at the back. The doors were open, but the house was strangely deserted and silent, reinforcing the dreamlike quality of the place. The only sound came from the chirping birds in the trees behind.

Just as we began to get paranoid and wonder if they had all been arrested, a friendly middle-aged couple appeared and told us that because the weather was so nice, everybody was camping in the woods. They gave us tea without milk and home-baked bread and showed us around the house, beginning with the huge walk-in freezer room and the baronial kitchen, then the public rooms hung with *thangkas* and paintings. In the hallway by the front door a huge noticeboard detailed the day's business: notices of concerts, local events, music and lectures in New York City. A neatly typed statement on psychedelically embossed paper proclaimed someone a newly elected Boo-Hoo of the Neo-American Church – slogan: 'Victory Over Horseshit'. The walls were hung with paintings, sculpture and bits of psychedelic paraphernalia. Cobwebby unravelling Gods' Eyes hung from the lofty ceiling. The vast living room was empty, the sun's rays shafting through the rising motes of dust, stirred up by our passage. In the gloom hung recently painted mandalas and ancient Tibetan *thangkas* on their Chinese silk banners. Everything was tinged with the faint smell of incense. It was very peaceful. Through the windows we could hear the leaves rustling in the slight breeze.

The house was not empty. Tim Leary was upstairs in his room on the third floor. We passed more paintings, Gods' Eyes and mandalas on the way to his enormous, comfortable sitting room. It was relaxed and untidy, with piles of books and papers stacked everywhere on the carpets, copies of the *Psychedelic Reader* and *Psychedelic Review* mixed in with *Time* and *Life*: dozens of books open face-down to keep his place. A pair of cream-coloured Lhasa apso puppies gambolled over the batik cushions. *Sgt Pepper* played quietly in the background. Leary motioned us to join him on the cushions.

He was a quietly spoken man, looking rather exhausted, his chin shiny and jutting forward a little in a determined manner. I noticed the profusion of laugh lines around his eyes; he smiled a lot and was probably older than one thought. He wore bushy sideburns, but his hair was otherwise neat and short. Some of his language seemed to me to be archaic, like suddenly finding oneself in an Elizabethan court. Some of it, however, was just plain corny.

'I'm writing a bible,' he told me, handing me a huge floppy manuscript. 'It's going to be called *High Priest*. Bible just means a history,' he said. Which is true. I remembered Ian Sommerville describing Leary's visit to Tangier, and how William Burroughs and his boys called him 'The Coach': 'It's because as soon as he enters a room he throws you some philosophical idea. First he'll bounce it around a bit, on the floor and off the wall, then he'll pass it to you, just like the coach tossing you the medicine ball.'

Tim wanted to know all about the Beatles, and had some rather far-fetched ideas about their intelligence and understanding of the political situation in America. To him they were prophets of a future age of enlightenment. I tried to explain that their genius lay almost entirely in their music and that their support of the underground movement was instinctive, not an intellectual decision, and due largely to the fact that they took drugs and so saw the hippies as natural allies. We had an interesting discussion that revolved around the significance of popular cultural figures and how his reading of the Beatles was determined by the political situation in America – something the Beatles themselves knew very little about.

Tim described a wedding he had conducted at Millbrook that spring between two of the residents. The League for Spiritual Discovery was a non-profit-making religious foundation that enabled him to conduct weddings and other services. In some strange way I felt like I was talking to the local vicar, a confident, self-assured paterfamilias. But this feeling was soon dispelled by his humorous descriptions of his involvement with Michael Hollings-head: how impossible Michael was to deal with, how he spiked everyone with acid, and how they eventually got rid of him by loading him up with copies of the *Psychedelic Reader* and *The Psychedelic Experience*, a large supply of LSD, and putting him on the *Queen Elizabeth II* to send him back to England. Tim showed me some of the letters that Michael had written him from Wormwood Scrubs. He was not busted for LSD, which at the time was not yet illegal, but for huge quantities of pot and amphetamines. The letters were amazingly funny and self-confident. He wrote his own story later in *The Man Who Turned On the World*.

As the day passed I found myself liking Leary more and more. I was a little concerned at the ease with which he switched around philosophical and religious ideas from wildly different cultures as if they were easily interchangeable. All the time, however, one was aware that Timothy Leary was a remarkable man, not for his six or seven PhDs, or for his many marriages (both of which he boasted about, just a little), but for his obvious awareness of what was happening and for the twinkle in his eye. I ultimately found him to be more European than American and he himself said that he felt a great affinity for the Irish character. This was certainly true; there was a side of Tim that was obviously at home propping up a bar and talking endlessly, for he really had the gift of the blarney.

Later he showed us his kitchen garden, where all the vegetables were planted in mandala patterns; we inspected the rows of meditation chalets in the garden, like the changing rooms at an English seaside resort, except that instead of being numbered they were all designated by a hexagram from the *I Ching*. A retreat-cum-summerhouse nestled in the trees. We were slightly unnerved by encountering several horses, painted in psychedelic colours, but were reassured that it was for a film and that it would wash off. Tim and Ken did get into an argument, however, when Leary revealed that he had given his dogs LSD. Ken did not believe in giving acid to any living creature unless they had asked for it. There was nothing furtive about Dr Leary, he was charmingly open, with wide eyes, a genuine smile and a smooth, even modulation to his voice; 'a charmer', as Ken put it. In a way I was surprised, having been exposed to the press stories about him, like everyone else. He was already famous in certain circles and notorious in others, but was not yet in trouble with the law.

A few days later, back in the city, Nigel and I had dinner in an Italian restaurant with Allen Ginsberg, Timothy Leary and a rude woman from *Time-Life*, who exasperated Allen with her assumptions about the hippies: their lack of hygiene, their loose morality and their use of drugs. As *Time-Life* was picking up the tab, Nigel made his contribution by seizing the wine list and engaging in a spirited discussion with the sommelier, this being one area where his upbringing clearly gave him superiority over the rest of us.

After the woman left, we walked a few blocks to the League for Spiritual Discovery store-front on Hudson Street, where tripping hippies lay all over the floor and a strong smell of incense drifted out into the street in a scene rather similar to the preconceptions of the *Time-Life* woman. An elderly Indian holy man sat in his white robes in the corner, rolling his eyes and tugging at his beard. A middle-aged woman with close-cropped hair knelt before him, washing his feet. Every inch of the ceiling and walls, door surrounds and windows had been painted with psychedelic designs, swirls and whorls of colour overlapping and seething, like the colours of a film of petrol on a wet road or the marbling on the endpapers of Victorian books. It created a total environment, a bit like fairground art. I never saw a more powerful example of 'psychedelic art', even in San Francisco; it was almost like being inside a living creature, and as such was not very pleasant.

Allen, Tim, Nigel and I walked slowly through the Village to the East Side, checking the record sleeves in the window of Discophile on 8th Street and the new books in the window of Bookmasters and the Eighth Street Bookshop. Allen and Tim were hoping to find their own books and records prominently displayed, which they were. We continued across Fourth Avenue to the St Marks and East Side bookstores. On St Marks Place they were treated to a series of nods, waves, smiles and approaches in the way that a popular padre might be received in a small Italian village. Tim seemed acutely embarrassed when a young hippie asked him for his autograph, proffering a magic marker and new pair of white Levis. Allen's reaction was the exact opposite, immediately asking the boy's name and where he was from. Allen and Tim kissed each other goodbye with genuine fondness. I noticed Allen's fingers entwined in Leary's wavy hair during their brief embrace. Allen fingered his Yoruba prayer beads and we went to order egg creams at Gem Spa.

All You Need Is Love

It looked very much as if *International Times* was done for. The staff hadn't been paid in weeks and some of them were turning to dope-dealing to get money. I reluctantly called Paul McCartney and told him that unless we raised about £400, we would close down. He cheerfully passed over the subject, saying it would all be okay, he'd fix everything, but he'd see us in the studio that night because something special was happening. They were going to simultaneously record and mix a new song on a worldwide TV link-up. As Paul put it, 'Getting the good news across', something about us all broadcasting the message in our own way. He wasn't being elitist. I knew that *IT* only reached a few thousand people, whereas the Beatles reached millions. In fact that TV programme, broadcast live on 25 June, was seen by hundreds of millions, not just in Europe and America, but in Japan and Africa as well.

Abbey Road Studio C was filled with flowers and the Beatles wore uniforms of green and pink and orange, similar to those on the *Sgt Pepper* cover. Waist-long scarves wafted from their necks, but the vaguely medieval look was marred slightly by the headphones they all wore, as well as by the usual studio clutter of microphones, headphone leads, instruments and music stands. Simon, Marijke and Josie wore fluid patchwork patterns, headscarves and coloured tights, very much in the exaggerated spirit of Dutch psychedelia. Keith Moon fooled around with Ringo on the drums as we all settled down crosslegged on the floor around the Beatles, waiting for the show to begin. It reminded me of storytime at primary school, all sitting expectantly around the teacher. The Small Faces, in new Granny Takes a Trip clothes, sat close to each other; and the Rolling Stones were headed up by Mick, who sat on the floor, close by Paul's high stool, wearing a silk jacket painted with a pair of psychedelic eyes, like the one Jimi Hendrix wears on his American *Are You Experienced* album sleeve. Mick had his white silk scarf and was smoking a very fat joint in front of the 200 million viewers, puffing away, laughing, singing along LOVE LOVE LOVE! He seemed unconcerned that he had a court appearance the next day. 'All You

Need Is Love!' streamers and balloons drifted down from the ceiling and we all sang along. People appeared carrying placards with the message written large in many languages and paraded before the cameras. Everyone appeared to be high on grass, acid, the colour, the excitement and the music. The music was good, very good and loud. And the message of flower-power was reaching millions of people.

After all the energy and excitement it really seemed a bring-down to remind Paul about the plight of *IT*'s miserable staff, but he took it well, called over Neil Aspinall and asked if he could borrow £400. Neal wrote a cheque as if he was paying the milkman. 'Remind me to pay you back,' said Paul. Neil nodded and went back to breaking down the equipment. In the control room George Martin played back the tape. I called Mike Henshaw to reassure him about *IT*, and Ian Iachimoe was credited in the staff box of the next issue.

Break a Butterfly On a Wheel?

While preparations were made for SOMA's advertisement in *The Times*, the trial of Mick Jagger, Keith Richards and Robert Fraser began at Chichester Crown Court on 27 June. Four days later Judge Block gave his sentences. They were draconian. Despite being a first offender, Keith was given a year in prison for allowing his house to be used for smoking cannabis, even though no drugs were found on his person. He was also fined £500. Mick was given three months in prison for possession of four amphetamine tablets, bought legally in Italy, and fined £300. They both spent one night in jail pending appeal. Robert Fraser was sent to Wormwood Scrubs for six months for possession of heroin.

It was if the Establishment had declared war on young people, and that night a spontaneous demonstration took place outside the hated *News of the World*, the first demonstration in Fleet Street since the First World War. The police set their dogs on the demonstrators, people were crushed and there were six arrests. Sue was bundled into a police van, but Michael X gave the policeman his business card and they set her free, thinking that he was her lawyer. What made the demonstration a uniquely underground event was that it occurred in the middle of the night, when all the Fleet Street newspapers were being put to bed; no one but young people would demonstrate at such a time.

Jagger and Richards appealed and were released on bail the next day. It was a Friday: UFO Club night. At midnight about a thousand people left the club, and made their way down Charing Cross Road and Shaftesbury Avenue in their hippie finery to the Eros statue in Piccadilly Circus, where hundreds more people had assembled from other London clubs. The combined crowd turned and marched on the *News of the World* building. The police again turned their dogs on them and one demonstrator was badly bitten. Demonstrators straggled back to the UFO Club around 3 am, and cheered as Tomorrow gave an inspired performance of 'Revolution'. The next night there were more demonstrations and this time a lot of people were arrested and beaten up by the police.

But the members of the underground were not the only people who saw the sentences on the Stones as a gross distortion of justice. The editor of *The Times*, William Rees-Mogg, wrote a leader called 'Who breaks a butterfly on a wheel?' condemning both the verdict and the sentences. In commenting before the appeal was heard, Rees-Mogg was in contempt of court, and had it been any newspaper other than *The Times* he might have found himself in court, but his leader was couched in terms of public interest and he got away with it. Following his lead, almost every national newspaper criticised the verdict and the harshness of the sentences, leaving the *News of the World* on the sidelines. Drugs were now a matter of public discussion.

Cavendish Avenue

You never knew who you might meet at Paul's house: it might be one of the Monkees, a bleary-eyed Brian Jones, up all night on acid, or members of Paul's family: his father inspecting the garden, his brother Michael, who had his own career in the Scaffold, or his Auntie Jin.

'You know why I like it here?' she asked me. 'It's because of the fairies at the bottom of the garden! It's just like magic. We go up to bed at night and leave all the crocks in the sink, dirty from supper, and when we come down in the morning, they're all clean. It's magic!' She polished her specs. 'We're down to watch Wimbledon on the colour telly actually.' She reached out and tugged at Paul's jacket. 'Since our boy's doing so well and can afford a colour set . . . It's quite a treat to see it on such a big screen. And in colour, too!' Paul said that he'd offered to get them tickets to see the tennis, but they wouldn't have it. 'Don't waste your money, lad! This is plenty good enough for us. What would be the good of us going to Wimbledon, really?' She had him beat. I liked his relatives, they were totally normal people, open, friendly and honest.

One of the people often to be found at Paul's at this time was Stash de Rola, Prince Stanislaus de Rola of Wattesville. A Frenchman from central casting, tall and arrogant, he wore his long black hair fringed in the medieval style and sometimes affected a cape. He had a very haughty air. He loved to discuss alchemy, a subject about which he knew a great deal – always hinting that he knew more than he was telling, that he was an adept, a secret master magician. In fact he was not French but Swiss, but his father, the painter Count Balthasar Klossowski de Rola, or more simply Balthus, was born in Paris. There was some doubt about the title, which originated with Stash's grandfather Erich Klossowski, a Polish art historian. His grandmother was a Polish Jew, the painter Elizabeth Dorothea, known as Baladine. I was impressed to find that the writer Pierre Klossowski was Stash's uncle.

Stash had made an undistinguished single, which went nowhere, but it was enough to give him the authority to call himself a pop-star. He was always about to 'get it together, man', but seemed never able to. He sometimes sold his father's drawings of young girls when money was short. His love of luxury, style and fashion seemed so inbred that his lack of money always seemed to be a temporary affair.

He never had a place of his own, but always stayed in the best of lodgings. When I first met him he was at Robert Fraser's apartment, but Robert somehow managed to pass him on to Paul McCartney, and Paul was unable to get rid of him. One day I visited him to drop off some albums and Paul was beaming with pleasure, 'He's gone, man!'

'Oh. Who?'

'Why, the Prince of Pop, of course!' Some money had appeared from somewhere and Stash had gone to Paris or Hollywood, to make a film or write a book. He was soon back, but this time comfortably ensconced with Lord Londonderry. Stash's twin claims to fame were that he was one of the percussionists on the Beatles' track 'You Know My Name, Look Up the Number', and that he was busted with Brian Jones.

Arts Lab

Jim Haynes opened his long-awaited Arts Lab at 182 Drury Lane in July 1967. 'If you like films, poetry, environments, paintings, sculpture, music "old or new", food, plays, happenings, People Show, warm flesh, soft floors, happiness; better things through chemistry, or what was once called art then you should probably join the arts lab at once.' Jim and Jack Henry Moore had taken over the derelict premises of an old printing company and together with a large group of volunteers had built a cinema, a theatre, an exhibition space, a bookstall and a café. Jim also had an apartment for himself at the back, reached by a separate door from Stukeley Street.

The basement cinema was the first space to be completed, with a floor of six-inch-deep foam rubber covered with fireproof carpet and stepped to provide lines of sight. You left your shoes outside.

The films were interesting and the sexual tension palpable, but the smell of dirty feet was overwhelming. Dave Curtis, who screened the films at UFO, was in charge of programming and a typical evening's viewing was Vsevolod Pudovkin's 1928 *Storm Over Asia*, alongside two films by Bruce Conner and three by Stan Brakhage.

Sue ran the restaurant on the first floor, a large church-like room with a high pointed ceiling, overlooking Drury Lane. Many of the UFO regulars worked there part-time including Karen Astley. It was more of a canteen than a restaurant, though there were blue tablecloths and wine glasses, but the food was of the organic hippie variety. The lab attracted its fair share of freaks and problem cases, who were irresistibly drawn to the restaurant. One of the most time-consuming and disruptive was Robin Farquharson, a South African who gave all his money away, but then expected to be fed and housed by other people. He was described on the jacket of his own book, *Drop Out!*, as a 'psychotic homosexual in a manic phase'. Sue couldn't ban him from the restaurant because he was an Arts Lab member and, as a qualified lawyer, he knew his rights; she could however refuse to serve him, and did.

A Chelsea Party

Christopher Gibbs lived in a splendid seventeenth-century house on Cheyne Walk overlooking the river, once the home of James McNeill Whistler who painted his famous 'Nocturne' series of views of the Thames while living there in the 1870s. Gossip columnists had given Christopher the title 'The King of Chelsea' and from Sloane Square to World's End and beyond he was deferred to on all matters concerning aesthetics and taste. He had a small antiques shop off the King's Road, filled with exquisite worn-out furniture salvaged from the attics of country houses; he was an expert on Elizabethan tassels, municipal floral clocks, newel posts and furniture of most periods. In his words: 'an enthusiast, a chaser and scholar of a rich diversity of works of art and man'. One would be summoned to afternoon tea and sit in the garden beneath a mulberry tree, sipping Earl Grey from porcelain cups as Christopher enthused over his latest find: a chair leg found at Knole ('You could build the rest of the chair around it'), or a medieval armadillo helmet with a chain mail face mask, ('I shall wear it to parties').

Christopher was very trusting and frequently permitted people to stay in Cheyne Walk when he was away. On one occasion he lent the house to some members of a New York ballet company. When he returned everything was in order, except that his 3,000-year-old mummified Egyptian shrew mouse had unaccountably disappeared. It seems that his guests had mistaken it for a block of hash and smoked it.

Sue worked at the shop as his assistant, fielding calls from *Vogue* magazine, which wanted to know where his monthly column was. He would write it at the very last minute, dictating it off the top of his head, word perfect. He always spoke in perfect sentences, his Etonian accent carefully modulating each syllable and bringing to the words a faint air of amused detachment.

On 10 July, Christopher held a summer party. The reception was held in a large panelled room with a view up the Thames. It was lit by a huge brass Moroccan drum-chandelier, flickering candles casting moving points of light through the holes pierced in its side. It was so dark that Sue mistakenly tried to eat some crystal incense from a glass bowl, thinking it was candy. People felt their way around the room, not wanting to trip over some priceless antique in the dark and rip a fifteenth-century tapestry from the wall as they fell. Dylan's voice emerged, rather scratched, from a sound system installed by Ian Sommerville. The plan was that after dinner we were all to go on to another house where Princess Margaret was dining, and we would all have a royal time.

At one point, a silver tray of chocolate brownies was brought around by a Moroccan boy with a gap in his teeth known as 'La Fenêtre Ouverte', and we all helped ourselves. Hash brownies take a long time to work and first timers often overdose, mistakenly thinking that they have not taken enough. These were made to the recipe given by Brion Gysin to Alice B. Toklas for her famous cookbook. Sue Miles had written it out for someone at *IT*, but the makers had inadvertently doubled the amount of hash, making them particularly potent, almost lethal. Bill Burroughs told me that it was one of Paul Bowles' favourite tricks to give unsuspecting visitors a large portion of *majoun* or hash candy, and then tell them, in their deranged state, that an overdose could result in permanent insanity or schizoid episodes.

I have only fragmented memories of the party: a long talk with Michael Cooper about his photographs of the Beatles and the Stones and the possibility of an exhibition at Indica. Michael Rainey in Sherwood green, tall, grinning as always, stoned, talking about UFOs. Mick Jagger and Marianne Faithfull: Marianne wearing a skimpy dress that showed her breasts from all angles except the front. She gave a broad smile and asked if I wanted some acid, her big eyes innocent as a nun's, freckles on her cheeks, long blonde hair smelling fresh-washed. Michael Cooper took some of the acid and ran out into the night. I remember talking earnestly with Mick Jagger and we were clearly in profound agreement about something as I remember us both nodding sagely, saying, 'Yes, yes, that's it!' for a long time.

Allen Ginsberg arrived, straight off the plane from Italy, where he had been reading at the Spoleto Festival. He brought Panna Grady with him; he was staying in her huge house in Regent's Park and we had arranged to meet him at the party. Panna unknowingly ate some of the brownies and soon began to shriek that it was all a big plot to get her there and trick her into getting stoned. She had never taken drugs before, not even a little toke on a joint. 'CALL THE POLICE THE HOSPITAL GET A STOMACH PUMP MY GAWD!' all in a piercing loud American voice. She raved all night, with Allen, stoned himself, talking her through her first high, sitting up all night with her instead of going to see Princess Margaret. Mick Jagger sat at his other side, so that he had some conversation during Panna's quiet periods. At one point Mick and Marianne left to run up and down Cheyne Walk to clear their heads a little. They returned and Marianne pronounced herself 'high but cool'.

Sue and I both felt distinctly ill and decided to leave. It was a cool night but I was sweating, my forehead was damp and the lights of Chelsea Bridge were smudged as I looked at them, as if rain were running over my eyes. Behind us a Mini-Minor was weaving down Cheyne Walk from one side of the road to the other in long easy loops. It reached us, stopped and stalled. Jane Ormsby-Gore, in an impeccably polite voice, enquired if we would like a ride back to her place in Westminster. Michael Rainey was sprawled in the back, seemingly unconscious.

We climbed the narrow red-carpeted stairs of 15 Lord North Street to the wood-panelled front room with its saffron-coloured carpet. The room was lit by candlelight and we all four sat, staring in silence at John Michel's huge painting of the execution of the Emperor Maximilian. The Emperor stood, blindfolded, against a brick wall. Each brick was carefully painted, and we had to examine every one of them. After a while Michael Rainey murmured, 'This is a very powerful high.'

Jane eventually replied, 'What we need is some vitamin C!' and left the room. After an age she reappeared with glasses of lemon juice and sugar. It *was* a very strange high, very cold, but it produced a lot of giggling from us all. In the end Sue and I felt strong enough to leave and somehow found a cab back to Southampton Row. I remember trying to count the change in my hand, but kept counting how many coins there were instead of adding up the amount. I finally gave the driver a handful, which seemed to satisfy him.

Somehow we climbed the stairs to the flat, but lying down proved to be a mistake: the ceiling spun round and round and would not stop. Sue was less affected than I, maybe her cookie was less potent. She was very pale but able to function and we discussed very seriously what was to be done. I telephoned Steve Abrams at about 3 am, then had to go down all eighty-six stairs to let him in. He arrived with a friend, who proceeded to pass out on our bedroom floor, having been to a similar party elsewhere. I retired to my bed and remember hearing Steve's disembodied voice saying, rather matter-of-factly, 'Oh dear, Miles doesn't seem to have a pulse any more.' I felt concerned at this news; it didn't seem to bode well. Later I remember hearing Steve talking to my doctor, Elizabeth Tate, his voice coming to me through waves of static, like a bad telephone connection. He was saying, in his usual donnish way, 'They appear to be suffering from poisoning caused by ingesting an overdose of tetrahydrocannabinol.'

She apparently replied, 'Silly buggers!' I began to feel a little better, and remember Steve's worried face as he asked me to mention the affair to as few people as possible, since it exploded his whole argument that pot was harmless and that there was no such thing as an overdose.

We later received reports about the party – of Members of Parliament freaking out and having their stomachs pumped; of a member of the House of Lords insisting that his friend's chauffeur take him to a Turkish bath and, once on the road, telling the driver that he was a 'worthless fellow and going the long way round just to get more on the clock'. A famous interior designer was in bed for a week, then politely asked for the orchestra to be taken from his room. 'It's very kind of them, but I've heard enough music, thank you.' But not everyone was so badly affected. The next day someone from the House of Lords telephoned Christopher to say, 'I say, Chrissie, thanks awfully for the party. And, uh, I suppose that was some of the jolly old LSD, eh? Um, you wouldn't happen to know where I could get some more, would you?'

Chez Panna

Allen Ginsberg lodged in the carriage house attached to Panna Grady's garden at 2 Hanover Terrace, a huge structure with a row of columns supporting a classical pediment with heroic statues, the windows looking straight out over the boating lake in Regent's Park. Panna was an American debutante, the daughter of the heiress Louise Marie St John and the Hungarian aristocrat Tibor de Cholnoky. She was attracted to difficult men with brilliant minds and in the mid-Sixties ran a literary salon in her enormous apartment at the Dakota, where Norman Mailer might find himself seated next to William Burroughs, Allen Ginsberg or Andy Warhol. In the June 1965 issue of *Fuck You / A Magazine of the Arts* Ed Sanders conferred on her the First Annual Fuck You Press Award for Distinguished Service to the Arts, saying:

> This year the award goes to Panna Grady for incredible generosity, kindness, tenderness, and benevolence in dealing with many freaky

215

neurasthenic artists, poets, moviemakers, magicians, etc. on the N.Y. scene. It often takes great patience in aiding writers, but her grace and squack-vectors have been fantastic.

One of the 'moviemakers, magicians' referred to was Harry Smith, compiler of the *American Folk Music Anthology* and certainly a contender for the title of tortured genius. He hit on Panna for money mercilessly, as did Gregory Corso and many other indigent poets and writers, until she could stand it no more. She had been having an affair with the Boston poet John Weiners, but there were many obstacles preventing a satisfactory relationship, the principal one being that Weiners was for the most part homosexual. Late in the summer of 1966 Panna began an affair with Charles Olson, and on 29 October they sailed for London.

It was fascinating to visit Charles at Hanover Terrace. He worked at night, after the visitors had all gone home to bed, and often did not get up until the early evening. We would visit at eight o'clock and Charles would enter the kitchen, yawning, stretching his massive frame and sitting down to a breakfast of four eggs, piles of bacon, toast and coffee. Charles was six feet seven inches tall, and big with it. He told me, 'The first time I realised that I was larger than the ordinary was once when I was running down a hill in Boston to catch a bus, and as I passed a little black boy he said, "My God, there goes Goliath!"' Charles roared with laughter.

Charles had been the rector of Black Mountain College, an experimental community which from 1933 until 1956 was the nurturing ground and sometimes home to Robert Creeley, Josef Albers, Robert Rauschenberg, John Cage, Merce Cunningham, Buckminster Fuller, Willem de Kooning, Franz Kline and most of the American avant-garde. He was the author of *Call Me Ishmael*, a celebrated study of Herman Melville, as well as many volumes of poetry. His conversation ranged from economics to continental drift, from Mayan ball-court statuary to the lineage of the early settlers of Massachusetts. He was the most stimulating conversationalist I have ever met. There would be visitors most evenings: Harry Fainlight (who knew Panna from New York), Alexander Trocchi, William Burroughs and assorted society figures, for Panna liked to socialise. Ultimately this was to be the undoing of Charles and Panna's relationship.

216

Characteristically, Charles went into hiding. In March 1967, after spending six months with Panna, he moved into the Mayfair Hotel on Berkeley Square where he remained incommunicado for several weeks while his friends frantically telephoned all over Britain and the States, not knowing if he was alive or dead. 'I have allowed myself to "disappear"' he wrote to the poet Robert Creeley, 'in order actually to recover freedom of all or any movement. Everything had gotten too conversational for the likes of an old winter bear.'

Charles next spent a month or so in Dorchester, researching the English end of the Gloucester, Massachusetts, fishing settlement in the museum. Eventually he responded to an ad in *The Times*, placed by his friend Harvey Brown, asking for news of his whereabouts, then returned to the States. Panna, meanwhile, turned her attention to William Burroughs whom she had courted previously in New York. William liked Panna, but refused even to acknowledge that she might be interested in him sexually. 'I always saw Panna with other people, I preferred it that way,' he said, pursing his lips.

Whenever Allen Ginsberg came to stay, the number of visitors tripled. It was very sensible of Panna to put him in the garden house where the interviewers and TV crews would not disturb her. Allen's sometime girlfriend Maretta Greer was in London with her English boyfriend Tony and they attached themselves to Allen. The Home Office had Tony's passport after repatriating him to Britain, and Allen paid to get it back. He also bought him a guitar. Within a week they had moved into the garden house with him, intending – though penniless – to leave for India any day via Marseilles. One sunny afternoon Allen was sitting in the garden beside a glass-topped table, being interviewed by a BBC TV crew, when the telephone rang in his garden cottage. Maretta emerged with the phone for him, trailing the extra-long telephone cord behind her. She was very pale, thin, with long blonde hair and wearing a necklace of Tibetan prayer beads. Apart from that she was completely naked. 'Film that!' Allen yelled, 'that's what's happening', but the camera was empty.

Allen was in London for two events, as a speaker at the Dialectics of Liberation conference at the Roundhouse to discuss world problems of anti-colonialism, Black Power and ecology, and for an Arts Council reading at Queen Elizabeth Hall. Also in London for the reading was Olson, who had reconciled his friendship, at least, with Panna and was back in his old room at 2 Hanover Terrace. Allen's first reading was on 12 July.

W. H. Auden began, shuffling onstage in his carpet slippers, followed by Stephen Spender and Charles Olson, who took several stabs at the material before he got into the rhythm. Allen led the Italian poet Giuseppe Ungaretti onstage for the second half and remained at his side to read the English translations after Ungaretti read in Italian. Allen finished the evening with mantras and recent poems. He had more time to stretch out three days later at his solo reading as part of the same festival. He attempted to dispel the formal atmosphere by laying out bananas and incense on the stage, and opened with his usual mantras, but though he read well, the reading was strained and not a great success. 'Horrible. So much like an opera singer's performance,' he said afterwards. 'I worked at it instead of just letting it come.'

It was raining and we couldn't get a cab in the windswept wasteland of the South Bank complex, so we took the tube to St John's Wood to visit Paul at Cavendish Avenue. On the train Allen was absorbed in his own thoughts. Then he suddenly asked in a loud voice, 'Does Mick Jagger make it with men?' The carriage went deathly silent, everyone straining to hear my reply. I took the easy way out and said I really didn't know. Sue backed me up. Allen obviously sensed that some peculiar British convention was being broken and didn't pursue the matter further.

We found Paul swatting up on Tantra from Ajit Mockerjee's *Tantra Art* when we arrived. He had invited Mick Jagger and Marianne over; they lived close by at Harley House on the Marylebone Road. Mick had his biggest, most arrogant, rude and lovable smile on and was leaning back in a rocking chair in front of the French windows, a long white silk scarf trailing from his neck down the back of the chair to the carpet. He had one of Eliphas Levi's books on magic with him and some of the discussion was about comparative religion and western mysticism as a more usable and culturally understandable alternative to eastern mysticism. Allen told us about the western gnostic traditions, but maintained that there was no western mysticism being practised and that only in the East could one find actual gurus and teachers. Mick revealed that he had optioned the rights to Frank Herbert's *Dune*: 'I quite fancy meself as a mad old monk with me cloak flappin' abaht in the desert,' he said.

We all sat around on the carpet just inside the door to the living room. Incense was burning from innumerable sticks in a holder. The huge Takis sculpture – 'My lights on sticks' as Paul called it – blinked on and off in the corner by the bookshelves. I was a little surprised at Mick's and Paul's attitude to Allen, which was quite deferential. Paul was in a very receptive mood and, though I knew he had many reservations about the things Allen said, he did not express them. Both he and Mick treated Allen as a visiting sage, much as I imagine they later treated the Maharishi. They put Allen at ease and wanted to hear what he had to say. Tea was served.

Paul sat close to Allen, crosslegged. Sometimes he would select a few of the packages on a table next to the door and open them – presents from his fans. The packages usually contained framed coloured photographs of chubby American girls, but some contained clothes. He found a red satin shirt and, gathering a collection of coloured felt-tip pens, began to doodle a psychedelic pattern all over it. He already had paisley patterns over his white tennis shoes, and now silver, green and metallic blue shapes began to spread over the bright-red shiny shirt.

Allen gave Paul a tape he had made of various mantras and chants, including the Hare Krishna mantra, which he proceeded to chant right there, accompanying himself with tinkling finger cymbals. Both Paul and Mick wanted to hear about acid, and expressed some reservations about Timothy Leary's activities. Allen in turn asked them about music and how to get his mantras on record. They gave him assorted advice, but did not offer to produce a record.

They discussed William Burroughs, whose face Paul had put on the sleeve of *Sgt Pepper*, but mostly Paul preferred to tell stories about the old days in Liverpool and about his family. He tried to explain to Allen the nature of British eccentricity and said that most of the exploits of the Beat Generation would have been regarded as perfectly normal in Liverpool. There was some talking at cross-purposes, but it was a friendly visit.

As we left, Paul, sensing that this was an occasion, folded up the red shirt, which was now decorated with intricate psychedelic patterns, and placed it in Allen's hands. 'A souvenir of Swinging

London,' he said. Allen seemed moved, and carefully stuffed it into his Tibetan hippie shoulder-bag before packing up his Indian harmonium.

Paul's chief memory of the visit was that Allen had advised him against using concrete to lay the foundations of the geodesic dome he was planning to have built in his garden. 'What if you ever want to move it?' asked Allen.

'He was right,' Paul conceded, years later.

The next day, 16 July, there was a rally in Hyde Park to demand the legalisation of marijuana. It was advertised by a red-and-gold Martin Sharp poster, flyposted all over town, which is now a collector's item. Brian Patten and Adrian Henri read their poems, but the crowd was excitable and few people heard them. Allen arrived late with Sue and me, wearing his red McCartney satin shirt, which was much too tight for him, and carrying a flower. Walter Cronkite immediately appeared with a camera crew and got in a quick interview for American television before Allen reached the podium. Allen began chanting, accompanying himself on the harmonium. A young policeman came forward and informed him that the playing of music was not permitted in a royal park. Allen obligingly stopped playing and gave the policeman the flower he had been carrying. The policeman blushed.

A few people smoked joints, and members of the Balls Pond Road commune danced and sang, their bodies and faces painted with psychedelic colours, but it was a small gathering and most people drifted away early, leaving Allen sitting on the grass surrounded by a group of friends and admirers, all chanting the Hare Krishna mantra. That evening BBC Television's national news carried the music, and the announcer made a *namaste* hand gesture as he said good night, a degree of levity never before seen on the channel.

Panna was having such a good time with all this activity that she decided to give a huge party for everyone involved in the Dialectics of Liberation conference and to invite the London literary crowd who had been at Allen's reading. Sue and I arrived early to help out and found her in a state of high anxiety: Maretta and Tony had seized a huge cut-glass bowl of strawberries and cream, intended for the entire party, had sat down on the floor and by the time they were discovered had eaten over half of it. Panna complained to Allen, 'They'll be sick, they'll kill themselves. Nobody can eat that much!' As usual Allen's uncouth friends had disgraced themselves. I never understood Allen's attraction to Maretta, whom he held in high regard as a spiritual teacher.

It was a wonderful party. Charles Olson led a heated literary discussion with Harry Fainlight and other writers and poets. Michael X circulated, dressed in a rollneck blue silk shirt with his Afro puffed out. At one point he came up to me and, opening his jacket, showed me the top of a cheque in his inside pocket. 'Another white liberal bites the dust,' he murmured. Michael was good at milking white guilt about the plight of the black man.

Tom Driberg and William Burroughs found they had much in common. Burroughs spent most of the time in an upstairs room with Ian Sommerville and a few other friends, coming down to investigate only when the police arrived. A fight had broken out between an Establishment poet and his wife's lover, and the police were summoned. They stood politely at the door, helmets in hand. 'There is nothing going on,' Burroughs assured them, pulling a grimace, meant as a smile. 'I can assure you that nothing ever happens at Panna's house. Nothing at all. Good evening.' He shut the door smartly in their faces. He made to return to the upstairs room. A party-goer asked him what was happening up there. Bill looked at him, 'Nothing at all! A complete void.' William stood on the stair, blocking the way, swaying slightly, staring drunkenly at the man until he left, defeated.

Allen greeted Mick Jagger with a hug, which Mick returned. Allen then took his string of prayer beads and threw the loop over Mick's head. Mick did the same with his beads, then they both hugged and jumped up and down. They ended up on a balcony, where Allen attempted to teach Mick some eastern chants and mantras that Mick wanted to record.

Mick and Marianne invited me to bring Allen over to their apartment in Harley House and to go with them to a Stones recording session in Barnes. When we arrived Marianne was there, but Mick had still not shown up. Marianne decided to try on some new dresses that one of the King's Road boutiques had sent over, so she gave us a fashion show. I remember a bright-yellow crocheted dress with large holes all over it. One of her nipples stuck through a hole. 'Oh dear, that will never do,' she said, taking the dress off. 'I'd have to wear something under it.' Allen, sadly, did not appreciate the show. Mick eventually appeared, but by now it was so late that I didn't feel like going all the way to Barnes for an all-nighter, so I walked home, leaving Allen to it.

The Stones were recording 'We Love You', their response to their legal difficulties, which opens with the sound of footsteps and a prison door slamming. The next day Allen was ecstatic. Through the thick glass of the control-room window, he saw not only the Stones, dressed in their flowing scarves and ruffled shirts, but John Lennon and Paul McCartney, who had come to sing in the chorus as a gesture of support. 'It was wonderful,' he said. 'They all looked like little angels.' Allen wrote to Peter Orlovsky: 'Last night I spent at recording studio with Mick Jagger, Paul McCartney and John Lennon looking like Botticelli Graces singing together for the first time. I conducted through the window with Shiva Beads and Tibetan oracle ring.'

The Dialectics of Liberation conference was organised by 'anti-psychiatrist' R. D. Laing and held at the Roundhouse, which had now been done up a bit. The distinguished group of speakers included Paul Goodman, John Gerassi, Mircea Eliade, Ernest Mandel, Paul Sweezy, Gregory Bateson and the 'leader' of the Diggers, Emmett Grogan, who was staying at Panna's at Allen's request. The conference was quickly dominated by the American Black Power leader Stokely Carmichael, whose plans for a separate black nation gave rise to many late-night arguments. These took place at 'Dialectics House', where the conferees met afterwards to discuss the day's events, while Ronnie Laing plied them with whisky. I remember one particularly violent shouting match, when Stokely claimed that if it was legitimate for the Jews to claim their own country on the grounds of persecution, then it was legitimate for blacks to do the same. It was hard to dispute his logic.

Allen's theme was 'Consciousness and Practical Action', and he began his speech by quoting at length from Burroughs' *Nova Express*, as an example of what happens when a planet goes out of control. He was responding to Gregory Bateson's exposition on the greenhouse effect, in which he accurately predicted that global warming would manifest itself within ten to thirty years. The entire conference was tape-recorded and released as a set of albums. Subsequently, a woman at the pressing plant, listening to a test pressing of Allen's speech to check for faults, was so upset by the quotes from *Nova Express* that she had to be sent home. The plant refused to press the record, and other means had to be found, holding up the release of the entire series.

The Times Ad

Meanwhile preparations for the 'pot ad' were going ahead. It was trailed by Philip Oakes' Atticus column in the *Sunday Times*, which revealed that all four Beatles would be among those contributing to the cost of the advertisement. On the eve of publication, when Steve Abrams went to approve the proofs, the advertising manager of *The Times*, a Mr Davison, got cold feet and delayed publication until he had checked that all those named had indeed signed. He also, not surprisingly, insisted on advance payment for the ad, and Steve Abrams called up Peter Brown at Brian Epstein's office. He sent round a personal cheque for £1,800 made out to *The Times*.

The 'pot ad' was published in *The Times* on Monday 24 July 1967. The full-page advertisement was headed 'The law against marijuana is immoral in principle and unworkable in practice', and presented informed medical opinion that marijuana was not addictive and had no harmful effects. The signed petition read:

> The signatories to this petition suggest to the Home Secretary that he implement a five point programme of cannabis law reform:
> 1. The government should permit and encourage research into all aspects of cannabis use, including its medical applications.

2. Allowing the smoking of cannabis on private premises should no longer constitute an offence.

3. Cannabis should be taken off the dangerous drugs list and controlled, rather than prohibited, by a new *ad hoc* instrument.

4. Possession of cannabis should either be legally permitted or at most be considered a misdemeanour, punishable by a fine of not more than £10 for a first offence and not more than £25 for any subsequent offence.

5. All persons now imprisoned for possession of cannabis or for allowing cannabis to be smoked on private premises should have their sentences commuted.

It was signed by sixty-five of the leading names in British society, including Francis Crick, the co-discoverer of the DNA molecule and a Nobel Laureate, the novelist Graham Greene (who was smoking opium in his flat at Albany when the petition was brought round for him to sign), and Members of Parliament Jonathan Aitken and Brian Walden; there were also artists, well-known medical and psychological doctors, and the Beatles. The media predictably reacted with outrage, and questions were asked in the House of Commons.

The Minister of State, Alice Bacon, gave a rambling, racist speech in which she blamed the use of pot and acid on the importation of 'negro music and Indian spirituality'. Nevertheless, she also said that the issues raised by the advertisement would be considered by the Wootton sub-committee, and she committed the government to taking the Wootton Report into consideration when framing new legislation.

A week after the advertisement was published, Keith Richards' conviction was dismissed on appeal, and Jagger's sentence was reduced to a conditional discharge. The ad had specifically asked for the premises offence to be abolished, and the ensuing debate may well have influenced the appeal court's decision.

When Baroness Wootton presented her report on 1 November 1968, the Home Secretary James Callaghan rejected it. This was perhaps not surprising. During his time in opposition Callaghan had been 'Sunny Jim, the Policeman's Friend', the paid parliamentary lobbyist for the Police Federation, and the police were doing very well with things as they were. Callaghan was under no legal obligation to publish the report, but there were stories in the press that some members of the committee were prepared to resign if it was not made public and he was probably also aware that Steve Abrams, *International Times* and other interested parties had already obtained copies of it and would certainly bootleg it and distribute it to the press if Her Majesty's Stationery Office didn't do so soon. HMSO published the report on 7 January 1969.

The report stated: 'The long asserted dangers of cannabis are exaggerated and the related law is socially damaging, if not unworkable.' The right-wing press reacted with fury; the *Daily Express* ran a famous headline calling the report the 'Junkies' Charter' and there was much huffing and puffing from the usual reactionary quarters. When the report was debated in Parliament on 29 January 1969 Callaghan said, 'I think it came as a surprise, if not a shock, to most people when that notorious advertisement appeared in *The Times* in 1967 to find that there is a lobby for legalising cannabis. The House should recognise that this lobby exists, and my reading of the Report is that the Wootton sub-committee was overinfluenced by this lobby.'

Sir Edward Wayne and Lady Wootton, the authors of the report, were outraged by the Home Secretary's insulting remarks and wrote a joint letter to *The Times*: 'We regard this statement as offensive to our distinguished colleagues and to ourselves, and particularly to the eminent medical men who signed our report, and we particularly deprecate the implication of the emotive word "lobby" in this context. We would also point out that after hearing the evidence no member of this committee recommended legalisation.'

Despite his unilateral dismissal of the Wootton Report, Callaghan was outvoted in Cabinet and actually had little option other than to implement its recommendations. New legislation controlling psychotropic drugs was drafted and, as he had asked the Wootton sub-committee to remain sitting in an advisory capacity, he now had to agree to their insistence on the difference between hard and soft drugs, a distinction not previously made.

The Labour Party lost the 1970 general election, but the legislation was re-introduced by Reginald Maudling for the Conservatives. The new act reduced the maximum imprisonment on

225

summary conviction to six months and magistrates were advised that minor offences did not merit prison sentences. They were told to treat pot smokers with 'becoming moderation' and to 'reserve the sentence of imprisonment for suitably flagrant cases of large scale trafficking'. The courts stopped imposing custodial sentences for possession.

Meanwhile there was another way to avoid being busted for pot. That autumn a number of doctors began prescribing it legally. A three-and-a-half-ounce bottle of tincture of cannabis cost seventeen shillings on the National Health when prescribed by a doctor. It was made from ganja and came as a liquid in a three-to-one alcohol suspension. William Burroughs got his from the famous Dr Dunbar. William used to dip his Senior Service into the liquid, allow the cigarettes to dry, then put them back into the pack. The problem was that the cigarettes were all stained an eye-catching green by the tincture and certainly smelled like pot when you smoked them. William insisted that no one ever noticed that they were not regular cigarettes when he lit up in a restaurant, and in any case they were legal. They were prescribed as a cure for paranoia – dope smokers were paranoid about being busted.

Neither legal tincture nor changes in the law helped Hoppy, and he found his time in jail very hard to deal with. Sue and I took Allen to Wormwood Scrubs to visit him. Allen did not have a visitor's pass, but the guards thought he must be Hoppy's rabbi and after some discussion they let him in. He spent some of his visit teaching Hoppy the rudiments of meditation technique. Hoppy had bumped into Robert Fraser a few times, who was also in the Scrubs, and we met a friend of Robert's in the waiting room, prior to our visit. Robert fared very well in jail, which he described as just like being back at Eton, but the other prisoners did not like Hoppy and it took him some time to recover from his ordeal.

It was the lack of a phone or reliable mail service that caused him the most anguish: 'The trouble with this place is that there is no communication whatsoever and I don't know what the hell goes on out there.' He had absolutely no outlet for his fertile mind, which continued to throw up scores of ideas for *IT* and UFO that he could not act upon. *IT* only reached him sporadically, so half the time he did not even know if it was still in existence. His letters were filled with requests for information, often in numbered paragraphs, and endless suggestions for advertising, distribution, finance, editorial content . . . 'Did Steve Stollman ever show? What news from Esam? Can we get stills from Stones film for *IT*? Now the time to interview Whitehead . . .' Sue and I visited him, as did Suzy and many of his friends, but we could never quench his thirst for information. He wrote to me: 'Jesus, if I was on the outside. I *know* what to do *now*!!'

Zappa

Frank Zappa came to Britain in August 1967 to promote *Absolutely Free* and used Indica as his unofficial base, somewhere that messages could be left for him and a place to arrange meetings. As MGM Records refused to print the lyrics on the album sleeve, Frank ran them in *IT* instead, writing a special introduction to each song for *IT*'s readers who might be unfamiliar with American teenage culture. It was for this feature that the infamous photograph by Bobby Davidson of him sitting on a toilet was taken. Danny Halperin at Osiris Visions had been hired as Zappa's publicist and had a poster made of it. The image was bootlegged all over the world, dogging poor Frank everywhere he went for many years. Frank wanted to meet Paul and, at the Mothers' press reception, I got Paul on the telephone so they could arrange to meet. There was an immediate cultural clash and they talked at cross-purposes. Paul thought Frank sounded very American record biz. 'He kept talking about "product",' Paul said, which surprised him. Frank may have been trying to sound more professional than he in fact was, but having scrabbled his way up through the record business he couldn't understand how Paul could know so little about the industry in which he was top dog.

Frank wanted Paul's permission to parody the *Sgt Pepper* cover on *We're Only In It For the Money* – permission he probably didn't need, since it has been done dozens of times since. At first Paul didn't see what he was getting at. As far as he was concerned it was fine, but he explained that the sleeve was EMI's copyright. He would be happy to call or write to them on Zappa's behalf if it was necessary, but he couldn't just say yes. Frank was astonished. He assumed that the Beatles, as the biggest band on earth, would be in a position to do anything they wanted. Frank did it anyway and included the *International Times* IT-Girl logo among the crowd on his cover as a reference to his visit.

UFO at the Roundhouse

In September UFO moved to the Roundhouse, which at last met fire regulations. But though the building had many associations with *IT*, the atmosphere of the old UFO Club did not travel. The Roundhouse required paid security guards, and bands like the Pink Floyd could now command high fees – they only played one UFO there. It was a vicious circle: the new venue cost a great deal more to rent and so more expensive acts had to be booked to attract bigger audiences, but the new crowds did not know each other and were mostly there for the groups. UFO was cold and dead, and the old crowd drifted away or were diluted by newcomers. The community spirit was gone and, on 6 October 1967, it was closed down. An *IT* headline that week announced 'UFOria is dead'. UFO was still just about breaking even, but there was no point in carrying on. I wrote to Hoppy, rather breathlessly it seems now, about the closing of his brainchild:

> Big building at high rent £150 including setting up time. Many doors all of which have to be open or unlocked for fire regulations, balcony stairs to be guarded, crowd control, bigger door problems and staff, people standing in bogs all night to stop people getting in window, etc. so staff bill of £200+ Joe's [Boyd] economics and interests says bigger outgoings require bigger crowds [true]. Of two ways of getting bigger crowds he chose bigger groups which failed. A festival there with Pink Floyd,

Move, Arthur Brown, Denny Laine and many others lost £500, ever since lost money. Organised trouble at door, one week eight staff members beaten up, Joy attacked twice, Hugh lip cut, Joe knocked down and kicked, friend of Mick Farren punched in face, etc. Answer was to get security people which Michael X provided at £200 for 20 of them. Nice people, no trouble, but even bigger outgoings. Meanwhile staff very uptight at first Simon [Barley, the manager] then Joe's handling of UFO culminating in a sort of staff meeting before a UFO in which Mike Henshaw and Joe explained everything about UFO's structure to the staff and they explained their grievances. This cleared the air a bit and the meeting the following week cleared all the air. But it was too late I'm afraid. UFO was the expression of *your* avant garde energies, it was a creative thing to you . . . UFO had a good life.

I hated UFO at the Roundhouse because it was my duty to bring home the money. At about 4 am we paid the bands, and the staff and I took whatever was left home to bank on Monday. One night in September I was robbed just as Sue and I reached our front door. The thieves must have done a dry run the week before and we were so naive that we didn't think of varying our routine. There were three of them. Two were waiting in the doorway with stockings pulled over their faces. As I stopped to find my key, one of them sprayed ammonia in my face while another knocked the briefcase from my hands with a pickaxe handle. At that moment a car came swerving across Southampton Row, they leaped in and were gone. Sue got the number of the car, which it turned out had been stolen specifically for the job.

Attendance had not been good that evening, and after paying everyone, there was only £62 in cash to take home. Fortunately the ammonia had largely missed my eyes, so I was able to see. We went straight round to the police station on Lamb's Conduit Street, where a bored night staff kept us waiting for twenty minutes before anyone could be found to take a statement. They refused to give us a cup of tea and acted generally as if we were the criminals.

Unfortunately my address book was in my briefcase with my phone number in it. The next day I received a threatening phone call: 'Take your business out of Camden Town, Mr Miles, or we'll cut you up.' They were clearly very disappointed with their £62 and had been expecting a great deal more. I reported the call to the police, who said they could do nothing. I explained that it was not my business, that I couldn't move UFO out of Camden Town even if I wanted to, and asked for police protection. The police found this very amusing, and that was my last dealing with them.

Michael X, on the other hand, immediately sprang into action and insisted on having one of his lieutenants outside the building whenever Indica was not open. The phone call had made me paranoid, and to be able to look out of the window at night and see a shadowy figure in the doorway of the post office across the street, in the RAAS uniform of blue-satin rollneck shirt from Do Do on Parkway, made me feel much better. On the other hand, I didn't want to become too obligated to Michael, much as I liked him, so after a couple of days Sue and I escaped to Amsterdam, a city I had always wanted to see, to visit Simon Vinkenoog. The whole experience had been very salutary, after all the parties with the beautiful people.

When we returned to London, Michael X offered to renew the surveillance but we no longer felt as threatened and declined. None the less I was very grateful for all he'd done. This was a period when we saw a lot of Michael. He regularly contributed articles and poems to *IT*, so he was often in the office or bookshop. He was a great cook and sometimes had Sue and me over for soul food. At one point Nigel Samuel was going to publish a soul-food cookbook that Michael had written. Michael said he enjoyed the company of the hippies he met through *IT* because they had no preconceived ideas about him. His father was Portuguese and his mother black, which meant that some West Indians accused him of being white. The white community, however, was under no such illusion – to them he was never anything but black.

At a lecture given in Reading in July, Michael gave an inflammatory speech, during which he referred to the Notting Hill race riots: 'In 1958 I saw white savages kicking black women in the streets and black brothers running away. If ever you see a white laying hands on a black woman, kill him immediately . . . Whitey is a vicious, nasty person. Fear of this white monkey is nothing . . .' About half of the audience was black, many of whom laughed when he suggested killing anyone who laid hands on a black woman, understanding the macho exaggeration and ghetto humour in his speech. Four days later, however, the Attorney General announced in the Commons that he had asked the DPP to investigate. Michael was charged with inciting racial hatred under section fourteen of the Race Relations Act, which had been passed the previous year. It was entirely typical of British justice that the first time the act was used was against a black person.

At his trial in November, most of the evidence came from a *Daily Sketch* reporter (a *Sun*-style tabloid that is thankfully no longer with us) who was covering the event. Michael conducted his own defence. He spoke quietly and told the jury about life as a black man in Britain. He reminded them of a recent case when 150 white racists attacked the house of a Jamaican family in Wolverhampton, just because they were West Indians. When six people appeared before the magistrate the next day, he dismissed the whole thing as a 'neighbourly dispute' and let them off. Michael was in every respect reasonable and unthreatening and the jury listened attentively, but the judge as good as told them that it was their duty to convict, which they did. Michael was given a year in Swansea prison. After sentencing, he told the judge, 'You represent white justice. Well, my people will have to deal with that.' Six months later the right-wing Cabinet minister Enoch Powell made his racist 'Rivers of blood' speech. He was not prosecuted.

I was beginning to feel deeply exhausted. For me, 1967 had been a year of insane activity. People pounded through the bookshop demanding information, contacts, Paul McCartney's phone number, somewhere to live, the name of a lawyer or, even worse, to show me their poems. In my capacity as a company director(!) I signed at least a dozen passport application forms, calmed the mothers of hippie children who telephoned Indica worried and anxious, talked people through bad trips, put up posters, wrote letters, columns for *IT* and other underground papers, and smoked too many cigarettes. Visiting poets and publishers had to be entertained with a cup of tea in the back room; journalists wanted to know all about the underground, but usually spent the time arguing instead of listening; and people from the Arts Council brought round visiting cultural dignitaries as if we were one of the London sights, which, in a way, we were. Each evening it was the same: people coming round, discussing plans, events, busts, the revolution. It was a fragmented period when I met literally thousands of people. It was both exhilarating and fatiguing.

Ley Lines

After the summer of 1967 we began to see more of the Chelsea people, a natural consequence of Sue working for Christopher Gibbs. The King's Road always seemed sunnier than the West End, with a proper village atmosphere, the Chelsea pensioners in their uniforms, the guardsmen at the Chelsea Cobbler, the pretty models in their mini-skirts running in and out of the boutiques from hastily parked sports cars and Mini-Minors. Here lived the people who hung out with Dalí at Port Lligat and danced the night away at Byblos in Saint-Tropez. There was quite a difference between the King's Road scene and the *IT* and UFO crew: the beautiful people had money. They were essentially an extension of Mary Quant's Swinging London, only with drugs. The people we knew there felt comfortable with that scene, but led double lives, experimenting with acid, spending entire evenings discussing flying saucers, ley lines and the court of King Arthur. Like most hippies they read Tolkien's *Lord of the Rings*, *Steppenwolf* and *Magister Ludi* (*The Glass Bead Game*) by Herman Hesse, and Kahlil Gibran's *The Prophet*. (None of these were recent books, but they summed up the reading habits of Sixties London.) In Chelsea, however, there was also a special interest in books about Camelot: *The Arthurian Chronicles*; Geoffrey Ashe's *Arthur's Avalon* and *The Quest for Arthur's Britain*; John Michell's *The Flying Saucer Vision*; Alfred Watkins' *The Old Straight Track*; books on magic, Aleister Crowley, standing stones. It was an important side of the English underground scene, informing the posters, the graphic art, the song lyrics and the poetry; it had no counterpart in the USA, except for the pioneer tradition.

The King's Road led straight to Glastonbury in those days (much as Brighton used to be the sea end of Wardour Street); everyone seemed to be travelling to Glastonbury each weekend and staying – those that were eligible – at Mrs Biggins' Aquarian Boarding House (those born under other signs stayed in bed-and-breakfasts, barns and haystacks), to seek the Holy Grail or plot ley lines. Other people waited patiently at Arthur's Tor for flying saucers to land. I asked John Michell, *IT*'s correspondent on such matters, what there was to see down there. He told me there were two Glastonbury sites to visit, the prosaic Ministry of Works site and the Pendragon Society one, which had a huge tent with banners flying from it. Both very good on acid. There was first a trickle, then an exodus of people from Chelsea moving to the West Country to study the Glastonbury Zodiac, the ley lines and to hunt for traces of King Arthur.

I didn't make it to Glastonbury for another decade, but Chelsea was not unknown to me. I used to buy my clothes from either Hung On You or Granny Takes a Trip, both on the King's Road. Granny's used to change the entire front of the shop on a regular basis: one time there was a huge flower-child girl's face painted right across the window and door; on another visit there was the stoic face of a Native American; for a while the back half of an American car protruded from the window, as if it had crashed through in an explosion of psychedelic Roy Lichtenstein stars – all painted by Michael English.

Once when I went there I found the owner John Pearce asleep on the floor just inside the door, next to a rack of yellow crushed-velvet trousers; a small pile of money had been placed by his side by a customer who had decided not to disturb him. He tried to sell me a lacy ruffled shirt, which was on special sale. There was a hole in the back the same size as an electric iron. 'No one would know if you were wearing a jacket!' It wasn't even reduced that much.

I always liked Michael Rainey's Hung on You because it was so uncompromising. The name, painted by Michael English, covered the shop window completely. The ground floor contained no clothes, just a huge blow-up of a grainy photograph of Chairman Mao swimming the Yangtze. There was a hole in the floor with a very steep ladder leading down to where the few clothes were kept. Even then there was very little to see: about six shirts and one or two jackets on a clothes rail. However, Barbara Allen in a fetching see-through top and micro-mini-skirt was usually there to advise. I succumbed to Rainey's insistence that Chinese-style clothing was the next big thing and for years wore a bottle-green Mao jacket with a high collar that he sold me.

I very much liked Michael's shop fronts, so when he suggested that he do one for Indica I was very responsive. He covered the side window with huge yellow stars, but the landlord almost immediately made us remove it. This was a pity. It would have been good to connect up the underground scene from the World's End to Bloomsbury with a recognisable graphic style.

15 Lord North Street

Jane Ormsby-Gore and Michael Rainey decided to follow the ley lines to Wales, and Sue and I took over their lease on 15 Lord North Street, a small Queen Anne house just round the corner from the Houses of Parliament. There were five floors including a basement, with a pocket-handkerchief garden in the back. The rent was quite high at £15 a week, so Graham Keen took one of the floors. The house was built in 1728 and still had its wooden panelling. I had a locksmith come to make door keys for the rooms, and the insides of the brass locks were shiny and clean as new, despite their age. The living-room carpet was bright yellow, supposedly the inspiration for Donovan's 'Mellow Yellow'; he can no longer remember, but he was a frequent visitor when the Raineys lived there.

The kitchen was in the basement, with an outside staircase in the area, which the 'tradesmen' insisted on using. I took the ground floor for my office and rather spoiled its look by installing big metal filing cabinets. The back half of the room had built-in bookshelves and became the library.

It was a very short street, but most interesting to live on. The very idea of living in that part of Westminster was amazing. I couldn't believe we were doing it. Being close to the Houses of Parliament meant that we were within the division bell, though our house, of course, was not connected. Rumour had it that there were brothels nearby where the bell was installed and, when it rang, half the clients scrambled into their clothes and rushed back to the House to vote. The Prime Minister, Harold Wilson, lived across the street – he never did bother to move properly into Number 10. My bank was in the lobby of Transport House, the Labour Party headquarters building at the end of the street on Smith Square, and the Conservative Party headquarters were also on the square. It was dominated by St John's, a wonderful four-towered Archer church sometimes known as 'Queen Anne's footstool'.

Next door lived Lady Reading, the head of the Women's Royal Voluntary Service. We got to know her through her housekeeper after she had put a boiled chicken to cool on her kitchen window. Our cat, Nadja, was found, her paws wrapped around it in a bear-hug, chewing contentedly on Lady Reading's lunch. We had a huge cheeseplant, which had grown too large for the miniature Queen Anne rooms, so we gave it to Lady Reading, who promptly cut it in half and had it strapped to the roof of her Rolls to be transported to one of her women's homes. From then on we received a bottle of claret at Christmas.

On the other side lived the actor Ralph Richardson, who had demolished his ground-floor corridor wall so that you walked into a wood-panelled reception room straight off the street. He was friendly and showed us his huge antique globe. Sir Laurence Olivier often visited. Our garden wall backed upon that of the editor of *The Times*, William Rees-Mogg, who once sent us a terse note asking us to please stop our cats from digging up his pansies. Lord Sainsbury lived next door to him. A huge Sainsbury's delivery van would block the street once a week while packets of sliced bread and toilet rolls were carried into his house on the corner of the square.

Across the street lived a friend of the Queen Mother, who would often visit her for tea. I remember watching her alight from her Bentley and the shock of recognition from a passer-by in pinstripe suit and umbrella who sprang to attention and saluted her. She gave a gay little wave and disappeared in a cloud of pink chiffon.

We used to see her daughter about once a week. My secretary, Sarah, used to drive me to Indica in the late morning after dealing with the day's mail at Lord North Street, and we frequently found ourselves passing the Queen on her way back to the palace as we drove the other way down the Mall towards Bloomsbury. I always used to try and catch her eye, because as soon as she saw someone looking she gave a wave. She must have had a regular coffee morning with friends.

We rather lowered the tone of the neighbourhood, particularly when H (my friend Howard Parker) came to stay, and we had Jimi Hendrix's Ford Transit parked outside, filled with Jimi's Marshall stacks. One of H's jobs onstage was to hold up the speakers from behind while Jimi pretended to fuck them with his guitar, rubbing it against them, writhing to the feedback while H strained to keep the whole stack from toppling over. In his second week at our house H was walking home late at night down Whitehall, and as he passed the Foreign Office a policeman beckoned him over: 'Wotchu doin' on my little patch then?' he asked, having seen H on several previous occasions. H explained that he lived at 15 Lord North Street. 'Oh, we know all about them,' said the policeman enigmatically. He probably thought Lord Harlech's daughter still lived there, which gave us welcome protection from police raids.

H was a wonderful conversationalist, good at 'givin' them the verbal' as he called it. In fact words came a little too fluently to him and one day he announced dejectedly that he was 'on Jimi's elbow list'. Early one morning at Copenhagen airport, when everyone was tired and hung over, he had spotted Jimi sitting on his guitar case. Without thinking H said, 'Cor, you look like a gorilla that's lost his bananas.' Though H was in no way a racist, Jimi quite understandably took umbrage and H was out.

H liked the rock 'n' roll nightlife and often found himself in strange company. One night he came in and said that Ronnie Kray had tried to pick him up at some nightclub. Ronnie's memorable pick-up line was 'I'm gay. More modern, enit?'

Betterton Street

IT was also on the move. Nigel Samuel bought a building in Covent Garden at 22 Betterton Street and installed his offices on the top floor. He gave *IT* the middle and ground floor. He carpeted the floors and bought electric typewriters. ECAL, the underground poster-distribution company part-owned by *IT*, had the basement. Nigel's decision to get more closely involved with *IT* and the underground did not go unopposed, with Lord Goodman in particular advising him to distance himself from us. But Nigel had retained Indica and *IT*'s lawyer, Keith Turner – who later went to work exclusively for Jimi Hendrix – and made his position very clear. Between them, Nigel and his mother owned the majority shareholding in the *New Statesman*, then the main intellectual organ of the Labour Party (and the paper that had accused *IT* of being 'American anti-socialist beatnikery'). Nigel's method of getting Goodman to back off was to convene a special directors' meeting at the *New Statesman* at which he and Keith Turner threatened to merge it with *International Times*, under *IT*'s editorial board, if Goodman did not stop meddling in his affairs. To Nigel's amusement, several of the *New Statesman* staff suddenly declared themselves in total favour of *IT*'s editorial stance and said it was time for a change. Nigel had his way and was able to buy the Betterton Street building. The *New Statesman* remained independent.

Sadly, Nigel was becoming more and more schizophrenic. Having had no experience of mental illness, I didn't recognise the symptoms when I saw them. I just thought Nigel was a bit spaced out at times. One such time was at Chez Victor on Wardour Street when, after their trademark steak tartare, which we all had, Nigel kept ordering green salads. He would nibble one leaf, then order another. The waiter looked despairing, but continued to serve him until the table was crowded with six of them. We all had another Armagnac and Nigel paid the bill as if nothing had happened.

Another time Nigel took us to Robert Carrier's flashy new restaurant in Camden Passage; the first course was caviar soup. After paying the bill, he insisted on inspecting the kitchen, pushing past the surprised waiter and peering into pots and pans, opening cupboards and running the edge of his hand over surfaces to see if there was any trace of dust. The staff stood and watched him, open-mouthed, thinking perhaps he was a food critic.

Nigel guaranteed the rent on the Arts Lab, but even here his illness began to show. One night he lobbed a house brick through the transom window, then walked calmly down to Bow Street police station. He informed the sergeant at the desk, 'A crime has been committed!' and explained that the window had been smashed.

'Do you have any idea who did it, sir?' the policeman asked.

'I did,' Nigel confessed.

At 6 am one morning I received a phone call from a distraught Nigel, asking me to come to his apartment immediately. He sounded terrible and had obviously been up all night. Thinking he might be suicidal, I hurriedly dressed and took a cab to Portman Square. I found him pacing the floor, a glazed look in his eye, watched by a very confused-looking black girl, naked except for her high heels. Nigel informed me that they were to be married that morning at Chelsea register office and that I was to be the best man. This was something of a surprise to me, and to the young lady. I demanded more details, but Nigel kept repeating, 'Everything is arranged, you'll see.' The girl finally got dressed and we took a cab to Chelsea Town Hall. Astonishingly, we were expected and the paperwork was in order. We were the first wedding of the day. Nigel had clearly been planning this for some time. No one else had been informed and there was a sudden panic when it was found that a witness was needed. I went out to the King's Road and tried to find someone, but the few people on the pavement were hurrying to work and looked at me as if I were mad. Eventually I found a hippie girl in a long silk skirt, who agreed. For some reason she was more nervous than the bride and groom and as soon as the register had been signed, she began drinking heavily – Nigel had thoughtfully brought a few bottles of champagne with him. By the time we had paid and settled everything she was completely drunk. I saw the bride and groom off in a cab and walked slowly back to the West End.

Lord Goodman annulled the marriage the next day.

1968

The overreaction by the police and the Establishment to the underground had its effect. Everyone knew someone who had been busted, planted by the police or fitted up; hippies were being stopped and searched on the street and taken to the station and strip-searched just for the amusement of the bored coppers. The police, 'the fuzz', became the enemy. The majority of the population still thought 'our police are wonderful' and so 'the straights', or 'the suits' as John Lennon called them, all became an ill-defined enemy too. Of course this was the kind of treatment that West Indians had suffered for years. Priest told me that he was stopped on the street at least six times a week – it was a normal part of the intimidation they had to endure – but for white, largely middle-class hippies it came as quite a shock.

There was a growing opposition to the Establishment in political matters as well as personal. There were anti-Vietnam War demonstrations outside the United States embassy in Grosvenor Square, where a cross-section of the underground, from Michael X and his supporters to Mick Jagger, were charged by mounted police. The events of May in Paris took many of the *IT* staff to France. A change came over the scene. Che Guevara posters proliferated, and *IT* began running interviews with political radicals like Fritz Teufel and others who later became involved with the Baader-Meinhof gang. The International Situationists targeted the *IT* building and sealed the front door with IS posters. *IT* carefully peeled one off and ran it as a front cover. In February *IT* supported Dick Gregory in his campaign for President of the USA and ran J. G. Ballard's controversial (and prescient) poem 'Why I Want to Fuck Ronald Reagan'. An interview with Rudi Dutschke ran next to 'Victory Thru Vegetables' by Greg Sams. There were long articles on macrobiotics, ecology, yoga, sex and meditation. Two distinct communities began to appear under the umbrella of the underground, one of which eventually produced terrorist groups like the Angry Brigade or the militant squatters' groups, while the other evolved into the pot-smoking, vegetarian, woolly-hatted hippies living in a commune somewhere in the Welsh hills, who emerge on market day with mongrels on the end of a length of bale twine to sell macramé and pottery to the suspicious locals.

The events that finally divided the two factions occurred in May in France where, for a few weeks, it really did seem as if the much talked-of 'revolution' was about to happen. France was in the grip of a general strike; the Bourse had been occupied and from its flagpole fluttered a white flag with a drawing of a huge reefer on it by *IT*'s Paris correspondent, performance artist Jean-Jacques Lebel. Students took control of the Sorbonne and held continuous teach-ins and discussions; the toll booths of the autoroutes were all occupied by strikers, who let drivers through free; there was a party atmosphere everywhere – even the staff of the Ritz occupied the building, then ran it normally, with the utmost civility, but as a collective. Back in London, *IT* was restructured as a co-operative, Hoppy got out of jail and started an underground information exchange called *BIT*, and a new wave of people appeared, politicised by May '68.

The hippies, as the press called them, were linked by a common love of progressive rock music and by marijuana; the fact that it was illegal united them as a group outside the law. Mick and Joy Farren personified the split on the scene. Joy identified with the macro-biotic-eating, tarot-card-reading, *I Ching*-consulting, horoscope-reading, apolitical hippies, who longed to leave the city and set up communes in North Wales. Mick, on the other hand, believed that a police state was coming and eventually set up an organisation called the White Panthers, allied to John Sinclair's White Panther group in Detroit, and of course in emulation of the American Black Panthers. Mick didn't see why hippies should take all the humiliation and abuse; he thought they should fight back. I remember quite seriously examining the outside balcony of his flat on Shaftesbury Avenue with him to see if it would be suitable for a machine-gun nest in the event of a police *coup d'état*. Unfortunately for Mick, his flat was next door to the Shaftesbury Theatre and Mick, with his enormous Afro, was often mistaken for an actor in the long-running musical *Hair*.

The underground divided into battling factions, with outside groups trying to wrest control of *IT* and half a dozen different promoters trying to become the British Bill Graham. The Arts Lab split over philosophical differences, with Dave Curtis and many other important organisers resigning, but the Lab continued, and in addition half a dozen other venues were presenting modern dance, experimental theatre and avant-garde films. Arts Labs opened in other cities and the ideas of the underground began to be discussed – or more likely argued over – in universities and schools across Britain. The 'What's Happening' columns in *IT* grew from issue to issue. On the music scene it was the era of the groupie and the in-club, as described by Jenny Fabian in her *roman-à-clef, Groupie*. Any evening of the week you could see the likes of Traffic, Dantalion's Chariot, Family, Blossom Toes, Fairport Convention, the Aynsley Dunbar Retaliation, Jeff Beck, the Graham Bond Organisation, the Action, Tomorrow, Junior's Eyes, the Moody Blues or Tyrannosaurus Rex. If 1967 was the summer of love, 1968 was best characterised as a year of political action.

Grosvenor Square

The Vietnam Solidarity Committee, headed by Tariq Ali, organised a massive demo outside the American embassy on Grosvenor Square for 17 March. The intention, as I understood it, was to occupy the building, if only briefly, as a symbolic gesture of solidarity with the Vietnamese. Whereas the American anti-war protesters were at least partly motivated by self-interest – the very realistic desire not to be sent to Vietnam to kill people and possibly be killed themselves – the British protest was much more in support of the Vietcong.

We fell in with Mick Farren and his group on the march from Trafalgar Square. At one point on South Audley Street the march was about twelve deep, but a policeman actually pushed his way through the marchers to aim a blow at Mickey's head before being engulfed by the crowd and making a rapid retreat. He must have known who Mickey was, or just didn't like the look of him. Mickey gave off a distinct anti-police vibe, which they picked up at a distance of some yards. In fact his Afro was so large by this point that it would probably have acted as a crash helmet and cushioned the blow. In his autobiography Mickey claims that it was at this point that I tried to kick in the headlights of a car, but naturally I have no memory of such an event.

In the square itself we ran into Frankie Y, one of Michael X's group. (Frankie didn't want to take the surname X like everyone else, so he went for the next letter in the alphabet.) Frankie, like Mickey, was another one whom the police instinctively disliked and made a beeline for, and he had already had to do some fast running to avoid being clubbed. 'Is okay,' he said, grinning. 'I'm a fast cat!'

After sealing off the square, the police charged into the crowd on horseback, wave after wave of them, crushing and injuring people who had no way of retreating. You only had to scratch the complacent surface of English life slightly before the full power of the state would attempt to crush you. After the demonstration the police received hundreds of letters expressing sympathy and concern for the horses injured in the attacks.

A few days later Mick Jagger came to Lord North Street to tape a conversation for *IT*. He had been at Grosvenor Square, but had decided against marching with Vanessa Redgrave, who invited him. I expressed my misgivings about the demonstration, saying that confrontations were not the way to change things, and that I felt very frustrated by the whole thing.

MJ: But that's what it should have been!

M: An expression of frustration?

MJ: But that's just fun, you see! Because that's your own inherent violence. That's our way out. 'Cause we love it! And it's our excuse, see? We can't be guerillas. We're so violent, we're violently frustrated. We haven't got enough violence, we've no opportunity. We don't want to be in the army, it doesn't do anything anyway . . . There's no guerillas, there's no, well, there's Welsh nationalists. You can go and join them, but what a joke! I mean there's nothing in this country, it's all . . . and there's all this violence . . . It's fun.

It was not long after that that Mick Jagger wrote 'Street Fighting Man'.

The Marriage of Suzy and Hoppy

Suzy Creamcheese came to meet me one day in Frank's bar on the corner of Cosmo Place, just up from Indica, where Harry, Nigel Samuel's gofer, was a regular. Suzy wore very short dresses and no bra. She was well built. Harry's reaction when he first saw her burst through the door was a shout of laughter and amazement. 'My giddy aunt,' he said to Tony, the barman. 'There's a girl here for our Frank. Just go and get a decko at 'er. There ought to be a law against it. They make me so excited.' When he realised she was coming to see me, he quickly wiped his brow and muttered, 'No offence, I'm sure.'

She came to tell me that she and Hoppy were getting married. She had had to promise the immigration authorities that she would marry within a week for them to permit her to stay in the country. Suzy and I did not get on all that well. Hoppy's incarceration had affected her very badly and I was not the only one who found her difficult. She had some kind of breakdown and ended up in the mental hospital, where she was very badly treated and only just managed to talk her way out of electric-shock treatment. But with Hoppy back on the scene they became, as the *Daily Sketch* put it, 'The cream of London's hippie society, the brightest lights among the flower people'. The press love a couple – Richard and Liz, Paul and Jane – and now they found a way to pigeonhole Hoppy.

The marriage was at St Pancras register office on 14 June, but they had not posted the banns early enough and it had to be postponed for a day. The *Express* duly reported it, 'The barefoot bride wore a short gardenia-white dress and very little else. The groom, in a red felt hat, orange shirt and lavender velvet trousers, had a placard on his chest proclaiming "Who needs a husband?"' It was too late to cancel the champagne reception, so it went ahead as planned, with 200 guests at the Open Space Theatre in Tottenham Court Road, where UFO used to be. Suzy told the press, 'I want to have a child, man, and keep a goat and a cow and live in the country.' John Lennon sent a bouquet and they cut a cake made from unleavened bread, nuts and dates by Greg Sams at the macrobiotic restaurant.

Everyone flowed out into the street and sat on the pavement to chant a Buddhist wedding mantra. The *Daily Mail* delightedly reported, 'They were led by American Miss Francie Schwartz, 23, on mouth organ. She wore a black see-through dress and said, "I took off my bra in honour of Hoppy. I hadn't met him before today . . . it was a magical meeting."' Hoppy and Suzy then went to see *2001: A Space Odyssey*, but that night she was rushed to hospital with appendicitis, so the marriage was yet again postponed.

They finally made it legal on 28 June, back at St Pancras register office. I signed the register as best man and Hoppy snapped open his metal children's Dick Tracy lunch box to produce his cheque book to pay. A steel band was playing on the steps of the Town Hall, and so many people were dancing that the police were called, but this time they shook hands and smiled for the press.

IT, like many other organisations, went through convulsive changes, energised by the events of May, and the long-standing problem of the paper's nominally capitalist structure was finally resolved. In July *IT* became a workers' co-operative, with the original board of directors acting as a board of trustees. This meant that for the first time I was to be paid for my articles and the staff were responsible for their own wages. I thought it was a great thing.

In fact the underground had now spawned the first crop of hippie capitalists, and headshops and psychedelic poster stalls began to appear in street markets. Import record shops and hippie boutiques sprang up across the country, and the major record companies rushed to capitalise on the new progressive music by launching 'underground' labels. The notion of indie labels was not yet in place in Britain, but the new groups did not want to be openly associated with the corporate giants – the 'men in suits': hence the Stable Label, Dawn, Direction, Harvest, Fly, Deram, and so on. Unlike the USA, there was never any separation of underground music from any other. (In Britain it is all 'pop music' and always has been. The Sex Pistols were number one with 'God Save the Queen' and Laurie Anderson made number two with 'O Superman', alongside hits by Mr Blobby and singing football teams.) The acceptance of underground pop music was immediate, and the only way to prove yourself as an art band was to release albums only. It was this sensibility that caused Led Zeppelin and the Pink Floyd to refuse to release singles.

In any case, all this new product needed to be advertised and under the editorship of Peter Stansill, the paper grew in size to twenty-four pages, thanks to 40 per cent of the space being taken up by ads. Otherwise *IT* still contained the usual mix of mysticism and revolution, anarchism and eastern religions. As *IT* approached its second birthday it ran a three-part series on 'Love and Fornication' by Theodore Faithfull, Marianne's father, and in November published the first letter written from the viewpoint of what was to become the women's movement. There were articles on Black Power, the Mexican student riots, the bare-breasted cellist Charlotte Moorman, student riots in Zurich, philosophical musings on a workless society, the CIA role in the Greek military take-over, Herbert Marcuse and underground rock – none of which were likely to appear in the Fleet Street papers. We were often astonished by our readers. A paragraph in the 15 November 1968 issue appealing for old spectacles for the Albert Bailey Mission for poor people throughout the world resulted in 1,575 pairs being sent by readers. Mr Bailey wrote, 'Christ would not be a stranger among you.' Subsequent donations weighed in at over 100 cwt. The police were also avid fans. When a potter in deepest Devon put in a small ad for a pugmill (used to process clay), he found himself visited by two plainclothes men armed with a search warrant.

Krishna Consciousness

When *IT* moved around the corner from Betterton Street to 27 Endell Street, the Radha Krishna Temple took over the space, which was convenient for their run up and down Oxford Street each day, chanting and ringing their bells. I already knew several of the devotees because they contacted me, through Allen Ginsberg, when they first came to London from New York. I put them in touch with George Harrison. They were nice quiet Americans, very polite and charming as well as good businessmen, and they often came into Indica. In January 1969 there was a ceremony in the basement shrine room at Betterton Street to welcome their guru, Swami A. C. Bhaktivedanta, at which I was asked to say a few words. The programme included 'films of rare moments of spiritual ecstasy', sitar music and a 'love feast'. I sat crosslegged on the floor next to George Harrison as the food was handed round and a bowl was placed before the statue of Krishna. Everyone began to eat and I heard one of the devotees whisper, 'George is eating Krishna's food!' I looked round as Mukunda, one of the leaders, whispered loudly in the devotee's ear, 'Shaddup!'

Zapple

By October 1968 Indica was in deep trouble financially, caused mostly by shop-lifting on a tremendous scale. There had long been a tendency for people to arrange to meet their friends in the shop, browse through a few magazines, then depart, presumably to buy their books elsewhere. Even now I meet people who cheerfully tell me, 'Oh yes, I stole loads of books from Indica when I was a student. You had the best bookshop in town.' I tell them that the reason it went out of business was because of people like them, and what is more, it's still not too late to pay me for the ones they stole. Of course, these were nice middle-class students who would have paid had they not been 'liberating' the books from the evil capitalists: John, Peter and me.

Rather apprehensively I went to Cavendish Avenue to see Paul, needing to have a serious meeting with him if Indica was not to fold. Years before, Paul had told me never to be scared to come to him if I was ever in dire need. 'Years from now,' he said. 'Twenty years from now!' We took tea in his living room like two English gentlemen. I asked for £3,000, which he quickly agreed to as if it was a bit of an embarrassment, then just as quickly changed the subject. A few days before we had been talking again about a series of very cheap spoken-word albums, issued if possible like a magazine. He saw this as a way of involving Indica with Apple. I now had a list of people I wanted to record, nearly all of whom were in the USA and many of whom, I suspect, Paul had never heard of. His response, however, was enthusiastic. 'Great!' he said. 'Get it together! Get an assistant and go out there and record them. Done. Just like that!' He laughed. I laughed. Paul rarely used his great wealth in gestures like that and we both found it funny.

A beautiful girl looked in to see what the laughter was about, but Paul said we were talking business and she pulled a face and left. There were several semi-clad girls walking about the house. 'It's terrible,' he said, gesturing. 'The birds are always quarrelling about something. There's three living here at the moment.' The jostling for position must have been something to see. 'And there's another one, an American groupie, flying in this evening. I've thrown her out once, threw her suitcase over the wall, but it's no good, she keeps coming back.' He gave a resigned look and laughed. He was obviously very pleased about something. 'Come and hear this,' he said, and we went upstairs to the music room. He put on a white label acetate of 'Back in the USSR'. 'How do you think the cocky Americans will like that?' We both laughed. It was superb.

The spoken-word label was called Zapple, named by John Lennon, not in honour of Frank Zappa, who was annoyed at what he thought was the appropriation and cashing in on his name, but in the same spirit that the original name was chosen: 'A is for Apple. Z is for Zapple'. It was the other end of the alphabet. Zapple was essentially another attempt at the cheap monthly experimental album that Paul had tried to launch when he set up the demo studio in Ringo's Montagu Square flat back in the autumn of 1965. My original list included Allen Ginsberg, Lawrence Ferlinghetti, Michael McClure, Richard Brautigan, Charles Olson, Kenneth Patchen, Henry Miller, Charles Bukowski, William Burroughs, Simon Vinkenoog, Ed Sanders, Ken Kesey, Anaïs Nin, Aram Saroyan and Anne Waldman. I also included a note to investigate the possibility of reissuing both Lord Buckley and Lenny Bruce.

I had always been fond of the album I made with Ginsberg, Ferlinghetti, Corso and Voznesensky at the Architectural Association, and planned to record a series of poetry readings, each featuring five or six poets, at places such as the Poetry Project at St Mark's Church in New York, or City Lights Books in San Francisco; or the 'Liverpool Scene' poets: Adrian Henri, Brian Patten, Roger McGough. Paul wanted to issue BBC radio plays, such as their production of *Ubu cocu* by Alfred Jarry, and we talked about setting up a deal with the BBC for a separate series. We wanted to record happenings, concerts of experimental music, lectures – anything offbeat, avant-garde or strange which would make people think, which would crack the mould a little bit and let new ideas through. We were after anything stimulating or provoking. One evening Paul, Peter and others were discussing how most people had no idea what Fidel Castro or Mao Tse-tung really believed. They were just presented as the enemy and their ideas were distorted by the western press. Boxes of Beatles albums and Apple releases were mailed to Mao Tse-tung, Fidel Castro, Indira Gandhi and others, with invitations to record a spoken-word album for Zapple to explain their philosophy to a worldwide audience of Beatles fans and young people. None of them even replied.

We also wanted to release recordings of conversations: William Burroughs talking about the effects of different drugs; the Beatles discussing their latest album. Paul thought this was a particularly good idea because it would help to publicise their records. It was a breakthrough to realise that *anything* could be released as a record, including out-takes and rehearsals. It was an idea that was in the air, and in fact six months later *GWW: Great White Wonder* by Bob Dylan, the first rock bootleg, was released. Had the Beatles actually released albums of conversations, they would have prefigured by many years the idea of journalists releasing their interview tapes, which began with David Wigg's *The Beatles Tapes* in 1976.

And so I became the label manager for Zapple, the spoken-word and experimental end of Apple, and found myself spending more time than ever over at Apple's Savile Row headquarters, much of it hanging out in Derek Taylor's famous press office, waiting to attend meetings with Ron Kass, the head of the record division, to discuss contracts, or with Peter Asher to work out the budget, or with George, John and Ringo. There were so many examples of people working at cross-purposes at Apple that I wanted to make sure that each of the Beatles was fully aware of what I was doing so that they would not countermand anyone's instructions. George said it was John and Paul's thing, nothing to do with him. Ringo said, 'Just get on with it.' John and Yoko said they were fully behind the project, and when I was in the States they sent a cable with more names of poets to record, including Gregory Corso and Anne Waldman. I telephoned Allen Klein in New York, and he yelled, 'I expected you here last week. Everything's arranged! Where were you?' It seemed that nothing could go wrong.

Allen Ginsberg was the first name on my list of poets to record. There were plenty of young kids with posters of Allen on their wall, but not many had actually read his books and even fewer had heard him read. I saw this as a chance to get his poetry out to the wide audience of Beatles fans. All four Beatles liked the idea, but when I approached Allen, he suggested that rather than poetry, he would like to release a recording of his musical versions of William Blake's *Songs of Innocence and Experience*. Blake used to sing them in taverns, but if there ever was any musical notation it was lost long ago. Allen sent me a tape of some of the songs, recorded at a poetry reading, and I was impressed. I had expected them to have an interesting rhythm because Allen's years of public reading had given a heightened sense of phrasing, breath length and balance to his delivery. The surprise came in the melodies, which were sourced from the songs themselves. Allen had discovered hummable phrases, even 'hooks'.

My first recording trip was set for January 1969. My plan was to hire a portable Nagra tape machine in New York and record Ken Weaver there, before flying to Gloucester, Massachusetts, to record Charles Olson. In Los Angeles I planned to record Charles Bukowski at his home, and in San Francisco I booked a studio to record Lawrence Ferlinghetti, Michael McClure and Richard Brautigan. I intended to visit Allen Ginsberg and plan his album with him, but wanted to delay the studio sessions for a separate trip later in the year when I could devote all my time to arrangements, rehearsals, selecting musicians and mixing.

I felt I was coming home when I arrived at Ken and Betsy's apartment on East 9th Street in late January. I had fond memories of my visit with Nigel Samuel two years before, and Ken had recently

stayed with us at Lord North Street when the Fugs toured Europe in
September and October 1968. It was a memorable visit, enough for
the band to feature prominently in Jenny Fabian's *Groupie* as the
New York Sound & Touch. The Fugs were having some success
and Ken now dressed the part. His already massive frame was topped
by a large, very heavy, leather cowboy hat. He wore hand-tooled
cowboy boots with Cuban heels and carried a large polished wooden
walking cane, so thick it looked like a club. His beard was now
enormous and his hair sat in great waves on his shoulders. He was an
impressive sight. He wanted to see everything, particularly an
English pub. The nearest one to Lord North Street was on
Horseferry Road, popular with nurses from Westminster Hospital
and civil servants from the government offices that filled the area.
The main bar was enormous, with several dozen customers, but as
we entered, the room went quiet and someone gasped, 'Good God!'

But Ken was used to this, so he strode to the bar and barked,
'Gimme a beer!' The publican quickly pulled him a pint without the
usual rigmarole of asking which brand he required and, as he set it
down, conversation resumed once more. 'Kinda quiet in here, isn't
it?' Ken asked, more to the publican than to me. 'I always imagined
English pubs as being noisier than this.'

Ken was a brilliant raconteur and I wanted to record an album
with him of Texspeak: bar conversation and humour in a Texan
accent. I hired a portable tape recorder through the Capitol Records
office, and we recorded hours of tape at East 9th Street. Street noise
leaked onto the recording, but that didn't matter; in fact I should
have probably gone for more ambient sound. Though the album was
not released, much of the material appeared in written form in his
1984 book, *Texas Crude. The How-To on Talkin' Texan*, which was
illustrated by Robert Crumb.

The Big O

The Nagra tape machine was costing $200 a week to hire, but I could not raise Olson on the telephone. I sent cables, and finally Olson called in the middle of the night, waking everyone up. He was prepared to be recorded the next day. I flew to Boston with Betsy Klein, the Nagra and a travel bag filled with tape. No one would rent us a car because I was paying and Betsy was driving, so we took a cab to Gloucester, now best known as the setting of Sebastian Junger's *The Perfect Storm*. Olson was not in when we arrived, but a note was taped to the windowpane of the back door saying that he would be back soon. It was written on the back of a threatening letter about an unpaid hospital bill. It was very cold and the low white-painted clapboard buildings of Gloucester were almost invisible under deep snow. All sounds were muffled and peaceful, broken only by the occasional crunch of a passing truck over the snow. Charles soon arrived with a large paper sack of groceries and climbed slowly up the wooden steps to his first-floor flat. I didn't expect the recording to take more than a few days, so first we socialised.

I knew him from the time he had stayed with Panna Grady in London, so the recording schedule that he suggested came as no surprise to me. Charles normally got up at about 8 pm, ate breakfast and talked. At Panna's the guests had all gone home by 2 or 3 am, so Charles had the rest of the night to work. At Black Mountain College, where he was the rector, his classes sometimes began at midnight.

Charles lived in a railroad flat on Fort Square. Wooden outdoor stairs led into the kitchen where, propped against a huge refrigerator, Charles used to hold forth. Everything was in a muddle, with books, dishes, jars of spices and a large storage jar of dried peyote buttons cluttering the shelves. The window frames had pencilled on them registers of ships and cargoes, the names of long-forgotten ships' captains and customs duties paid – long lists, fading in the sun, obscured by a thin film of grime. The boats arrived at Gloucester harbour, visible over a few rooftops through the snow-flecked glass.

The living room was like a used book store, the bookcases full to overflowing, jammed with coffee-ringed first editions, magazines and journals piled on the floor to table height. One book I pulled from a shelf had a letter from Ezra Pound used as a bookmark, with several manuscript poems included.

The bedroom felt unused, with motes of sun-warmed dust falling through the musty air as we disturbed the books. It was the end of January so we couldn't ventilate the apartment without freezing. In the warm rooms it was strange to feel the frozen window panes. I searched for the right place to record. In the silence of the snow, our voices were clear, even though all the books tended to absorb some of the edge. On our first night we did nothing but talk over a delivered Chinese take-away. There was so much to say. Charles ranked along with Oscar Wilde as a conversationalist, his talk ranging from geological time to the importance of a sense of place, the trade between England and New England in the eighteenth century, and gossip about Allen Ginsberg, Tim Leary and other mutual friends. He discussed Truman and Melville, the Fugs, Janis Joplin – whom he loved – and *Origin* magazine.

We eventually set up the Nagra in Charles' bedroom. He sat in a chair that creaked alarmingly if he leaned forward. The room was dominated by a long trestle table covered two deep in books, arranged spine up, mostly on maritime history. The table sagged under the weight, so I put the tape recorder on the floor and positioned the microphone among the books, as close to Charles as I dared. Not too close, because Charles gesticulated while reading and would have knocked it. I sat on the floor with my headphones and followed the text.

The first thing Charles found was that his speaking voice was not at all how he expected it to sound. To him it was terribly dry and boring. The room's acoustics did make it drier than usual, but I explained that we could fix this to a certain extent in the mixing. We did a lot of takes that first day, and Charles listened carefully to each one, head cocked to one side, attentive. We marked up the text with the musical notation indicating 'speed up' or 'slow down', used in this case to indicate volume, and underlined words for greater emphasis. I conducted him by waving my arms about and pursing my lips to get him to give certain words more stress or to raise his voice. After a night's work, he got the hang of it and we knew how to do it. He insisted, however, that we erase the tapes, which I did. Sometimes he would catch himself sounding boring and laugh out loud. I left one such occasion on the record I finally produced from the sessions, at the beginning of 'I Am the Gold Machine'. Mostly we recorded material taken from his new book *Maximus IV, V, VI*, which, fortunately, I had brought with me. He had not yet received his copies from Cape Goliard in London because of a British postal strike. At my request we also taped some sections from *Mayan Letters*, one of my favourite books.

The following two nights we sailed through everything I was hoping to record, getting most things in one or two takes, all except 'I Am the Gold Machine', which for some reason took a dozen or so attempts. Charles did not seem to mind our intrusion on his privacy; in fact he appeared to welcome it. The whole time we were there he received only one telephone call, from his daughter. He said he was worried that he would not be able to leave her anything and was shocked when I suggested that the Ezra Pound letters and first editions were worth a tidy sum.

He was not in good health. He lived alone, and because many people regarded him as unapproachable, he was often lonely. He said that his output had halved when his wife died twelve years before. We talked about his maritime charts, and he spoke at length about a huge chart of Gloucester harbour pinned to the wall behind him, which he had annotated extensively. He sat on the bed, and became obviously irritated that I could not understand what he was referring to. When he turned to indicate what he meant, he realised the chart was almost blank. The sun had bleached it away, and now it was a large, yellowing sheet of dust-marked, fly-spotted parchment, attached to the wall by only three corners. This jolted him and he made a joke, but I could see that deep down he knew he was dying.

The recordings were a success. They sounded as I had wanted them to, as if Charles had simply read them off with no preparation, in spontaneous performance. We left after four days and he gave me a copy of the *hors commerce* edition of *Human Universe* as a commemorative gift, with his annotations on some of the essays. I was very touched. Charles died a year later.

Cherry Valley

Next I went to Allen Ginsberg's farm in upstate New York, about eighty miles from Albany, to discuss the project. I took the 6 am Greyhound from the Port Authority to Cherry Valley and Peter Orlovsky met me many hours later at Crane's Drugstore, where we had a malted milk before he drove me to the farm in his '56 Chevrolet. Though this part of the state was very poor, it was like walking into a *Saturday Evening Post* cover, with white picket fences and wooden clapboard houses, all covered in deep snow. Allen had 100 acres of meadowland surrounded by state forest. The farmhouse was in the middle of the land, a two-storey house with four bedrooms upstairs and a room for Peter and his new girlfriend, Denise, in a separate wing off the kitchen. A traditional red-and-white barn stood next door, where the horse and milk cow lived. There was no electricity, but the telephone company had been compelled by law to install a line, albeit a party line. Allen bought the place to get Peter out of the city and away from his amphetamine dealers, and also entertained hopes that Kerouac might move there to dry out, but Kerouac would never leave his mother.

Allen was on crutches, the result of a car crash in early December which had hospitalised him with a fractured hip and four broken ribs, but he still managed to show me around. Peter and Gordon Ball, the farm manager, had winterised the bedrooms by installing wooden tongue-and-groove panelling in each one, but with no heating system the rooms were still bitterly cold. Luckily the Aladdin oil lamps gave out a lot of heat as well as light. Allen's room could have belonged to Walt Whitman, whose portrait was framed on the wall; there were oil lamps on his desk, a coat rack behind the door, a big seven-drawer chest, a wooden-framed bed set off the floor, boxes underneath filled with underground papers, lots of shoes and dead flies on the floor.

When it was quiet, the seventy-times-an-hour click in the pipes could be heard as the gravity pump shot water by the cupful up the hill to the tank buried above the house, using no gas, electricity or windmill, just the weight of the water in the spring itself. Allen was

254

immensely proud of this and it was one of the first things visitors were taken to admire.

The living room had a big, comfortable busted old settee and rugs from barn sales. By the window hung a Tibetan *thangka*, brought back from India by Allen in 1963, the only one not stolen by junkies. There was an out-of-tune upright piano and an old-fashioned wooden pump organ, used by Allen in the composition of his music. Lee Crabtree from the Fugs had taught Allen the basics of musical notation and a series of basic chords. All through the afternoon and evening Allen sent halting, windy notes whistling into the run-down old room to accompany his deep basso voice. As evening fell, the oil lamp was lit and a solitary moth circled its glass shaft. After a break for dinner we continued, the tootling, wheezing organ perfect for Allen's hesitant playing. Peter Orlovsky sang duet on some songs in an enthusiastic, wildly out-of-tune screech. It grew late and Julius, Peter's silent, catatonic brother, came in from the kitchen and arranged his work boots neatly side by side next to the settee before retiring up the creaking stairs to bed. I loved what Allen had created and relished the thought of working on it, but I could foresee endless problems.

Hollywood

I landed in Los Angeles just after the Capitol Tower had closed for the weekend. I had made no plans, so no one was expecting me and I had no accommodation arranged. I telephoned the local underground newspaper, *Open City*, and said I was from *IT*. 'Come on over,' they said. The paper was located in a low industrial building on Melrose, like a converted automobile body-shop, and had a huge psychedelic mural covering the whole of one wall. There was something strangely unconvincing about the painting: it was too crude, too exaggerated. John Bryan, the editor, noticed my puzzlement and explained. In one of those situations that can only happen in Hollywood, the building had been used as the set for an underground newspaper in a cheap exploitation movie about hippies. Then, in a classic reversal, a real underground newspaper had moved into the space.

The staff there were very friendly. I was immediately offered a bed and every kind of hospitality. California seemed very foreign to me compared with New York, which had a familiar European feel to it. I loved the climate, the palm trees, the laid-back way they did things. It all seemed magical. It struck me that in Los Angeles people think of space in terms of time, of time in terms of routes and of automobiles as natural and essential extensions of themselves. One girl at *Open City* said, 'I don't want to be bumped in the night', relating directly to her car. Few of my friends in London had vehicles; they were too expensive. I was particularly impressed by the sunsets, and the fact that Los Angeles has no weather. I wrote about it all enthusiastically in my column in *IT* and was delighted, and flattered, to find that Reyner Banham later used several of my comments as epigrams in his wonderful book *Los Angeles, the Architecture of Four Ecologies*.

The Capitol Tower, at Hollywood and Vine, looked like a stack of singles: at any moment you expected the bottom floor to be whisked away and all the floors to slide down one storey. I was particularly struck by the sign in their parking lot: 'Caution: Severe Tire Damage!', which pertained if you drove in the wrong direction over a set of vicious-looking spikes at the entrance. Apple rented offices there and I was the first person from London to visit them. They were desperate for information, but I could not answer most of their questions. I was given a huge office and two female secretaries but, aside from booking studios and hiring a tape recorder for me to record Charles Bukowski, there was nothing for them to do. As I had a few days before I went to San Francisco I asked them to show me the sights.

I was taken for taquitos on Alvira Street – the reconstruction, probably in the wrong place, of the original pueblo of Los Angeles. I saw the bubbling La Brea Tar Pits and the LA County Museum. We went to the beach at Santa Monica Palisades, where I was impressed by the amount of equipment that my assistants deemed necessary, including a portable hi-fi with separate speakers for full stereo and a cold box for drinks. The Beatles had placed an ad in the newspapers asking for tapes and there were hundreds waiting in the office for someone to play them. One was from the country-rock band Poco, then still called Pogo. I liked it and went to see them play on the Strip. They were great and I forwarded their tape to Peter Asher in London recommending that he hear them. They eventually signed with Epic. In the evenings we went to clubs where, being from Apple, we were given the best seats and the owners came to schmooze and ask about 'the boys' and give us drinks on the house.

The person I was particularly pleased to meet was Eve Babitz, who starred in the famous photograph of Marcel Duchamp playing chess with a naked girl. She was making collages, some of which were used for sleeves by Warner Brothers Records. She said the reason her breasts were so large in the photograph was that she had just gone on the pill when the picture was taken and it had made them swell right up.

The Zapple label was launched on 3 February 1969, shortly after I arrived in California. Apple's West Coast publicity agency, Jim Mahoney & Association, sent out a press release, presumably written by Derek Taylor. It was strange to see the outcome of all the stoned conversations about experimental audio-magazines turned into an American business press release:

> Beatles to introduce Zapple, new label and recording concept.
>
> On May 1, just two weeks short of the first anniversary of the formation of Apple Corps Ltd. and its Apple Records division, the Beatles company will introduce a new label and recording concept.
>
> The label will be called Zapple and it will emphasise a series of 'spoken word' albums and some music releases of a more wide-ranging and esoteric nature. Price of the Zapple albums will generally be $1.98 or $4.98 depending on the type of release.
>
> Zapple will be a division of Apple Records, which is headed by Ron Kass, who is also chief executive for all Apple music activities. Supervising the Zapple program will be Barry Miles, a British writer-intellectual in his late 20s.
>
> The first three releases on the Zapple label are now being pressed and include:

1. A new John Lennon–Yoko Ono album entitled *Unfinished Music No. 2 – Life With The Lions*;
2. A George Harrison composed-produced electronic music album which was recorded with a Moog;
3. A spoken-word album recorded by poet-writer Richard Brautigan.

Other well-known writer-poets already committed to Zapple releases include: Lawrence Ferlinghetti – America's best selling 'serious' poet; poet-playwright Michael McClure; veteran literary figures Kenneth Patchen and Charles Olson and poet-essayist Allen Ginsberg. Additionally, Zapple will release one of the late Lenny Bruce's last concerts as an album.

It is the hope of Apple Corps Ltd. that the new label will help pioneer a new area for the recording industry equivalent to what the paperback revolution did to book publishing.

The company is now studying new market ideas for the label, which it hopes to eventually retail in outlets where paperback books and magazines are sold, University and College outlets will also be emphasised in Zapple's distribution plans.

Discussions are now in progress with several world figures as well as leaders in the various arts and sciences to record their works and thoughts for the label. The Beatles plan to tape several discussion sessions amongst themselves as an album release – probably for the fall. It is assumed that Zapple will have little difficulty attracting those people who might not normally record albums because of the general educational tone of the project . . .

Buk

I had been an admirer of Charles Bukowski's work since 1965 and with Zapple I finally had a chance to record him. I pulled up at 5125 1/2 De Longpre Avenue in a slummy part of East Hollywood in a rented green Mustang driven by number-one secretary, Pat Slattery.

The street looked shabby, but not dangerous. Slums in Los Angeles are not like those of other cities. During the Watts riots a few years before, the foreign press had driven straight through Watts looking for the slum because, to European eyes, these were reasonable houses: everyone seemed to have a large car and a television, it was sunny and there were palm trees lining the streets. It was not the South Bronx, it was only a slum in contrast to the aspirations proffered by television.

De Longpre was a silent, empty street made from large uneven blocks of concrete, lined with scruffy palm trees and a web of utility cables. The single-storey wooden-framed houses had peeling paint and there were holes in the screen doors. Bits of cars lay in front yards and rubbish blew about. Buk's house had a hedge to one side and a '57 Plymouth on the ruins of his front lawn. Beer cans overflowed the garbage bin.

Buk stood filling the doorway, a large man with thin hair, a grey face, ravaged and pock-marked from severe acne in childhood, and colourless lips which broke into an expressive smile. He was vital, friendly, humorous; he seemed to burn with life. The screen door opened straight into his living room. The shades were drawn. Rickety shelves were overloaded with books, magazines, old newspapers and racing forms. The settee had a hole where the stuffing was bursting out. There was a pile of car tyres in the corner and many empty beer cans, and in another corner was Buk's desk. Here was his typewriter: a pre-war, battered, sit-up-and-beg, cast-iron Remington; dusty but for the carriage and keys, it was surrounded by cigar butts and ash, crumpled paper, extinct beer cans. Hundreds – perhaps thousands – of poems had emerged from that old machine; countless stories, columns for *Open City*, which had been running his 'Notes of a Dirty Old Man' column since May, and letters to every little mimeographed poetry-magazine editor who contacted him, from Germany to Japan, Midwest farmboys to slick New Yorkers – hundreds and hundreds of them.

Immediately after finding seats for us he was off, slipping like a shadow through the door, across the porch and away. Soon he returned with another six-pack, a smile on his face, a bottle of Miller Lite in his hand. He rummaged in the messy kitchen until he found a glass for Pat, whom he seemed particularly pleased to meet, then

259

settled down to talk. He described the race-track and told us of his admiration for his publisher John Martin, he spoke about little poetry magazines and his worries and fears in trying to make it as a professional poet. He was still working for the Post Office. Essex House, the pornographic book publishers, had just released a collection of his pieces from *Open City*, called *Notes of a Dirty Old Man*, as a mass-market paperback (or as mass market as a company that published books with titles like *Thongs* was likely to get) and Buk was encouraged by this latest development.

We talked about the record. He was casual, relaxed and said that he had made a lot of home recordings before: 'Sure, just show me how the machine works and come back in a few days. I'll just curl up on the rug with some packs of beer, my books, turn on the machine and . . .' I wired up an Ampex 3000, arranged a microphone stand and microphone, headphones and a dozen reels of blank tape. He refused to allow me, or anyone else, to be present to supervise the recording, claiming to be too shy. He had not yet done any public readings.

San Francisco

Once I had set Bukowski up with a home studio, I took off for San Francisco. It felt familiar and European. There were shops on the streets and sidewalks filled with people, as well as buses and, of course, the famous trolleycars. I headed first of all to Richard Brautigan's apartment at 2546 Geary. Richard was tall and gangling, and affected the image of an old prospector or western pioneer, with a huge moustache and long hair past his shoulders, tight pants and cowboy boots. Allen Ginsberg had always dismissed his work as shallow and contrived and used to call him 'Bunthorne' behind his back – a reference to Reginald Bunthorne, the aesthete in Gilbert and Sullivan's *Patience*. It was an obvious bachelor pad, scruffy but pleasant, with Communication Company handbills, and posters for concerts and poetry readings, most of them featuring him, tacked on the walls. His big high-ceilinged kitchen served as the living room and we sat around the table and discussed mutual friends and the London scene. Richard had a close male chum, his 'best buddy', Keith Abbott, who seemed to be his constant companion: Abbott, as he was known, made continual runs to the fridge for beer. Richard's girlfriend, Valerie, was also there, but Richard was intent on annoying her and came out with such lines as 'I don't want my daughter to be educated. I think women should just be decorative.' Valerie raised her eyes and said, 'Oh, Richard, don't start all that again.' The trouble was, Brautigan really did think women should be subservient to men.

At Richard's suggestion I hired Valerie as my assistant, and it also seemed practical to move into her apartment on Kearny, near Coit Tower, and pay rent to her rather than check into a hotel. I slept on a couch next to the front window in the living room, surrounded by brightly coloured objects brought back from her South American travels. I visited Lawrence Ferlinghetti at his office in City Lights Books, and met Michael McClure. I booked studio time at Golden State Recorders on Harrison Street, intending to juggle the times and dates among the three poets, depending on how well each of the recordings went.

I had already planned the structure for Richard's album so we worked on his first. I wanted to capture the whimsical, almost precious, innocence of Richard's work, and create an accessible public surface to the record, to draw people in and make them listen. To do this we recorded, in stereo, the actual stream that featured in *Trout Fishing in America* and overdubbed a ringing telephone. We set up microphones in Richard's kitchen, bought a pile of six-packs and taped hours of conversation between Richard and Abbott, and of Richard talking on the telephone, to use as fillers between tracks. For one very short poem, we got in dozens of Richard's friends to read the poem, repeating it over and over on the record in their different voices and intonations. Richard even got Herb Caen, the *San Francisco Chronicle* columnist who coined the term 'beatnik', to deliver the poem in his hard staccato Chicago accent. Richard enjoyed recording and I enjoyed his company, but the friendship was not to last.

Michael McClure

Michael McClure was the Prince of the San Francisco poetry scene: he was a friend of Bob Dylan and of Jim Morrison; he had written 'Oh Lord, Won't You Buy Me a Mercedes Benz' for Janis Joplin, and was known as much for his plays as his poetry. He was acutely self-conscious, very aware of his classic profile, and very self-absorbed. I wanted to record him after hearing a tape of his 'Lion Poem', where he roared at the lions in the San Francisco Zoo, and they roared back. It was a very powerful recording and I wanted to use it on the album. One of the first things we did was transfer it to 15 ips tape and remaster it. Unfortunately Michael decided that he wanted Freewheelin' Frank from the Hell's Angels to appear on the record, which was to consist of himself playing an autoharp given to him by Bob Dylan, and Frank banging a tambourine and reading his satanic poetry. Frank insisted on having his chopper with him in the studio, which caused one or two delays in the recording. With studio time at three dollars a minute, I eventually took Michael for a walk around the block, and explained that his plans for the album were just not clear enough and we were wasting time and money. 'That's the first time I've actually heard what someone has said to me in a very long time,' said Michael. I liked Frank, but he couldn't sing and he couldn't play the tambourine. He gave me a signed copy of one of his psychedelically embellished satanic poems. I repositioned Michael's album to be the last, to give us time to decide exactly what was going on it, and moved on to Lawrence Ferlinghetti instead.

In many ways Lawrence's work was designed more for reading aloud than for the page, so this was a good opportunity for him to get out his recent work. In the Fifties he had pioneered poetry with jazz, and he was very aware of the problems of recording and live performance. Working with him was easy and we soon had an album's worth of tape, including one long track with a classical musician backing him.

Golden State had other acts booked in, which gave me some free time, which I used to get Valerie to show me around the Bay Area. We hired a shiny green Mustang, a car that Americans thought of as tacky, but which was regarded as the height of cool in London. As we pulled out of the Hertz lot, I felt a wonderful sense of freedom. We could go anywhere! Radio on, surging over the hills of San Francisco. We climbed Mt Tamalpais and walked on Stinson Beach in the rain, we explored Muir Woods and found a waterfront bar in Sausalito. Inevitably we began an affair.

To avoid being seen together by Richard, other than on business, we spent many of the nights in LA commuting by air between San Francisco and Los Angeles. It was fortunate that I had recorded Richard's album first because it was already at mixing stage by the time he found out what had happened. The affair strained relations between us so much that his final approval of the mix came via his lawyer.

It had been nine days since I left Bukowski with a room full of recording equipment, so Valerie and I went over to see how he was doing. Buk was there, a bit hung over, and so was a woman: middle-aged, wearing black fishnet stockings and a black slip. She disappeared into the bedroom without speaking, emerging some time later ready to leave, looking tired and worn. Buk crushed some notes into her hand. 'Car fare,' he said, as much to me as to her. Nothing in the room had changed. The Ampex was where I had left it, but it was done; every reel was filled with Buk's careful selection from his writing: six hours of his favourite pieces. He said to be sure to listen to the one called 'The Firestation' as he liked that best of all. Unfortunately he had attempted to record 'on the other side' of the tape as well, and had wiped a few things before he realised what was happening. Then we had a few drinks. He told us a long story about his '57 Plymouth and about his crazy landlord, flirted with Valerie, and eventually we got everything packed up and he helped carry it out to the car.

Valerie took me to visit her friend Steven Schneck whose novel, *The Nightclerk*, I had always admired. His lawn was set back from the road on a steep hillside and was covered with the Sunday editions of the *LA Times*, great round bundles in various stages of decay, left where the newspaper boy threw them. After a year or two they turned into brown heaps, like fallen monoliths, but the decay was only skin-deep, for the pages were intact quite near the surface. I asked him why he liked living in LA. 'It's like living nowhere,' he said. We discussed the idea of a sense of place, and both of us agreed that this is something LA is severely lacking.

We visited the offices of *Open City*, where I'd first gone on arriving in Los Angeles, and John Bryan and his wife took us to dinner at El Coyote on Fairfax. John asked us how long we had been married and was embarrassed when we revealed that we had only really been close for two days. His question came as a shock because it suggested that maybe this should be something more than a two-week affair, ending with me returning to Sue and Valerie going back to Richard.

After dinner we went with John and his wife to the Whisky-a-Go-Go because I wanted to check out Alice Cooper, who had not yet recorded, but had been recommended to me by Frank Zappa who was considering signing him for his new record label, Straight. There had been a lot of fuss the previous week because Alice had bitten off the head of a chicken onstage, or so it was claimed, but the act that night was uncontroversial. Being from Apple Records got us all in and free drinks all evening. It was pouring with rain, and in the Whisky parking lot John demonstrated the LA parking tradition of pushing other cars aside with your own to make enough space to park. He was not the only one doing it and cars were rolling in all directions, headlights cutting through the rain and mist creating stark black-and-white images, like the *cinéma noir* lighting of the old Warner Brothers movies that were made not far from there.

Phil Ochs

Late the next morning we drove up into the Hollywood Hills to 8575 Franklin Avenue for lunch with Phil Ochs. I knew Ochs from London, where he'd shown up out of the blue at Lord North Street. When Dylan went electric, it was his friend Phil who took over as the leading male singer of the protest movement. Their arguments and subsequent split are part of Greenwich Village folk-music legend. The morning sun was brilliant and the rain had cleared away the smog. We climbed the final forty-degree slope and killed the engine. The view from the top was spectacular, with the city ending in the wide curve of the ocean at Santa Monica. It was silent. The first occupant of the premises that we saw was a monkey, running round the high perimeter fence, but soon Andy Wickham appeared and we began talking. Andy was a skinny, freckle-faced Englishman with a mop-top haircut, who looked as if he should be part of an English invasion duo, like Chad and Jeremy or Peter and Gordon. He worked for Warner Brothers where he had just produced an album with Fats Domino and was very excited about the work he was doing with Van Dyke Parks. Andy ushered us into a huge living room with a view out over the city.

Phil Ochs was there, seated at his grand piano, which had a candelabrum on top, like Liberace's. He wore glasses and a little peaked cap that reminded me of a Cotswold farmer. He was one of the most open, honest, friendly and socially responsible people I ever met in the music business, but I was surprised by his attitude towards women, which was quite Neanderthal. Just like Richard Brautigan, he and Andy held incredibly reactionary women-belong-in-the-kitchen-and-bedroom views. It seemed strangely out of sync with Phil's otherwise progressive opinions. The women's movement was just emerging – *IT* was just starting to run articles on the New York end of the movement, and debate in the letters column was beginning, but there was not much intellectual discussion to work with yet; Germaine Greer's *The Female Eunuch* and Kate Millet's *Sexual Politics* were a year away from publication, but it was obvious that this relegation of women to second-class citizenship was wrong. It was the subject of heated discussions, particularly in the next few years. After Phil and I agreed to fundamentally disagree, we talked a lot about the Vietnam War and police violence and what could be done to stop both. He and Andy were like army buddies, like Kerouac and Cassady, closer to each other than to any women friends, mystified and threatened by the new world around them that Phil, at least, had helped to create.

We drank wine from huge, heavy cut-glass goblets and he showed me a photograph of the gold lamé suit he had commissioned from Nudie, similar to the one he made for Elvis. Phil had recently seen Elvis play Vegas and was filled with admiration, hence the gold suit, which he intended to wear on the sleeve of his next album, *Phil Ochs' Greatest Hits*, even though he had never had a hit. I suggested that his folk followers might not get the humour in the sleeve, but he just laughed.

Big Sur

Valerie and I drove back to San Francisco up the Pacific Coast Highway, stopping off to see Larry Lewis, my old friend from art-college days, *en route*. Larry and his girlfriend, Sheila Silverman, lived deep in the redwoods outside Santa Cruz, and took some finding even though I had a map drawn by Larry. He had spent more time embellishing it with extraordinary birds and flowers than marking all the relevant turns and intersections. But we got there. Larry had become very pure in his asceticism. He was now a vegetarian and ate only raw vegetables, most of them weeds that I had no idea were edible. Thus when he announced lunch, he walked through the trees to the small plot of land he cultivated, randomly grabbing a handful of leaves from here and there until his salad bowl was full. There was no dressing, but he added a generous dollop of brewer's yeast to the top to make the whole thing even more unappealing. There was no prospect of a drink. Even a cup of coffee was out of the question. Larry allowed himself one cup of warm – not hot – herbal tea every week or so, but even that was seen as tempting fate: 'Warm drinks send me off into head trips,' he explained. The top of Larry's head had gone orange. This was from his massive consumption of carrot juice. He had invested in a three-quarter horse-power industrial carrot juicer, of which he was inordinately proud, though it seemed to me that too much carrot juice was probably bad for you. He and Sheila had a baby girl. Sheila was still breastfeeding and her T-shirt had great wet patches on the front from her leaking breasts. She was the original Jewish earth mother, warm, generous, loud and all-embracing. The child crawled naked in the yard. When it shit, their German shepherd rushed up and ate the faeces. It was presumably the only protein it got, since there was no likelihood of Larry buying canned dog food.

The Coach

I took Valerie with me to visit Timothy Leary in Berkeley. I had received a letter from Tim giving me his daughter's telephone number and instructions that someone would collect me after I had telephoned her and been given Tim's secret number. I called a week or so after arriving in San Francisco and was given his address. The subterfuge had been in case someone else saw the letter. On the way we saw Angela Davis' car on the Oakland Bridge being openly followed by two carloads of FBI men, so maybe Tim's paranoia was justified.

Tim lived, in some splendour, in Queens Road, Berkeley. The doors were open, so we wandered in and found him in an ante-room. As usual, he had loads of friends visiting, meeting, discussing projects and plans, both with Tim and with each other. I had a long talk with Max Scherr, owner editor of the *Berkeley Barb*, whom I liked very much. He used a lot of my stuff from *International Times* in his paper. Ralph Metzger was there too, tall, thin, nervous and detached. He looked like a myopic scientist who had wandered into the wrong room at a hotel and joined the wrong party. He and Leary had worked together for many years. Eugene Schoenfeld was there, filled with the joys of sexual liberation, puffing his rosy cheeks out like a chipmunk. He told me he had just recorded his latest radio programme while taking a bath with his two secretaries. He must have had a large bath. He wrote a sex advice column under the name of Dr Hippocrates, which dozens of underground papers syndicated; he asked me why *IT* didn't run it. I told him it was because *OZ* took it and we had the same readers, but he complained that *OZ* didn't always run it. It was something we never resolved. He was very taken with Valerie, saying how he would love to hire her as one of his secretaries, and tried hard to get her to stay on when it was time to leave.

The house was decorated with expensive Tibetan *thangkas*, mandalas and eastern religious objects. Strong incense burned in a large burner on the coffee table. One whole side of the living room was a glass wall, with a door leading to a deck with a fantastic view out over the Bay to San Francisco. The house was on a steep incline, so the hillside fell away dramatically below us. Rosemary Leary was playing the perfect hostess, bringing round tray after tray of canapés, but I confess I was careful to eat only things that I thought would not have been spiked.

Tim took me to his bedroom for a talk, and gave me a copy of *The Beatles Book*, an anthology of essays, one of which was by him. It was typically hyperbolic; Tim was never one for half-measures: 'This essay is a logical exercise designed to prove that the Beatles are Divine Messiahs. The wisest, holiest, most effective avatars (Divine Incarnate, God Agents) that the human race has yet produced . . .' He believed that they were prototype mutants of a new enlightened human type. We tossed the idea around for a bit, and from his viewpoint I could see that he was right, though from mine he wasn't.

He told me again about his six PhDs and his six wives, then he told me the story of Mary Meyer, the wealthy aristocratic mistress of President Jack Kennedy, who came to Tim when he was still at Harvard to learn how to give LSD sessions. She was the estranged wife of Cord Meyer, a top CIA policy-maker, and told Leary about the CIA's experiments with drugs. He said that he took a number of trips with her and supplied her with acid, which she told him she would use to turn on the President. One year after Kennedy's assassination she was murdered on a towpath in Georgetown, in what looked suspiciously like a professional hit. James Angleton, the CIA's counter-intelligence chief, took charge of her diaries and personal papers after her death and revealed that he had destroyed some of them. He also revealed that her bedroom had been bugged and her telephone tapped. The murder was never solved. Tim thought the CIA did not want the President fooling with LSD in case he was on a trip when the Russians attacked, but of course by the time Meyer was killed, JFK was already dead. It occurred to me that Tim's involvement with Mary Meyer might well have been the root cause of many of his later legal problems.

Meanwhile, Back in Blighty

It was raining when I landed at Heathrow and there wasn't enough daylight. I was given a small room next to Peter's at the Apple offices on Savile Row and there I completed the mix of the Brautigan and Ferlinghetti albums, which were to be released as Zapple 3 and 4. John and Yoko's *Life With The Lions* and an album of George Harrison learning to play the Moog Synthesiser were already out. *Listening to Richard Brautigan* reached test-pressing stage. The cover featured two photographs, one of Richard holding a telephone, and another of Valerie answering it. Most of Richard's books had front-cover photographs of him with his latest girlfriend. For this album there were two separate photographs. I began to edit the Charles Bukowski album on a Revox tape machine at Apple, but did not get very far. George Harrison invited some Hell's Angels to visit from California and Ken Kesey arrived with them. Kesey borrowed my Revox without asking and I never saw it again. At least the master tapes had been locked safely in Peter's office. Not having a machine of my own made editing very difficult, so I postponed the Bukowski until after my next recording trip.

That March, George Harrison was busted by the notorious Sgt Pilcher, who vindictively chose Paul McCartney's wedding day to raid Kinfauns, making George and Patti late for the reception. Pilcher 'found' a block of hash on the floor, causing George to comment, memorably, 'I'm a tidy person, I keep my socks in the sock drawer, and my hash in my hash box. It's not mine.' George telephoned Caroline Coon at Release, the twenty-four-hour emergency service to call if you were busted for drugs, and they fixed him up with a lawyer specialising in such matters. Set up in 1967 by Caroline and Rufus Harris, Release was probably the most important of all the underground organisations. Caroline had been filled with indignation at the treatment her Jamaican boyfriend received at the hands of the police when he was busted for pot, and her involvement in his case led her to form a charity to help defend everyone who found themselves in similar circumstances. Release eventually handled one-third of all drugs cases in Britain, a tremendous workload involving dozens of lawyers and daily court appearances.

The outcome of George's case was successful, so Caroline asked Derek Taylor at Apple if it would be all right to write to George through him, explaining Release's needs and submitting a formal application for funds. She was given an appointment to see George, and Derek brought her up to George's office, where Peter Asher and I were also present to give support. It was a friendly meeting, ending with George opening his desk drawer and producing his cheque book. He handed a cheque to Caroline, who dared not look at it until after I had taken her downstairs to the front door. She was expecting something like £50 and was 'gobsmacked' to see it was for £5,000, enough to enable Release to move from its cramped office in Princedale Road to a larger one in the next-door building, which they bought. A photocopy of George's cheque was displayed on the wall of the office for all the years Caroline worked there. I was very pleased to see the Beatles move closer to the underground scene by offering such practical support.

Hotel Chelsea

Ken Weaver moved to Arizona, so when I arrived in New York that June I checked into the Hotel Chelsea. 'This is obviously where you belong!' Allen Ginsberg told me, as he chatted amiably with the owner, Stanley Bard, and insisted on coming with me to room 420 to make sure it was not too ratty. I knew the moment I entered the lobby that I wanted to live there: paintings by Larry Rivers, Christo, Karel Appel – all previous residents – filled every inch of wall space and while we were waiting for Bard to appear, Allen ran into Arthur Miller, an old friend of his who had first moved to the hotel when he broke up with Marilyn Monroe. The Chelsea was to become my home away from home for the next three years. Sarah Bernhardt, Thomas Wolfe and Dylan Thomas had all lived at the Chelsea and the composer Virgil Thomson, couturier Charles James, writer Arthur C. Clarke, actress Viva, songwriter Leonard Cohen and singer Janis Joplin still did. This was where Dylan wrote 'Sad Eyed Lady of the Lowlands', and where Burroughs stayed in 1964. Warhol made *Chelsea Girls* there. I had not really put together all the references before, but I should have known, the place was a legend.

Allen took me to visit his old friend Harry Smith who lived there. He had described Harry to me as a 'magician-artist', but he was much more than that. Harry was a skinny gnomic fellow, about Allen's age, with a straggly untrimmed beard and long tangled hair pulled up into a bun at the back. He had a hunched back, probably caused by years of bad posture rather than a disability. He fixed you with his eye and cocked his head like a parrot, but the gaze was fierce, not funny, and his smile was a grimace.

Harry showed us his portfolios of artwork, beautiful Egyptian glyphs painted in a technically complex rainbow of colours on cards that could be arranged in different orders to make larger designs. He had cards with black-and-white designs, each complete in themselves, but which also joined together to make larger shapes, no matter in which order they were arranged. He explained that these linear arrangements came from his interest in Eskimo string figures, or cat's cradles. He had cardboard shoe boxes of index cards showing the progression of most of the main string figures, notated using a system of his own invention. He explained how each string figure told a story and then demonstrated: 'See, here's the whale . . .' and with a few twists of his fingers we could see a whale shape move across the web of string. 'Here comes the hunter . . . Here he is raising his spear . . . and this is the kill.' Harry moved his fingers and thumbs to make the string picture change, his eyebrows arched, his eyes bulging. 'Now the hunters are going to cut up the whale . . .' He said that he had to practise every day in order not to forget the moves.

Crammed into Harry's dusty room were the products of years of anthropological studies: entire collections of objects. Each year at Easter he bought all the hand-painted Ukrainian Easter eggs that he could afford. There was a shop on East 7th Street, across from the First Ukrainian Church of God, that sold them. He compared each year's output and could identify the work of a number of these anonymous artists. He explained the stylised patterns to me: 'See, here is the forest, and this is a wolf . . .' and a simple row of triangles became a row of pine trees. He had assembled a collection of traditional Native American dresses, each garment neatly preserved in a plastic wrap, which so completely filled his wardrobe that the doors could not close. This was the most complete collection in existence of Native Seminole patchwork – so he claimed – with an example of every traditional pattern. Harry knew the symbolism of each. His chest of drawers was filled with Native beadwork. Harry's own clothes were dirty and worn and thrown in the corner of the room.

For a time he collected the paper aeroplanes made by the children of different New York public schools, comparing the system of folds and noting the racial backgrounds of the children who made them, but he was eventually driven away by the school guards who thought he was a pervert.

Industrial metal shelving held his collection of rare anthropology books and tapes. In the early Fifties he had assembled the legendary *Anthology of American Folk Music*, a set of three double albums with extensive scholarly sleeve notes by Harry, including a summary of the plot line of each song written like a *Variety* headline. Thus an obscure version of 'Froggie Would a Wooin' Go' by 'Chubby' Parker and His Old Time Banjo was described as 'Zoologic miscegeny achieved in mouse frog nuptials, relatives approve'. In 1991 he received a Grammy for his work in promoting American folk music.

Piled high on the table were film cans containing Harry's various works in progress, as well as the famous animations, which are now regarded as being at the forefront of the avant-garde American cinema. Harry's light-shows pre-dated the psychedelic era by decades and he not only originated many of the special effects in use today, but also invented a special cheap projector for the purpose. His film activities were more or less continuous – whenever there was enough money he would shoot more footage. Apart from the advantage of being able to lead an active social life without actually leaving the building, the main reason Harry lived in the Chelsea was that by standing in the lobby he would encounter a constant stream of fresh people with money.

Harry loved the Chelsea; something that some of the transient residents could not understand. One night Marty Balin of the Jefferson Airplane was coming on very strong to Harry at the hotel bar, the El Quixote. Balin told him that for $400 a month – Harry's rent – he could have a fabulous house in the Bay Area. Harry's defensive reply was, 'Yeah! And have to pay the rent.' Harry owed about $4,000 in back rent. Stanley Bard admired Harry's work, and liked to have 'artistic' people living in the hotel, some of whom, inevitably, were going to stiff him for the rent.

One night in the El Quixote, Harry and I were sitting, rather stoned, discussing reality. When I suggested that the bar might not really exist, Harry burst into tears and between sobs said, 'Don't ever suggest that the Chelsea doesn't exist! Can't you understand that it's all I've got!' Mostly, however, Harry did his best to make other people cry, believing that if people saw his very worst behaviour and were still prepared to accept him, then a relationship might be possible; a form of avuncular hazing. He homed in unerringly on people's weaknesses, seeking their Achilles heel. To a young Jewish girl, daughter of a friend: 'I see you're old enough to grow a moustache!' To a confident young black teacher: 'Tell me of your unfortunate experiences of being black.' Some people, like William Burroughs, couldn't stand his rudeness. Others, like Allen, or Harry's best friend Peggy Biderman who lived in the hotel, were prepared to put up with even his most extravagantly bad behaviour in the belief that Harry was a genius.

Harry believed that it was the duty of wealthy people to support artists, and, as many of the residents of the Chelsea were there because of the artistic ambience, he was usually able to finance his projects. One evening Harry appeared at my door with a tall young man, cowboy hat in hand. 'Come and have a drink!' he said. 'Look what I found in the lobby, a rich Texan. I'm just taking him to my room before anyone else sees him. Come along and he'll give you $1,000!' I felt tired and didn't go. Next day I saw Harry in the lobby. He showed me his $1,000, all in $100s. 'Why didn't you come?' he asked, puzzled. Many of the residents of the hotel were also artists and they sometimes resented being asked for money. One evening at the bar, Harry badgered a photographer from *Life* magazine for hours for money, and when the exasperated man finally gave in and passed Harry a twenty, Harry promptly burned it.

Claude and Mary

Also living at the Chelsea were Claude Pelieu and Mary Beach. I wanted to meet them because I sold *Bulletin From Nothing*, their cut-up magazine, at Indica. Allen told me a wonderful story about Claude to give me an idea of what to expect. Several years before, at a party given by Panna Grady at her apartment in the Dakota, Norman Mailer and Claude had been standing, waiting, outside the door to the bathroom, both getting more and more desperate. Mailer knocked urgently on the door, but to no avail. Claude was drunk and could wait no longer, so he pulled out his penis and pissed in Mailer's pocket. Mailer was initially unaware of what Claude was doing, then jumped back in horror. Enraged, he grabbed the door handle and virtually tore the bathroom door from its hinges. Out fell a heap of mops and brushes. They had been waiting outside the broom cupboard. 'Now,' said Allen, gleefully, 'every time Norman sees Claude, he puts his hands in his pockets!'

I called Claude and Mary and went to visit. They had a one-bedroom suite overlooking 23rd Street with double French windows opening out onto a balcony. The walls were gleaming white, recently painted, and books were piled high on the marble mantelpiece. At the right-hand end of the mantelpiece were piles of blank paper and an old office typewriter where Claude wrote, standing up. The walls to the left of the door and the right of the window were covered by huge collages of cut-outs taken from underground newspapers and magazines, particularly from *Evergreen*, Robert Crumb cartoons from *EVO* and *Zap*, and sex pictures from *Pleasure*, *Screw*, *New York Review of Sex*, *Kiss*, et cetera. Words were collaged all across it as well as political jokes, with Nixon peeping between the spread legs of a naked girl. A Sony portable television to the right of the door was always on, and static coursed across the newsreader's face. Claude and Mary had very European manners and immediately offered ice-cold beer, coffee or spirits. They seemed in every way a respectable middle-class couple. Claude wore his hair in a neat Beatle cut, which was restrained by the standards of the time, and Mary dressed as the middle-aged Yankee heiress that she was.

Two bookcases were filled with modern literature, new copies of paperbacks often sealed in cellophane to protect them. Claude and Mary conversed together in French and all my visits had this background of the French language, as Mary translated items of conversation that Claude misunderstood, or when she asked him to bring more beer or to roll more joints. They did a tremendous amount of work here, translating Burroughs, Ginsberg, Leary, Ferlinghetti and others into French. They did not often go out; a trip to Greenwich Village to buy all the new sex papers and paperbacks was quite an event for them.

To an outsider their relationship seemed at first to be antagonistic, with Mary constantly criticising Claude in rapid staccato French, accompanied by a grimace, and Claude continuing at great length to describe, in as derogatory a manner as possible, the defects and qualities of Mary's clitoris and cunt. This use of shock language was characteristic of Claude and he lovingly bestowed it on everyone. Mary's great friend Peggy Biderman would have been surprised if Claude didn't refer to her at least once as a 'Jewish cunt' during her daily visit. They were all very open and friendly and showed me all their files and books on Burroughs and Ginsberg. They made me as welcome as possible and I was very grateful for it.

A few days later, in the El Quixote, I saw Claude and Mary eating at one of the centre tables. Claude looked up as the waiter approached. He had on full Egyptian eye make-up. The waiter started back in shock. 'You want to fuck me, eh, motherfucker?' Claude asked the

275

waiter. 'You think I'm a goddamn fag?' The waiter knew Claude and on this occasion actually smiled. The manager, Gil, frowned in magnificent Spanish disapproval from behind the bar.

Another time I was with a large crowd of Chelsea residents, sitting at the huge table at the back of the bar, next to the door which led through to the Chelsea lobby. Leonard Cohen, Harry Smith, Peggy, Claude and Mary and a few others were all there drinking. A Polaroid photograph was passed around of Claude lying flat on the bed, his feet on the floor, his erect cock stuck through the middle of a dollar bill. Everyone laughed because Claude and Mary looked *so* respectable otherwise.

Conversation with Claude and Mary was about Abbie Hoffman, Jerry Rubin, Ed Sanders, Allen Ginsberg, William Burroughs, the Black Panthers, Jean-Jacques Lebel, the underground press, counter-culture and dope. We drank Miller Highlife and smoked pot. They were not well informed about music except the Fugs and the MC5, which had reached them through literature. Once, sitting in our favourite large booth just inside the El Quixote, Claude and Mary were trying to find a name for a new literary magazine they intended to put out. They had a list of Ed Sanders-type names like *Moist*, but none of them was really suitable. I passed Mary the menu, closed my eyes and pointed at random to one of the items, in the best Dadaist tradition. They called the magazine *Fruit Cup*, and dedicated it to me.

I once ran into Claude in the lobby looking rather pale. He had just come down in the elevator. Normally one or other of the elevators was out of service and neither of them exactly inspired confidence. Claude had entered the elevator and had been joined by the maid who cleaned their room, a very large black lady from Haiti. Claude was more than six feet tall and well built. As the doors slowly closed, she grabbed him in a bear hug and began jumping up and down with him, shouting at the top of her voice, 'I – don't – like – small – men!' Although flattered by her attention, he none the less felt a certain consternation because each time they landed, the elevator cable seemed to stretch and the car shuddered and groaned. Claude was sure he was about to die and said he planned to cushion his fall by throwing himself on top of her if the cable broke.

Klein

Allen Klein

My first task in New York that summer was to sort out Allen
Ginsberg's contract with Apple, which we had to clarify before
recording could begin on his album of Blake songs. Even though all
four of the Beatles and Ron Kass, the head of Apple Records, had
said that they wanted the album to happen, Allen Klein, Apple's
newly appointed business manager, insisted on a deal that would give
Apple the rights to everything, including the publishing. Allen and I
went to see him at the offices of his company, ABKCO, on the top
floor of 1700 Broadway. It was a financial office. You could see that
they were unused to having actual artists visit, even though their
publicity office was there. We were shown through doors made
from heavy beaten copper, which looked like something Klein had
picked up from the auction of the *Cleopatra* set in Hollywood. It was
a corner office with spectacular views of other midtown skyscrapers
and Central Park through windows on two sides. The furnishing was
opulent and utterly tasteless, like the copper door. Klein sat in a
grubby white T-shirt staring at us, his hands on the desk. My
impression was that, for Klein, everything was confrontation, was
screwing the other guy. Writing a contract to allow two parties to do
something together was anathema to him.

Ginsberg held out and demanded a say over his rights. 'Assuming I
trust you,' he said, 'how do I know you're always going to be here as
head of Apple? You might go down into Central Park one afternoon
and rape a little girl on her way home from school.' He gestured out
of the plate-glass window towards the park. 'Then you'd go to jail
and I'd have to deal with a stranger who didn't understand the nature
of our deal.'

Klein was visibly upset; he spun around in his leather armchair.
'That's absurd!' he shouted. 'I have a wife and children. I wouldn't
do a thing like that. You're just saying that to try and shock me, to
be obscene!' Klein, though obviously opposed to Allen's political
opinions and philosophy, was still fascinated by him. Klein met
plenty of famous people, but Allen was famous for his words, and his
conversation was of great interest to Klein. For some reason he then

277

insisted on talking about pornography and censorship. The meeting dragged on for more than an hour, with one short break while Klein barked at someone in Australia. Allen and I finally emerged, but there was no deal in place. Another outline contract was going to be prepared, but in the meantime Klein said go ahead and start recording.

First came the selection of musicians to use on the album, followed by rehearsals at Robert Frank's West Side apartment. Though we had no signed contract, we decided to begin recording. We went into Capitol Records' midtown studios. The room was too big, there was no atmosphere and the engineers wore white coats and carried scissors in little leather holsters for splicing tape. We cut several tracks before disaster struck. Allen Klein finally got complete control of Apple and began firing people *en masse*. The staff at Apple resigned by the dozen and no one knew what was happening. Capitol would accept no more studio bookings and refused to hand over the existing tapes. Zapple was folded without anyone even informing me and I was stuck at the Chelsea with unpaid hotel bills and rehearsal costs. Derek Taylor very kindly made it his responsibility to get approval from one of the Beatles – I think it was George – to wire me enough money to settle up with everyone.

I felt a responsibility towards all the people I had recorded and gradually found ways to release most of their albums: EMI–Harvest brought out *Listening to Richard Brautigan* in 1970 and Folkways released Charles Olson's *Maximus IV, V, VI* two years later. Ferlinghetti's tapes appeared on a number of different Fantasy albums, but the original album, as envisaged, never appeared. The Bukowski tapes were finally released on CD in 1998 as *At Terror Street and Agony Way*. The Ken Weaver and Michael McClure tapes were never edited. The head of Apple Records, Ron Kass, and the head of A&R, Peter Asher, both moved to MGM Records to take up the same positions there, and asked me if Allen would like to bring out his Blake record with them. This time Allen decided to pay for the sessions himself and lease MGM the completed masters. That way he retained complete control.

Allen took over my hotel bills and I began looking for an

independent studio. Frank Zappa suggested that I use Apostolic Studios at 53 East 10th Street, which was where he recorded *We're Only In It For the Money* and *Lumpy Gravy*. I went to have a look at it. It was perfect.

Apostolic was named after its tape machine, a prototype twelve-track Scully about six feet long. The rates were reasonable – $95 an hour and $115 an hour after midnight – because everyone had said that no one would go downtown to record. The studio had an in-house astrologer who sometimes decided that the signs were so bad that no recording should be done that day. It was funky and relaxed, but the staff were really professional and became creatively involved in the project, unlike the Capitol Records staff who made no effort to disguise their contempt for the material we were trying to record.

I thought that each track needed to be considered separately, with its own line-up and production, rather than assembling a group of musicians who would accompany Allen on the songs like a regular pop group. There were other considerations as well: Allen's time-keeping was unconventional and changed from line to line according to the meaning of the text. A traditional rhythm section was therefore out of the question, which is why there are no drums on these tracks. The time-keeping duties fell to the keyboards or bass, who could drop in or out whenever needed but could also be used to strengthen Allen's voice. Much of the charm of Allen's renditions came from his untrained, somewhat uncertain singing, though I hoped we could correct some of the more out-of-tune notes with overdubs and double tracking. A number of other devices were used to strengthen his voice: a bass following the vocal line instead of keeping time, an organ swell to distract from a flat note, a trill or sweetener to balance a certain dryness. This was Allen's first musical outing on record and in later years his voice and microphone technique improved immeasurably. However, I have a great fondness for these early recordings, which I feel get closer to how Blake would have sung the songs than any of the 'serious' classical musical settings of them.

It was obvious that we needed top-flight musicians to carry Allen through the more difficult musical passages. He suggested that Charles Mingus might play bass. This seemed too good to be true, but Allen called him and we arranged to meet at the Village

Vanguard on Seventh Avenue where he was playing. After catching a superb set, we met him backstage and Allen outlined his ideas for the album. Mingus said that he needed to hear some of it, but that this was not the place. We were to stop by his apartment the next afternoon. Mingus lived on the dead-end block of East Fifth Street off Avenue C. Little kids had the hydrants open on the corner and tried to soak us as we picked our way to his apartment through overflowing garbage cans and burned-out cars. It was very hot and Mingus came to the door wearing just a pair of shorts, sweat running in rivulets down the operation scars across his stomach. He seemed out of it, punch-drunk, but we may have roused him from sleep. It was a railroad apartment, each room leading to the next, the first room piled high with old newspapers and cardboard boxes, leaving a corridor to walk through. Mingus and Allen gossiped a little about Tim Leary – Mingus was married by Leary at Millbrook and Allen was one of the guests – then Mingus said, 'Okay, let's hear it.' Allen had his harmonium with him and sang his way through four of the Blake tunes.

Mingus listened carefully but didn't think it was for him, though he was supportive and sympathetic. He gave us the phone number of Herman Wright, who had played with Yusef Lateef, Clark Terry and Ron Carter. Mingus assured us that Herman was the man for the job – and he was.

Stonewall

After a Sunday-night recording session, Allen and I decided to walk over to the Stonewall Inn, where riots had broken out two days before. On Friday, 27 June, eight policemen from the Morals Squad had raided the bar in a more-or-less routine piece of police harassment – liquor laws forbade public drinking by overt homosexuals. But this time, instead of meekly accepting intimidation, the gays fought back with bottles and beer cans. The window of the bar was smashed, the police car had its windscreen broken and a parking meter was used as a battering ram. Out of the incident emerged Gay Power, a term probably coined by Lucien Truscott IV in his *Village Voice* article 'Gay Power Comes to Sheridan Square'.

The next night a large crowd gathered outside the boarded-up windows of the bar. There was a lot of taunting from both sides of the police barriers, which eventually turned into bottle-throwing. The police were determined from the beginning to quell any demonstration and twice broke ranks and charged into the crowd, flailing their batons and beating people to the ground. It was all over by about 4 am.

It was hot and humid when Allen and I walked over to Sheridan Square the next night at about 1.30 am. Quite a crowd had gathered, police barricades lined the sidewalks and officers stood around in shirt sleeves, swinging their truncheons, as if they were just looking for someone to beat on the head. The Stonewall was open for business again, but you had to cross the police line and have your ID checked to get in. The Mattachine Society, a gay-rights group that had always avoided confrontation and believed that quiet integration and assimilation into society represented the best route for gay liberation, had pinned a notice to the boarded-up window pleading for calm. Someone had scrawled GAY POWER next to it.

The atmosphere seemed tense, and both sides were trading insults. Allen immediately attempted to defuse the situation. He flashed a peace sign at the crowd and shook hands with the policemen guarding the barricade, exchanging pleasantries. They knew who he was, of course, and appeared to be pleased to meet him. The bar was on the right of a large, more-or-less square room, mostly taken up by a dance floor, with the far wall covered in a grid of coloured squares which flashed different colours to the music, like the dance floor in *Saturday Night Fever*. The room still showed evidence of the riot, but they had cleaned it up and were trying to get their customers to cross the police line and give them some business. I bought a beer while Allen danced with one of the few customers, 'like a galleon in full sail' as he put it, when I complimented him on one or two unusually well-executed twists and twirls.

A *Voice* reporter asked him his opinion of it all. 'We are one of the largest minorities in the country. Ten per cent. It's about time we did something to assert ourselves . . . They're beautiful. They've lost that wounded look that fags all had ten years ago.' Allen signed a few autographs, leaning on the police line, and I left him there, chatting, to walk back to the Chelsea.

Singing Blake

We ended the album with a poem not in *Songs of Innocence and Experience*: 'The Grey Monk', Blake's great fulmination against tyranny, as apposite now as it ever was:

> The hand of Vengeance found the Bed
> To which the Purple Tyrant fled;
> The iron hand crush'd the Tyrant's head
> And became a Tyrant in his stead.

For this we needed a deep powerful drum roll to end. This time Allen's address book produced Elvin Jones, possibly the world's greatest drummer (the John Coltrane Quartet, Miles Davis, etc.), whom Allen knew through Thelonious Monk. Jones strolled casually into the studio and immediately discussed his fee. When that was settled he glanced over his shoulder and a tiny Japanese woman – his wife, I think – staggered in through the door carrying his drumkit, which she then proceeded to set up. He did his bit in one perfect take, collected his money and was gone, all in under an hour.

Songs of Innocence and Experience by William Blake Tuned by Allen Ginsberg was released by MGM Records in June 1970, and naturally didn't sell, though we got a great review by Lester Bangs in *Rolling Stone* as well as one in *The Blake Newsletter*, which thought that Allen got closer to Blake's actual voice than any of the classical settings of the work.

Woodrow Wilson Drive

The tapes mixed and safely copied, I flew to Los Angeles to deliver them to Peter Asher at MGM. I went up for a drink with Ron Kass. Ron had originally been head-hunted from Liberty Records to run Apple Records and must have had a good contract with them. We stood in his office with Picasso prints on the wall, looking out over the Hollywood Hills, and he expressed relief at finally being free from Allen Klein's meddling, and the interference and uncertainty of the Beatles – from John in particular. In fact Ron's career with MGM didn't last long and he received another golden handshake when the company was taken over by Mike Curb.

Frank Zappa had invited me to stay and after a couple of phone calls I located him at TT&G studios at Sunset and Hollander. I took a cab, enjoying the familiar warm air, the palm trees and the incredible billboards. The view from the twenty-four-hour snack bar on the second floor of TT&G was of a vacant lot. Beyond that, past the black silhouettes of a row of skinny mop-topped palm trees, was a crude floodlit psychedelic mural, claimed to be the biggest in the world, which the Fool had just finished painting on the side of the hanger-like building that housed *Hair*. And beyond all that was the night sky, clear and clean enough for a smattering of stars to show through, crisscrossed by the blinking strobes of aircraft heading for Burbank airport.

Don Van Vliet, aka Captain Beefheart, was examining the automatic vending machines, muttering criticisms in a gravelly voice. We were taking a coffee break while Frank rewrote some of the parts for his latest album, *Hot Rats*, which he was making in the studio downstairs. 'I can break glass with my voice,' Don told me conversationally. 'I once blew out a twelve-hundred-dollar Telefunken microphone.'

'Really?'

'BLAAAAAAAAAAAHHHHH!!!'

We inspected the window. Not a crack.

'I'm feeling a little bit tired.'

'What the fuck was that?' yelled Zappa, running into the room. He had heard the noise in his soundproof control booth and come to investigate.

'We were just seeing if Don's voice could break the window,' I said, but Don was already thinking about something else and Frank's sudden entry seemed to have disturbed his train of thought.

'Come and listen to this,' said Frank. 'We'll be able to put your vocal on tonight, it looks like.' But Don didn't think so. His voice wasn't on top form, and it wasn't until the next night that he sang 'Willie the Pimp' so nicely for the album.

Johnny Otis was the conductor for *Hot Rats*. He had been working for the Musicians' Union for the past few years, but he was soon to make a comeback. It was through Otis that Zappa was able to locate Don 'Sugarcane' Harris to play violin on the album – Otis located him in jail on a drug bust and Zappa bailed him out. He also brought along his son Shuggie to play on some of the tracks. 'Let's get this group moving,' he shouted, bursting into the studio. He wore shades, knife-creased trousers, black silk socks held up with black calf-suspenders, high-shine shoes, a black shirt and a little voodoo image worn as a necklace. His hair, black as a Lincoln Continental, was sprayed into place with thick lacquer, and not a single hair moved out of place as he bobbed his head to the music. He stamped his foot ferociously, just a fraction ahead of the beat. A little bead of sweat appeared on his brow as he grinned and grimaced with the beat, leaning over and clapping his hands within inches of the drummer's ear, driving him into the music. The drummer did not look pleased. Johnny's massive injection of energy soon made the band move and it wasn't long before Frank was twiddling with the knobs on the mixing board and explaining, 'I'll just make a test mix before we go.'

Over the years I spent some time observing Frank at work in the studio and I always found his hands-on production of extreme interest. On this occasion he was working with keyboard player Ian Underwood, a consummate professional. Frank interrupted Ian in the middle of a passage to dictate a rewrite of the whole centre section. 'Change the A to A-flat, the B to C . . .'

Short silence.

'Okay, I got it.'

They did another take. Ian Underwood played the new passage flawlessly. On the second take, Frank decided that he had a master and went to the studio to discuss the position of the microphones for the next part. 'We'll put the Electrovoice there, pointing upwards to catch the sound of the saxophone as it bounces off the wall. That's how they made it sound so greasy in the Fifties!'

Frank's cigarette burned another brown line in the Formica as he balanced the various tracks and made a test mix. Some time in the middle of the night Frank's wife Gail showed up in her big Buick and drove us home. She steered the car with the palm of her hand, her fingers splayed, and the huge air-conditioned monster surged up the twists and bends of Laurel Canyon Boulevard until we made the final turn at the top and caught a catherine-wheel glimpse of the necklaces of light laid out below, before plunging into the dense foliage that concealed all the Laurel Canyon inhabitants from each other.

'He's burned them all,' muttered Frank.

'You didn't have photocopies?' asked Gail.

'No. Years of work.'

'Are you sure he's done it?'

'Yes, he told me tonight. He did it two weeks ago.'

Captain Beefheart had just burned the only copies of hundreds of songs he had written since he and Frank were at high school together in Lancaster, California, in the Mojave Desert. Frank continued to lament, and I realised that Don was just about the only contemporary of Zappa's whom he openly regarded as a genius. Fortunately, a few days later there seemed to be some doubt as to whether or not the songs were burned.

Captain Beefheart, the name given him by Zappa when they were in their high-school band the Soots, had a business meeting with Zappa and his business manager Herb Cohen while I was staying at the house. Beefheart recorded for Frank's record company, Bizarre Records, and had recently completed the double album called *Trout Mask Replica*. Their famous friendship had been severely strained by the making of this record. In particular Frank was offended by such unorthodox recording techniques as singing in the studio with the microphone set up in the soundproof control booth, so that Don had to bellow through the glass while Frank pushed the record levels up to maximum, with all the hiss that entails, in order to record anything at all. When I asked Don about this particular effect he shrugged, 'Well, to me, that's just the way it is.'

One track was recorded when Don began singing a song to Zappa down the phone line. Frank quickly plugged the phone into the board and started the first tape that came to hand, some empty tracks on a Mothers of Invention tape, then had Don start again. On the album the Mothers provide the backing, though Don could not hear them on the telephone.

Don, in turn, was offended by the way that Zappa and Herbie Cohen were marketing the album, 'They were selling me like a freak alongside that madman Wild Man Fischer and the GTOs.' Wild Man Fischer was a street person who sang songs for a quarter to make a living; Zappa recorded a whole album of his a cappella singing. The GTOs were five LA groupies whom Frank named Girls Together Outrageously, or GTOs for short, and planned to record.

Frank and Don were closeted for hours. When Don emerged we went for a stroll on the back lawn by the pool. Don removed his grey top hat. Georgia, Frank's German shepherd, sniffed around us. The stars were twinkling. It was 3.30 am. 'Everyone is out to burn,' Don told me. 'D'you know what I mean? All artists get burned. All art gets burned!'

I told him that I thought Frank was honest and respected Don very highly as a composer and musician, and regarded him as one of his few personal friends. Don listened carefully, then conceded that this might be so with Frank, but that Frank was not the only one involved in Bizarre. This led to Don giving me a hair-raising description of the financial goings-on surrounding his first two albums, before he signed with Frank, *Safe As Milk* and *Strictly Personal*.

I made sympathetic noises.

Don said he would like to live in England because the police didn't wear guns there. Also, the English audience appreciated his music better than the Americans. Unfortunately he was broke and would have to stay in LA.

I tried to console him by saying that at least he was where the sun was.

'I hate the sun. I only go out at night!'

I looked closely at his face. It was deathly white. He told me that he was a better poet than Allen Ginsberg and a better saxophonist than Charlie Parker, because he was totally free whereas they were trapped in form. His art was one long B-L-O-W. Tentatively, I ventured to say that his painting owed a lot to Abstract Expressionism, especially De Kooning and that his sax playing was not totally dissimilar to that of Ornette Coleman, but Don replaced his top hat and said that it was time for him to continue his discussion with Frank and Herb Cohen, the master of Bizarre business.

Frank and Gail Zappa lived in a large mock-Tudor house on Woodrow Wilson Drive, high in the Santa Monica Hills overlooking Hollywood. Parked in the driveway when I was there were a white Jaguar (bought off Captain Beefheart and with the seats all slashed by the LA police in a fruitless search for drugs), a gleaming fully automatic red Buick Riviera (the type referred to as a 'soft car' by the GTOs) and a business-like panel truck in which the Marshall amplifiers were kept. The house sat back off the road, cut into the side of the hill so that the front ground floor was the back basement. The windows were shuttered and the only indication that it was anything other than a nice middle-class Hollywood household was the double-door loading bay on the ground floor to enable bulky studio equipment to be brought in and out.

The kitchen was, by English standards, something from the future, with surfaces littered with blenders, mixers and choppers, an eye-level oven, a triple-door fridge, deepfreeze, twin sinks with waste-disposal units and an ice-water dispenser with its own little paper dixie cups. I loved it! All around the walls, above the kitchen units, hung Frank's ever-growing collection of hotel keys, and the walls were covered with lots of weird photographs and drawings, many of them sent by fans to United Mutations, the nearest thing that the Mothers had to a fan club. There were Polaroids, clippings and trivia, including summonses from the City of Los Angeles for putting garbage out on the street too early. The kitchen was where everyone hung out: it was Gail's domain, but there was an invisible presence, the man in the basement: everything was focused on Frank and his work, and was designed to make sure he could function smoothly and efficiently; food appeared when he wanted it, roadies and business people were ushered in and out, and his appointments kept track of.

The house was like a medieval court, functioning twenty-four hours a day. On a given afternoon you might find the GTOs planning a concert in the kitchen; Herbie Cohen demanding coffee and cupcakes; two-year-old Moon Unit with her continual eating, washing and walking needs; Pete, a girl from the Midwest who followed 'her Mothers' to the coast and now seemed to be living in Frank's house; Captain Beefheart restlessly pacing up and down; Kansas the roadie, perched on a kitchen stool, fielding long-distance calls from girls in Montana, Michigan and Saginaw – wherever the Mothers' last tour took them. Most of the time he spent 'fixing the wheels . . .' All the girls adored him. Then there was Carl, Frank's younger brother, who lived in the changing rooms by the pool, and did all the things that Frank used to sing about: worked at the car-wash and as a short-order cook. Frank got him to demonstrate the LA Flop and the Pachuco Hop for me, looking on adoringly as his brother flopped about, humming to himself. And there was more: Mother-maniacs who just wanted to be there to listen to tapes, or journalists who got caught up in the Zappa time-warp and found that days had gone by and they still hadn't interviewed anyone. There were groupies who lay in wait for people in the living room: 'Your bed looks awful narrow. If you like you can come and sleep in mine.' Endless visitors; all presided over by Gail, who never appeared to sleep at all and whose contented liquid smile was only ever clouded by her super-sensitivity to the slightest criticism of Frank or by anyone jumping on his bandwagon. Gail ran the court and the king remained invisible, hidden beneath it all, crouched over his tape machines in the basement. He was a workaholic, rarely emerging from his lair unless he wanted company: 'There are a steady stream of interesting people walking through the door – all I have to do is sit here, man.'

On the door leading to the basement was a small black card on which was written, in white, DR ZURKON'S SECRET LAB IN HAPPY VALLEY. The basement was huge. It had thick baby-blue carpet, like walking through long grass, and shuttered windows covered by soundproof screens. Two huge speakers stood five feet high and between them an assemblage of plastic, wood and a car hood by Cal Schenkel covered the hatch through which films were projected from an anteroom. The carpet was littered with instrument cases, an electric organ, an antique wheelchair and further assemblage material. Paintings, concert posters and a framed broken plaster plaque, proclaiming 'Zappa's Grubby Chamber' in large white paint on a green distemper backing, covered the walls. The sunlight was completely excluded and some areas of the room, notably the ones people sat in, were very dark. It was impossible to read while sitting on the settee. The permanent shutters locked out time as well as light, so the room was still until someone moved, and then time was measured by that.

A row of cupboards contained Frank's collection of 7,000 R&B and doo-wop records. We spent hours playing them. I noted down ones I wanted to get: 'Valerie' by Jackie & the Starlites on Lana; 'Little Darlin'' by the Gladiolas on Excello; the Spaniels' 'Goodnight Sweetheart' on Vee Jay; and of course 'Rubber Biscuit' by the Chips. The cupboards also contained tapes: thousands of them, mostly on 10 inch NAB spools to fit the Scully 280 two-track machine which was the centre of Frank's life. It stood by the wall connected to a TEAC A1200U for making tape transfers and had its own small patch-board for making connections between the record player and amplifiers in the small adjoining record room. Scattered around were piles of tape boxes, leads, guitars and more tapes: tapes of concerts, 'Here's one which has a crazed groupie from Miami'; test mixes, 'Like to hear *Absolutely Free* without the vocal overdubs?'; conversations and oddments, final mixes and out-takes.

Some days I would take Moon for a walk in the garden. We would wander round the pool and play with Georgia and on one occasion we walked down the street, but Woodrow Wilson Blvd has no provision for pedestrians so we didn't make it any further than the first intersection. Moon's baby brother, Dweezil, spent most of his time sitting in a bassinet on the kitchen counter, staring at a flickering portable television. On 20 July 1969 Gail, Dweezil and I watched as Neil Armstrong set foot on the moon and bounced about in slow motion on the sandy surface. Dweezil watched without comment.

One evening I went with Frank and his family to their favourite drive-in burger stand, a circular building where the waitresses wore rollerskates and clamped a little table on your car window. On another occasion Frank took me to one of the cultural highlights of Los Angeles: Canter's, two blocks north of Beverly Blvd on Fairfax; a twenty-four-hour corned-beef and pastrami restaurant and cocktail lounge that was a particular favourite of the local rock musicians, and consequently of the LA groupie set. We sat watching the street, Frank drinking his habitual black coffee while I nursed a Miller's.

'See those fat cars?' Frank asked. Fairfax was a busy street, but there was a preponderance of shining new Cadillacs, slowly bouncing and jerking along in the slow lane next to the restaurants. Just visible, trying to see up over the dashboards, were the drivers; tiny little old Jewish men, clinging desperately to the steering wheel, trying to control their expensive toys. 'They're all out looking for pussy!' said Frank, a happy smile on his face. 'They know there are a lot of hippie chicks along here, but I don't think they ever score.'

One of the GTOs invited me to their recording session, so I went with them to the studio. Frank was producing the album and was already there. The girls had no studio discipline and all talked at once, then all giggled at once. Frank thought their lyrics were interesting from a sociological angle: the groupie viewpoint, something that he explored again later when Flo and Eddie joined his line-up. As far as Frank was concerned, the GTOs were as good as most of the other girl bands, perhaps better because they were so weird. Herb Cohen thought their album, *Permanent Damage*, was garbage and predicted that no one would release it. He was right and a few months later Frank put it out on his own label, Straight Records.

My friend Howard Parker, 'H', came to stay at Frank and Gail's. Frank very much enjoyed H's quick-witted roadie humour and his use of cockney rhyming slang. Frank sometimes made notes of it, but when he used it, he always got it wrong. For instance, he took the word 'poofter' from H, but didn't realise that it referred to a homosexual, so when he used it as a place-name on the track 'Poofter's Croft, Wyoming', he came in for a lot of abuse as a homophobic.

Frank loaned H and me Beefheart's slashed-up white Jag and we chugged around town in it until we got pulled over by the Pollution Squad, who demanded that we get the car off the road until we had fixed the exhaust. H gave them a torrent of cockney verbal, which charmed them sufficiently to save us from getting a summons.

Summer in the City

I flew back to New York and checked into the Chelsea. The rooms were stifling hot. You could rent an air conditioner for your room, but it cost extra and Percy had to come and install it. (Televisions also cost extra, but as the quality was so terrible, most residents bought their own.) The only air-conditioned space in the hotel was the El Quixote bar and it enjoyed better-than-ever business. Peggy Biderman and a group of residents formed the Chelsea Sand 'n' Surf club, which met on the roof, near the central chimneys. There were several gardens on the roof of the hotel in those days, one for the use of residents, but the club members chose to meet on a baking-hot section of the tarred roof, where they rolled out their towels, set up their cool-boxes of cold beer and settled down to work on their tans. The Chelsea was once the tallest building in New York – before the Flatiron Building went up – and still had a great view: south to the Statue of Liberty and Jersey, north to the Empire State and the midtown towers.

Many residents rarely left the building and that summer Peggy, Harry, Claude and Mary could always be found at the bar of an evening. Several times we were joined by Leonard Cohen, who also lived there. Leonard was always very generous. One evening he joined a huge table of us, all of whom had eaten and who were rapidly filling the table with more empty bottles. Leonard only had a few drinks, but he picked up the tab for the whole table, eight or nine of us.

Jerome Ragne, who wrote *Hair*, lived in the Chelsea. He usually sat at the end of the bar near the door where the jukebox was, so that he could play foreign-language versions of 'The dawning of the age of Aquarius . . .' and laugh and laugh at his success. Claude and I once met another resident, Florence Turner, sitting on a stool at the bar. She was sobbing. She wrote pornography for a living and had just subjected her heroine – of whom she had grown rather fond – to an undignified act. 'They put pencils up her bottom!' she moaned. Claude found this so funny that Gil, the maître d', threatened to throw us out.

There were a lot of drug casualties around that summer. I once rang for the elevator and the doors opened to reveal a naked girl with eyes that were so large it was frightening. I don't think she was registering anything. I reached in and pressed the button for the ground floor, then stood back as the doors closed. She wasn't there when I rang again a few minutes later.

On another occasion the elevator doors opened in the lobby and standing there blinking was a skinny hippie holding two large paper carrier bags by their handles, both filled to the brim with marijuana, which stuck out of the uncovered tops. He wore a refraction lens stuck to the centre of his forehead and the pupils of his eyes were like pinpoints, caused by something stronger than his luggage. 'Wanna score?' he asked me. He made no effort to leave the elevator and before I could reply, the doors closed again.

There was also an amphetamine freak who hung around outside the hotel. He must have lived nearby, maybe at the YMCA across the street. He reeked of cheap perfume, his face was painted with garish symbols and his long hair was hopelessly tangled into a fuzzy burr. He liked to whirl like a dervish, arms outstretched, outside the rusting metal security grille of Interesting Records, dancing over the broken flagstones with an ecstatic smile on his face. Interesting Records, the imaginatively named used-record store next door to the Chelsea's main entrance, was where all the record critics, myself included, sold their review copies. You could get most of the latest albums there at half-price.

H showed up in a hire car and we raced around Manhattan. One evening we pulled up in front of the Chelsea and both leaped out, slamming the doors and locking ourselves out, with the car double-parked and the motor running. After trying everything we could think of to open the doors, I walked down the block to the prowl cars parked outside the Horn and Hardart Automat, where the police liked to gather for coffee and doughnuts. One of them laughed uproariously at our dilemma, then accompanied me back to the hotel. He went to the desk and asked for a metal clothes hanger. Mr Gross, one of the owners, tried to charge him a dollar for it, but the cop soon set him straight, indicating that they knew full well what went on in the hotel. 'Now don't look at how I do this,' the cop told us. A couple of twists and he had the door open. It took about two seconds. We were effusive in our thanks and only afterwards did H remember that he was carrying a huge block of hash in his pocket.

Meanwhile, Back in Blighty II

IT was at last looking healthy, at least for the moment. The print run was now 40,000 with a readership of perhaps four times that. It was running at thirty-two pages, with lots of record-company advertising; the staff were getting paid and for the first time some of them had been able to take paid holidays; the paper even bought a van. And all this was in the face of continued opposition from the police and authorities. On 28 April the police had raided the paper for the second time and once again thousands of back issues were seized, along with all the small-ad files and sealed letters, replies to small-ad box numbers. Charges were finally brought nine months later: two serious conspiracy charges relating to the 'males' column in the small-ads section. The police also visited the printers, disrupting the printing schedule, not only of *IT* but of *OZ* and the UK edition of *Rolling Stone*. The printer was intimidated and subsequently refused to print any further issues of *IT*. Weeks were wasted trying to find another but, as one potential printer said, 'The word is out.'

However, commercial considerations won out and the paper continued; a regular fortnightly is a nice little earner for a printer.

Inspired by my descriptions of New York and LA, Nigel Samuel wanted to visit New York again that October and suggested we go at once. In fact it took him a few days to get the tickets, but in the meantime he enlarged the party to include his younger sister Nicola, and Caroline Coon from Release. I was used to Nigel's unpredictable behaviour, but even I was surprised at his display at Heathrow where he got rapidly drunk at the bar and then began talking complete nonsense – not the nonsense of a drunkard, but disconnected, rambling thoughts culminating in the idea that he would not come with us. The flight was called and still he would not come. He did, however, insist that we went and so, at the last minute, we did, assuming, correctly, that he would manage to get back into the centre of London unscathed.

We were flying first class, with Air India, 'the hot one' as they called it in Laurel Canyon, not because of the food, but because the lavatories had a vacuum suction in the sinks for the waste water, which meant that if you smoked a joint in there, bending low over the taps, the smoke would all disappear down the plughole. We were discussing Nigel's behaviour when Captain Shastra sat down beside us and began telling us how much fuel the plane needed to get from Bombay to New York. Nicky, who was next to him, said, 'Fascinating, but don't you think you should be in the cabin driving it?' The captain laughed very loudly, startling some of the other passengers, and said that the plane knew how to fly itself better than he did. I wondered if he was drunk.

I sat next to Caroline, talking underground politics all the way and getting to know her. I first met her in 1967 when she and Rufus Harris started Release, the twenty-four-hour legal hotline to call if you were busted. She trained as a ballet dancer, boarding at a ballet school from the age of five until she grew too tall. She was at Central St Martin's School of Art, just round the corner from Indica, and was the first person I met who knew about Georgia O'Keeffe.

Caroline had been invited to stay at the West 12th Street apartment of Johnny Morris, the manager of the Fillmore East. He picked us up at the airport and drove us into the city. I called the

Chelsea to reserve a room and got 420, where I stayed before. I had lunch with Caroline the next day. We took a Checker cab back to the Chelsea and stayed together for five days. I showed her my New York, not that I knew it that well yet. I introduced her to Allen Ginsberg, and he invited us to fly with him to Albany to hear him read at Skidmore. There was an overflow audience and speakers had to be installed in an adjacent room. Allen was a big hit with the students and the English department, but was a bit miffed at the attention Caroline received at the dinner afterwards. The *Nickel Review*, the college newspaper, ran a photograph of her in their report on the evening.

We were put up in an old house on campus, cold winter rain outside. As we were getting ready for bed Allen politely asked if he could sleep with us, but didn't take it badly when we said no. The house was warm and comfortable; it creaked and groaned in the night; an old casement clock ticked away the time downstairs in the living room.

Cherry Valley

I was sad to see Caroline leave, but she had to attend a Commonwealth drugs conference in London, so I went with Allen to the Cherry Valley farm to finish work on the detailed sleeve notes for the Blake album. We sat in the kitchen and talked about the Woodstock Festival. He and I had been at a meeting at Abbie Hoffman's apartment that summer and listened as the Yippies plotted to break down the fences and make it into a free festival. We discussed the fundamental human need to congregate: the old reason for fêtes and festivals and celebrations. He described the two-million-strong 'Kumbh Mela' held every twelve years in Hardwar, India, where holy men from all over the country congregate to wash in the Ganges. He was there with Gary Snyder and Joanne Kyger in 1962. We agreed that festivals like Woodstock should be free, possibly paid for by merchants, food concessions and film and record rights.

Afterwards I sat in the musty attic, dusty copies of *Playboy* and *New Yorker* in boxes on the floor, flies buzzing at the window, the space between the storm window and the screen deep with their withered little corpses from summers past. Through the window, thick mist obscured the lake. A large lion skin with a snarling head and yellowing fangs lay spreadeagled on the dirty rug, bagged in Africa by the father of Belle Gardener, one of Gregory Corso's girlfriends. Now its glass eyes stared out through the cold mist at the barn, painted the traditional rust-red colour, where Bessie the cow lived.

Someone was playing ragtime piano below. Allen was coughing in his wood-panelled room as he read Spiro Agnew's McCarthyite speech on network media distortion. It was hard to believe man had landed on the moon and that on the other side of the world American napalm was falling on Vietnamese villages.

Bessie the cow came into the kitchen and had some cake, fed to her by an ecstatic Peter, who kissed her and slapped her all over. Even Peter's catatonic brother Julius smiled. Bessie ate some red apples before leaving. Her shy calf wouldn't come in, but peered frightened round the open kitchen door with sad brown eyes, a perpetual little tear on her cheek.

Allen talked about death. He said he didn't want to have children; how could he perpetuate the pain of human existence? He was looking forward to the escape of death and said that life for him was not a search for happiness but the avoidance of pain. 'Life is very much shorter than anyone thinks.' He had recently returned from Jack Kerouac's funeral, and his old lover Neal Cassady had also died the previous year. Specks of dust rose into the pale sunlight that entered the room. Through the window Gordon passed carrying pails to the barn. Peter shouted for Julius to join him outside. It was a secure refuge, but not for Allen, who seemed to feel the pain physically with furrowed brow as he read the war news in the *New York Times* and groaned. Each evening the meadow outside the kitchen was filled with glow-worms.

I exchanged the return half of my first-class ticket to London for an ordinary-fare return and a Miscellaneous Travel Voucher, which I used to buy a return ticket to California to see Valerie.

Chelsea Evenings

Back at the Chelsea, I was getting to know many of the permanent residents, largely through Peggy Biderman, who acted like a house-mother to all newcomers and was friends with virtually everyone in the hotel. She had been there for years and raised her two daughters in a tiny room with a bathroom down the hall. She took me to see George Kleinsinger, the composer of the Broadway musical *Shinbone Alley*, but known to me as the composer of *Tubby the Tuba*, a children's opera narrated by Danny Kaye that was played constantly on BBC Radio's *Children's Favourites* when I was little. George lived in a huge, double-height penthouse on the tenth floor with a grand piano in the centre. There he sat, puffing at his pipe, surrounded by palms and trees filled with chirruping birds – thrushes, parrots, a mynah bird, a toucanette and a Chinese nightingale – which flew freely around the room. Along one peeling wall were huge water tanks containing long-necked turtles, which swam gracefully from end to end, the inspiration for one of his ballets. Another corner of the room had a re-creation of a swamp, and it was there that the North American coot lived. George bought one, and the other, unbelievably, came pecking at his window, trying to get in. He had a pair of spider monkeys, exotic fish, snakes, spiders and an alligator, which Percy the bellman used to walk each day down the corridors until one day it tried to bite him. George had a beautiful black girlfriend called Bahni, much younger than him, who was a model. She used to entertain us with stories about life on Seventh Avenue. She kept her own apartment in the Village, and one night someone broke in and strangled her. It was a brutal murder and George never really recovered from her death. His face turned a permanent grey, and though he always drank, he now became an alcoholic.

One day I ran into Peggy in the lobby, where she was talking to two skinny young people dressed in very colourful clothes; the man had on a white sailor suit and the girl wore green tights with ribbons tied round her legs. I thought maybe they were mime artists or actors. Peggy introduced me to them, Robert Mapplethorpe and Patti Smith. Robert was making collages and Patti was a poet. They obviously adored each other. They looked alike, with wide mouths and large features, and they moved with restless youthful energy, hopping about, twisting and turning as they spoke. The Chelsea was the perfect place for them.

They had been in the hotel for several months and already knew a lot of people there, including the film-maker Sandy Daley. Sandy's room was painted a dazzling white and contained nothing but a mattress, a vase of flowers and, rustling slightly, a group of Andy Warhol's 'Silver Clouds', helium-filled, pillow-shaped balloons bobbing against the ceiling. There must have been a cupboard or shelves in her bathroom for her clothes and papers. Sandy made a number of films with Patti and Robert, which were screened at the Chelsea. There were many film-makers in the hotel and a lot of residents had projectors in their rooms. It was a common event for half a dozen people to gather for an impromptu screening. The films were usually silent or accompanied by records.

Stanley Amos exhibited some of Robert's collages in his room, and a bit later Robert and Patti rented a half-studio over the Oasis Bar, a few doors down the street, where Brendan Behan used to drink. Robert made collages of fetish objects, crosses, underwear, with bits of red cellophane or lace, which he framed and exhibited on the walls like an art gallery. His and Patti's room at the Chelsea was tiny and they spent most of their time in the studio, which overlooked 23rd Street and had very good light. Eventually they took over the whole studio and moved in; their possessions were piled untidily behind a curtain at the back.

Patti was the biggest rock 'n' roll fan I had ever met. She wanted to know everything about the London music scene and had very fixed ideas about Jeff Beck, the Yardbirds, the Kinks and the Beatles and would argue with me about little details that she had picked up from the teen magazines, which she took as gospel. She talked excitedly about Rimbaud and Burroughs with a wide-eyed, infectious enthusiasm that impressed me. I had never previously considered grouping rock musicians with writers, but Patti regarded them all as gods. She was great for breaking down compartments and of course later transferred effortlessly from one genre to another. At this point, however, both she and Robert were young and ambitious and busily engaged in networking, as we now call it.

New York, New York

It was on this trip that I realised that New York was where I would most like to be. What attracted me was the idea that every possibility was open to you – you didn't need anyone's permission. It was the energy, the sense of familiarity, even though most of the images came from films and TV shows; it was the twenty-four-hour city that we had campaigned for in *IT*, the twenty-four-hour city we had dreamed of. Not that the Chelsea area was in any way attractive in those days, except for the hotel itself. I remember going to visit Robert and Patti once and there was a pool of blood on the sidewalk outside the Oasis. But I liked to see the police collect their billycans of hot coffee from the Horn and Hardart Automat, all shiny-arsed with sinister police equipment weighing down their belts, their battered blue prowl car parked next to the hydrant outside. You could sit next to a cop in a coffee shop and engage in small talk if you wanted, for they were just part of everyday life, whereas in Britain the police live in a parallel universe, not even allowed to use public toilets, divorced from reality.

I relished going down to the corner store at 2 am to buy frozen 'Sarah Lee' cheesecake straight out of the freezer and a cup of coffee to go. I enjoyed the way the passing subway sent blasts of hot air up through the street grilles, making gusts of dust, dirt and crumpled newsprint rise spectrally in the air at the corner of 22nd Street and 7th Avenue. I liked the steam seeping from cracked pipes, or erupting from manholes in the middle of the streets as if hell was just beneath the cracked tarmac, and the battered chimneys Con Ed put on those that smoked too much. At 4 am they looked beautiful; a row of chimneys at crazy angles, plumes of steam catching neon or passing headlights and red tail-lights as dirty yellow cabs crashed blindly through the clouds of steam over the pitted, potholed roads.

In the daytime I liked the aural storm of music from cabs and hand-held radios, or piped out of shops by loudspeakers in a high-compression static rain of sound: salsa, soul, solid funk, rock 'n' roll and 1001 Strings. I loved the ever-present sirens: the klaxons of fire trucks, and the deep honk of an articulated ten-wheeler, the high-pitched strobe bleeps of an ambulance or blue cop car with its big red light revolving, the car horns and cabs bleating like lost sheep.

Harry Smith's friend Frank Berke lived on 22nd Street in the next block. At 3.30 am one night Peggy, Harry and I went to visit him. The Bronco Burger System's lights lit up the north side of the street like Las Vegas, a visual nightmare going round and round, twenty-four hours a day. The red neon sign of the Oasis bar was still on. A drunk muttered something incoherent to Harry, who stopped dead in his tracks, outraged, and asked if the drunk believed in God. The drunk clearly gave the wrong reply because Harry upped and heaved a New York City trash bin at him. The bin rolled out across 7th Avenue, waste paper spilling from it. Harry, the genius, rendered crazy as everyone else by drink and drugs. The Empire State loomed tall and dark over us, clouds swirling past its television antenna. Frank was still up, as we thought he would be; it was too hot and humid to sleep. He was refreshing and full of energy without being frantic and made us all feel good. Harry did not even make one of his comments about Frank being black. Frank showed me one of Harry's paintings, a Tree of Life, drawn in meticulous detail and coloured in what were no doubt the correct symbolic colours. On the walls were a series of calligraphic Chinese wall hangings, all hanging upside-down. Frank was a good friend of Cecil Taylor, the great jazz pianist, and when I asked where Taylor was working these days, hoping to see him play, Frank said he had a job as a short-order chef in a burger joint on Times Square. I had not yet understood the down side to New York.

Here to Go

Through the bedroom window of the house in Lord North Street, the Victoria Tower of the House of Lords loomed over the rooftops, the Union Jack flying in a cold clear winter sky from the flagpole. I was jetlagged and missing America in an almost physical way.

England seemed so intractable, social change seemed almost impossible. It all seemed hopeless to me, even though *IT* and the 'underground' were now a force to reckon with. There was now a real movement – more of a community of spirit than a political entity – concerned with questioning the authorities, questioning the laws. Suddenly people were talking: opening a debate on the treatment of mental health patients (the subject of a long-running series of articles and letters in *IT*); about the rights of schoolchildren (another controversial subject in the days when children could still be caned); about the emerging women's liberation debate; the embryonic ecology movement; and the long-running support for activists in the black community; as well as trying to put a bit of spirituality back into an increasingly materialistic society. But looking out at the House of Lords served to reinforce the idea that British society was not likely to change, the inertia was too great, and most people were content with what they had. 'Mustn't grumble' was still in force.

IT also had an enemy within. In October a few part-time members of *IT*'s distribution staff, led by Ian Dallas, who had guest-edited a couple of issues, staged an occupation to take over *IT* 'for the people'. Not having the wit or intelligence to start something of their own, they somehow thought *IT* came out all by itself. Just like the police, they 'liberated' a few thousand back issues, though unlike the police they did not bring them back. They invited in the London Street Commune, a squatters' group, to act as unofficial security guards and by the time the whole debacle was over, the office had been smashed to pieces, the files were missing, the IBM electric compositor, the answering machine, an amplifier belonging to a staff member and a load of other stuff had been stolen. They were finally evicted and brought out their own paper, called *International Free Press*, which folded after one issue.

The police raid in April 1969 resulted in two charges being brought against the paper and its three directors: conspiring with persons inserting small ads to induce readers to resort to the ads for the purposes of homosexual practices, and thereby to debauch and corrupt public morals contrary to Common Law; and conspiracy to outrage public decency by inserting ads containing lewd, disgusting

301

and offensive matter, contrary to Common Law. Though homosexuality itself had been made legal in 1967, the gay age of consent was twenty-one, and younger people had been placing ads. It was to be a long and expensive court case, very traumatic for the individuals involved, who faced a possible prison sentence.

I was no longer a director; *IT* was published by a different company, set up when it became a 'workers' co-operative', and the new directors were Graham Keen, Peter Stansill and the business manager, Dave Hall. After five days at Wells Street Magistrates Court in January 1970 the case was moved to the Old Bailey. They were found guilty and the fines bankrupted the company that was then running the paper. *IT* continued, as ever, and one of the charges was thrown out on appeal two years later. By then the paper had changed totally. Mick Farren was editor and very few of the old staff were still around. *IT* folded with issue 164 on 5 October 1973, just in time to see Chief Inspector Victor Kelaher of the Drugs Squad in the dock at the Old Bailey along with five of his fellow detectives, on charges of conspiracy to pervert the course of justice. *IT* reappeared for three issues in May 1974, financed by John Lennon, but couldn't sustain the effort. To my knowledge *IT* has started again in at least seven incarnations since, throughout the Seventies and Eighties, running for half a dozen issues and then disappearing until some other group picks up the name and logo.

The attack on *IT* by a breakaway group depressed me more than it should have done; after three years the paper still seemed to stagger from one crisis to another. In addition Indica was insolvent, largely because of the high level of theft and permanent under-capitalisation. Piles of dusty underground papers, a year old, sat unsold, and we were forced more and more to accept large consignments of books on sale-or-return – books we would not normally have stocked – just to keep the shelves full. The gallery had closed the year before. John put on great shows, but was just not cut out for the stroking and flattering needed to run a commercial art gallery or for the need to keep office hours. He missed three meetings with buyers from the *QE2*, even though he was living in the back of the gallery.

I didn't want to ask Paul McCartney for yet more money for Indica. He had his own problems. Years later Paul told me, 'That was a very difficult period. John was with Yoko full time, and our relationship was beginning to crumble. John and I were going through a very tense period. The break-up of the Beatles was looming and I was very nervy. Personally it was a very difficult time for me. I think the drugs, the stress, tiredness and everything had really started to take its toll. I somehow managed to miss a lot of the bad effects of all that, but looking back on this period, I think I was having troubles.'

I felt the same way: tired, stressed, as if I was cracking up. Allen Ginsberg invited Sue and me to come and live on his farm in Cherry Valley and unwind. We had been going through a hard time together and this seemed the ideal opportunity to sort things out. Nick Kimberley and Ann Shepherd were offered jobs at Compendium, the new counter-cultural bookshop in Camden Town, so I didn't feel too bad about closing the shop. We put Indica Books Limited into voluntary liquidation, and I resigned from the poster-distribution company Effective Communications Arts Limited. I was a director of two of Nigel's companies, Bibliomania Limited and Parsimony Limited, so I resigned from them as well. As for Lovebooks Limited and ESP Disc Limited, they were already dormant. Graham Keen still lived at Lord North Street, so I assembled all my books and papers and anything we regarded as valuable and locked them in the ground-floor office, freeing up the rest of our part of the house for Claude Pelieu and Mary Beach who wanted to move to London from the Chelsea Hotel.

Before leaving, I guest-edited the 27 February 1970 issue of *International Times*, a farewell gesture wrapping up my day-to-day involvement with *IT*, by returning to my original concept of the paper: hard underground news that could not be read elsewhere, and essays designed to fuel public debate: William Burroughs on mind control, Allen Ginsberg on the dangers of speed, Alexander Trocchi on Sigma, an interview with John Lennon and Yoko Ono, John Michell on pollution, and a piece I wrote on my pet peeve, London as a twenty-four-hour city, as well as, of course, the Furry Freak Brothers. A few days later Sue and I flew to New York.

Many of the people in the British media today came up through the underground press, though mostly they are from the next generation

– those who worked on the Seventies papers, such as *Ink*, *Friends*, *Time Out*, or the Seventies issues of *IT* and *OZ*. The majority of the Sixties editors of *IT* moved abroad: Jim Haynes to Paris, Jack Henry Moore and Bill Levy to Amsterdam, Alex Gross to New York, David Mairowitz first to Berkeley and then Avignon, Peter Stansill to Seattle, Mick Farren to New York and then LA, and it was the same story with *OZ*, as Richard Neville, Martin Sharp and many of his co-workers returned to Australia.

What we did may have been naive, distorted, arse-backwards and hopelessly idealistic, but we were stumbling towards something better. Out of the Sixties underground scene grew the ecology movement, with Greenpeace, Friends of the Earth and the Greens; the women's movement; an official, if not a public, acceptance of a 'multi-cultural society'; equal rights for homosexuals; and in general a greater tolerance for alternative lifestyles (hippies are no longer jeered at by construction-site workers – who are liable to wear earrings, piercings or even ponytails themselves); and a greater public understanding of victimless crimes, be they in one's choice of drugs or sexual practice, even though these remain on the British statute books.

Though Britain is more of a meritocracy now, it is still not a land of equal opportunity. The richest people on earth may work an eighty-hour week in the USA, but in Britain most of the really serious money is still in the hands of those born to wealth and privilege. There is still no written constitution or Bill of Rights, there is no Freedom of Information Act and Britain still censors more of what its people can read or view than any other European nation. I welcome the day when Britons are citizens, not subjects, when we celebrate the boundless potential of life instead of finding reasons for inaction. As Buddy Holly sang: 'That'll be the day . . .'

Selected Bibliography

Aitken, Jonathan *The Young Meteors*, London, Secker & Warburg, 1967

Albrecht, D. *Happenings & Fluxus*, Cologne, Kolnischer Kunstverein, 1970

Appleby, John *38 Priory Street and All That Jazz*, Westbury-on-Trym, Bristol (privately published by the author), 1971

Babitz, Eve *Eve's Hollywood*, New York, Delacorte, 1974

Bakewell, Michael *Fitzrovia: London's Bohemia*, London, National Portrait Gallery, 1999

Ball, Gordon *'66 Frames*, Minneapolis, Coffeehouse, 1999

Becker, Jürgen & Wolf Vostell *Happenings*, Berlin, Rowohlt, 1965

Berke, Joseph (ed.) *Counter Culture*, London, Peter Owen, 1969

Bernard, Barbara *Fashion in the 60s*, London, Academy, 1978

Black, David *Acid: the Secret History of LSD*, London, Vision, 1998

Brown, Robin 'The beautiful people', *Mayfair* Vol. 2, No. 10, October 1967

Calas, Nicolas & Elena *Icons and Images of the Sixties*, New York, E. P. Dutton, 1971

Charters, Ann *Olson/Melville: A Study in Affinity*, np (Berkeley), Oyez, 1968

Clark, Tom *Charles Olson: The Allegory of a Poet's Life*, New York, Norton, 1991

Coon, Caroline & Rufus Harris *The Release Report on Drug Offenders & the Law*, London, Sphere, 1969

Dwoskin, Stephen *Film Is: the International Free Cinema*, Woodstock, N.Y., Overlook, 1975

Edinger, Claudio *Chelsea*, New York, Abbeville, 1983

England, Peter 'Oh! Oh! What a Gal. A girl called Suzy forgets her wedding banns', *Daily Sketch*, 15 June 1968; 'Oh, Oh, Suzy What A Wedding Day!', *Daily Sketch*, 29 June 1968

Etchingham, Kathy *Through Gypsy Eyes: My Life, the Sixties and Jimi Hendrix*, London, Victor Gollancz, 1998

Fabian, Jenny 'All Change', *Queen*, 5 February 1969; 'What did you do in the sixties daddy?', *Tatler* Vol. 279, No. 6, June 1984

Fabian, Jenny & Johnny Byrne *Groupie*, London, New English Library, 1969

Faithfull, Marianne *Faithfull*, London, Michael Joseph, 1994

Fallows, George 'The Wedding (At Last) of Suzy Creamcheese', *Daily Mirror*, 29 June 1968

Farquharson, Robin *Drop Out!*, London, Anthony Blond, 1968

Farren, Mick & Edward Barker *Watch Out Kids*, London, Open Gate, 1972

Farren, Mick *Get On Down*, London, Futura/Dempsey & Squires, 1976

Farren, Mick *Give The Anarchist a Cigarette*, London, Jonathan Cape, 2001

Fido, Martin *The Krays: Unfinished Business*, London, Carlton, 1999

Fiegel, Eddi *John Barry: a Sixties Theme*, London, Constable, 1998

Fordham, John 'What's IT all about?', *Unit*, University of Keele (not official), December 1967

Fryer, Jonathan *Soho In the Fifties and Sixties*, London, National Portrait Gallery, 1998

Fryer, Peter 'A map of the underground, the flower power structure & London scene', *Encounter*, October 1967; 'Inside the underground', *Observer Magazine*, 3 December 1967

Galpin, Christine 'The disturbing world of the flower children', *News of the World*, 30 July 1967; 'Weekend with the flower children', *News of the World*, 6 August 1967

Gilbert, Richard 'The emergence of the London underground', *Town*, March 1967

Gitlin, Tod *The Sixties: Years of Hope and Rage*, New York, Bantam, 1987

Glessing, Robert *The Underground Press In America*, Bloomington, Indiana University Press, 1970

Graham, Peter *A Dictionary of the Cinema*, London, Tantivy, 1964

Grant, Linda *Sexing the Millennium*, London, HarperCollins, 1993

Selected Bibliography

Green, Jonathon *Days In The Life: Voices from the English Underground 1961–1971*, London, William Heinemann, 1988

Green, Jonathon *All Dressed Up: The Sixties and the Counterculture*, London, Jonathan Cape, 1998

Hamblett, Charles & Jane Deverson *Generation X*, London, Tandem, 1964

Haynes, Jim *Thanks For Coming!*, London, Faber & Faber, 1984

Hebdige, Dick *Subculture: The Meaning of Style*, London, Methuen, 1979

Hewison, Robert *Too Much: Art and Society in the Sixties, 1960–75*, London, Methuen, 1986

Hickey, William 'Out comes the "underground" to see Suzie wed', *Daily Express*, 15 June 1968

Hollingshead, Michael *The Man Who Turned On The World*, New York, Abelard-Shuman, 1974

Horovitz, Michael 'Stirring Times' (letter), *The Times Literary Supplement*, 2 September 1965

Hugill, Barry 'We are all children of '67', *The Observer*, 25 May 1997

Igliori, Paola (ed.) *American Magus Harry Smith*, New York, Inandout, 1996

International Times (IT) 1–70, 14 October 1966–17 December 1969

Jarman, Derek *Dancing Ledge*, London, Quartet, 1984

Jones, D. A. N. 'Psychodelphic oracles', *New Statesman*, 17 February 1967

Joyce, Mary 'Sex, freedom or not', *Knave*, Vol. 3, No. 3, April 1971

Judson, Horace 'The right London number for youngsters in trouble', *Life*, 15 September 1969

Keeler, Christine (with Douglas Thompson) *The Truth At Last: My Story*, London, Sidgewick & Jackson, 2001

Kent, Patrick 'Would you like your daughter to go to parties like this?', *The People*, 30 July 1967

King, Michael *Wrong Movements: a Robert Wyatt History*, London, SAF, 1984

Landesman, Jay *Jaywalking*, London, Weidenfeld & Nicolson, 1992

Le Parc Represente La Republique Argentine (Exhibition catalogue), XXXIIIe Biennale de Venice 1966, Paris, Galerie Denise René, 1966

Logue, Christopher *Prince Charming: a Memoir*, London, Faber & Faber, 1999

Lyders, Carole 'The psychedelic bride celebrates in the park', *Sunday Mirror*, 14 May 1967

Malik, Michael Abdul *From Michael de Freitas to Michael X*, London, André Deutsch, 1968

Marowitz, Charles *Burnt Bridges: A Souvenir of the Swinging Sixties and Beyond*, London, Hodder & Stoughton, 1990

Marwick, Arthur *The Sixties*, Oxford, Oxford University Press, 1998

Maud, Ralph 'The Christine Kerrigan Affair', *Minutes of the Charles Olson Society* 12, Vancouver B.C., February 1996

Melly, George *Revolt Into Style: The Pop Arts In Britain*, London, Penguin, 1970

Metzger, Gustav 'Damaged nature, autodestructive art', London, Coracle, nd (1999)

Michael, Thomas 'Lord Buckley is dead', *Penthouse*, Vol. 2, No. 11, October 1967

Michell, John 'Ufos and the message from the past', *Albion* 1, May 1968

Miles, Barry *Pink Floyd: A Visual Documentary*, London, Omnibus, 1980

Miles, Barry *Frank Zappa: A Visual Documentary*, London, Omnibus, 1993

Miles, Barry *The Rolling Stones: A Visual Documentary*, London, Omnibus, 1994

Miles, Barry *Paul McCartney: Many Years From Now*, London, Secker & Warburg, 1997

Miles, Barry *The Beatles: a Diary*, London, Omnibus, 1998

Miles, Barry & Charles Perry *I Want To Take You Higher: The Psychedelic Era 1965–1969*, San Francisco, Chronicle/Rock and Roll Hall of Fame and Museum, 1997

Mitchell, Alexander 'Do the police play fair?' *Sunday Times*, 16 March 1969

Morgan, Ted *Literary Outlaw: the Life and Times of William S. Burroughs*, New York, Henry Holt, 1988

Morton, James *Bent Coppers: A Survey of Police Corruption*, London, Little, Brown & Co, 1993

Neville, Richard *Hippie Hippie Shake*, London, Bloomsbury, 1995

Selected Bibliography

Neville, Richard *Out of My Mind*, London, Bloomsbury, 1996

Nicholl, Charles 'It, Oz, and all the others', *Daily Telegraph Magazine* 465, 28 September 1973

Obst, Lynda (ed.) *The Sixties: The Decade Remembered Now, By the People Who Lived It Then*, New York, Random House/Rolling Stone, 1977

Palmer, Tony 'The voice of the underground', *London Magazine*, Vol. 7, No. 12, March 1968

Pearson, John *The Profession of Violence: the Rise and Fall of the Kray Twins*, London, Granada, 1973

Peck, Abe *Uncovering the Sixties: the Life & Times of the Underground Press*, New York, Pantheon, 1985

Pilkington, Norman 'Busy summer in London', *Los Angeles Free Press*, 25 August 1969

Pooley, Leana 'Buried Underground', *Evening Standard*, 27 October 1976

Quattrocchi, Angelo 'Letter to a dying underground', *New Statesman*, 13 February 1970

Rexroth, Kenneth 'Making the rounds of literary London', *San Francisco Examiner*, Section 2, 4 December 1966

Roberts, John 'The raving revolves around LSD', *Tit Bits*, 25 March 1967

Robins, David & Liz Béar 'Underground Voices: Jim Haynes, David Medalla, Jack H. Moore', *Circuit*, 5, Winter 1968

Scala, Mim *Diary of a Teddy Boy, A Memoir of the Long Sixties*, Dublin, Sitric, 2000

Schaffner, Nicholas *Saucerful of Secrets: The Pink Floyd Odyssey*, New York, Harmony, 1991

Selerie, Gavin (ed.) *The Riverside Interviews 6: Tom McGrath*, London, Binnacle, 1979

Sinclair, Iain *The Kodak Mantra Diaries*, London, Albion Village Press, 1971

Singh, Rani (ed.) *Think of the Self Speaking. Harry Smith – Selected Interviews*, Seattle, Elbow/Cityful, 1999

Spencer Neil 'The underground press', *Arrow* 95, Sheffield University, Union of Students, nd (1968)

Stansill, Peter & David Zane Mairowitz (eds.) *BAMN, Outlaw Manifestos*, London, Penguin, 1971

Swinfield, John 'The Non-wedding of the year failed to take place yesterday, but the reception went on as planned.' *Daily Mail*, 15 June 1968

Tennant, Emma *Burnt Diaries*, Edinburgh, Canongate, 1995

Thomas, Harford (ed.) *The Permissive Society: The Guardian Enquiry*, London, Panther, 1969

Travis, Alan ' "It's porn if the ink comes off on your hands" ', *The Guardian*, 14 September 2000

Turner, Florence *At the Chelsea*, London, Hamish Hamilton, 1986

Turner, Steve 'Peter Pan and the mid-life crisis' (in three parts), *The Times*, 11, 12, 13 August 1986

Vestey, Michael 'Raving London', *London Look*, 11 February 1967

Vyner, Harriet *Groovy Bob: the Life and Times of Robert Fraser*, London, Faber & Faber, 1999

Wallace, Christine *Germaine Greer: Untamed Shrew*, London, Richard Cohen, 1999

Watkinson, Mike & Pete Anderson *Crazy Diamond: Syd Barrett and the Dawn of the Pink Floyd*, London, Omnibus, 1991

Wheen, Francis *The Sixties: a Fresh Look at the Decade of Change*, London, Century/Channel 4, 1982

Widgery, David *Preserving Disorder*, London, Pluto, 1989

Wilcocks, Dick 'sTigma – a kick at soporifics', *Peace News*, 12 March 1965

Index

BM is Barry Miles.

Index